Social Conflict within and between Groups

Intergroup competition and conflict create pervasive problems in human society, giving rise to such phenomena as prejudice, terrorism, ethnic cleansing, and interstate war. Citizens, policy makers, social workers, schoolteachers, and politicians wrestle with these problems, and with difficult questions that these issues pose:

- What causes conflict to escalate?
- How should we manage conflict within communities, and also in society at large?
- Is conflict always bad, or does it have other more beneficial consequences?

Social Conflict within and between Groups provides an overview of contemporary research from the social sciences on these questions. It brings together the research output of a number of leading researchers in psychology, management and economics, sociology and political science, and draws on the outcomes of ten prominent research programs conducted over the past five years. The chapters cover a range of fascinating topics, including prejudice and discrimination in multi-ethnic societies, and conflict and negotiation in the field of industrial relations. The authors also consider the possibilities for intervention at the interpersonal, intergroup, and societal level.

This is the first volume to provide an interdisciplinary overview of the various scientific approaches to studying the origins and consequences of social conflict. It will be of great interest to researchers, graduates and upper-level undergraduate students from across the social and behavioral sciences.

Carsten K. W. De Dreu is Professor in Psychology at the University of Amsterdam, the Netherlands. He is fellow of the Royal Netherlands Academy of Arts and Sciences, and was President of the European Association for Social Psychology. His research is concerned with the neural and psychological underpinnings of human cooperation and conflict, decision making, and creativity and innovation.

Current Issues in Social Psychology
Series Editor: Arjan E. R. Bos

Current Issues in Social Psychology is a series of edited books that reflect the state-of-the-art of current and emerging topics of interest in basic and applied social psychology.

Each volume is tightly focused on a particular topic and consists of seven to ten chapters contributed by international experts. The editors of individual volumes are leading figures in their areas and provide an introductory overview.

Example topics include: self-esteem, evolutionary social psychology, minority groups, social neuroscience, cyberbullying and social stigma.

Self-Esteem
Edited by Virgil Zeigler-Hill

Social Conflict within and between Groups
Edited by Carsten K. W. De Dreu

Social Conflict within and between Groups

Edited by Carsten K. W. De Dreu

Ψ **Psychology Press**
Taylor & Francis Group

LONDON AND NEW YORK

First published 2014
by Psychology Press
27 Church Road, Hove, East Sussex BN3 2FA

and by Psychology Press
711 Third Avenue, New York, NY 10017

Psychology Press is an imprint of the Taylor & Francis Group, an informa business

© 2014 Carsten K.W. De Dreu

The right of the editor to be identified as the author of the editorial
material, and of the authors for their individual chapters, has been asserted
in accordance with sections 77 and 78 of the Copyright, Designs and
Patents Act 1988.

British Library Cataloguing in Publication Data
A catalogue record for this book is available from the British Library

Library of Congress Cataloging in Publication Data
Social conflict within and between groups / edited by Carsten K.W. De
Dreu. -- 1 Edition.
pages cm
Includes bibliographical references and index.
ISBN 978-1-84872-295-8 (hb) -- ISBN 978-1-84872-296-5 (softcover)
-- ISBN 978-1-315-77274-5 (ebk) 1. Social conflict. 2. Multiculturalism.
3. Intercultural communication. I. Dreu, Carsten K. W. de.
HM1121.S62987 2014
303.6--dc23
2013049360

ISBN: 978-1-84872-295-8 (hbk)
ISBN: 978-1-84872-296-5 (pbk)
ISBN: 978-1-315-77274-5 (ebk)

Typeset in Times New Roman
by Saxon Graphics Ltd, Derby

Contents

List of Contributors

Hillie Aaldering
University of Amsterdam, Department of Psychology, the Netherlands

Agnes Akkerman
Vrije Universiteit Amsterdam, Department of Sociology, the Netherlands

Hajo Boomgaarden
University of Amsterdam, Department of Communication Science, the Netherlands

Brian Burgoon
University of Amsterdam, Department of Political Science, the Netherlands

Carsten K. W. De Dreu
University of Amsterdam, Department of Psychology, the Netherlands

Sarah de Lange
University of Amsterdam, Department of Communication Science, the Netherlands

Bart de Vos
University of Groningen, Department of Psychology, the Netherlands

Claes de Vreese
University of Oxford, Lincoln College, United Kingdom

Catherine de Vries
University of Amsterdam, Department of Political Science, the Netherlands

Evangelia Demerouti
Eindhoven Technical University, Department of Organizational Behavior, the Netherlands

Bertjan Doosje
University of Amsterdam, Department of Psychology, the Netherlands

Naomi Ellemers
Leiden University, Department of Psychology, the Netherlands

Maurice Gesthuizen
Radboud University of Nijmegen, Department of Sociology, the Netherlands

Josette M. P. Gevers
Eindhoven Technical University, Department of Organizational Behavior, the Netherlands

Ernestine H. Gordijn
University of Groningen, Department of Psychology, the Netherlands

Hedy Greijdanus
University of Groningen, Department of Psychology, the Netherlands

Louk Hagendoorn
Utrecht University, Faculty of Social Sciences, the Netherlands

Fieke Harinck
Leiden University, Department of Psychology, the Netherlands

Kai J. Jonas
University of Amsterdam, Department of Psychology, the Netherlands

Elanor Kamans
University of Groningen, Department of Psychology, the Netherlands

Alex Lehr
Radboud University of Nijmegen, Department of Political Science, the Netherlands

Ram Manikkalingam
University of Amsterdam, Department of Political Science, the Netherlands

Borja Martinovic
Utrecht University, Faculty of Social and Behavioural Sciences, the Netherlands

Marte Otten
University of Amsterdam, Department of Psychology, the Netherlands

Tom Postmes
University of Groningen, Department of Psychology, the Netherlands

Sonja Rispens
Eindhoven Technical University, Department of Organizational Behavior, the Netherlands

Andrea Ruggeri
University of Amsterdam, Department of Political Science, the Netherlands

Michael Savelkoul
Radboud University of Nijmegen, Department of Sociology, the Netherlands

Ozum Saygi
University of Amsterdam, Department of Psychology, the Netherlands

Peer Scheepers
Radboud University of Nijmegen, Department of Sociology, the Netherlands

Susanne Täuber
University of Groningen, Department of Psychology, the Netherlands

Kirsten Thommes
Aachen University, Department of Human Resource Management, Germany

René Torenvlied
Twente University, Department of Public Administration, the Netherlands

Marc van de Wardt
University of Amsterdam, Department of Political Science, the Netherlands

Wouter van der Brug
University of Amsterdam, Department of Political Science, the Netherlands

Daphne van der Pas
University of Amsterdam, Department of Political Science, the Netherlands

Kim J. P. M. van Erp
Eindhoven Technical University, Department of Organizational Behavior, the Netherlands

Marijn van Klingeren
University of Amsterdam, Department of Communication Science, the Netherlands

Martijn van Zomeren
University of Groningen, Department of Psychology, the Netherlands

Maykel Verkuyten
Utrecht University, Faculty of Social and Behavioural Sciences, the Netherlands

Rens Vliegenthart
University of Amsterdam, Department of Political Science, the Netherlands

Preface

Wherever one looks, the world appears to be in turmoil and seems to struggle with a multitude of changes and social problems. Political and religious conflicts rage in various countries, and ethnic tensions causes violent eruptions in suburbs of European cities. Technological development as well as global media coverage appears to aggravate conflict, and relatively localized conflicts spill over to countries elsewhere in the world. The legal and illegal drift of people, goods and ideas across the globe shakes up social orders and creates or intensifies insecurity and injustice. Internet and e-mail have opened a potential for bringing opposing groups of people together as well as for polarizing debates. Across the world, the fear of terrorist attacks galvanize discriminatory prejudice and stereotyping against immigrant populations, and groups of different faith; and writers and journalists censor themselves because they fear hostility and violent reactions. While the multitude of changes in the work-place require employees to negotiate their conflicts of interest with their supervisors and colleagues on an almost day-to-day basis, the growing tendency to privatize and create competition to serve customers ameliorates choice conflicts both for citizens looking for new health insurance and better transportation, and for competing firms, companies, and institutions providing these products and services.

Together, globalization of economy and business, and the rise of a diversified and exceedingly multicultural society appears to converge with a variety of conflicts at all levels, of different degrees of intensity and urgency, and of different form and shape. Indeed, citizens, policy makers, social workers, schoolteachers, and politicians all wonder how to deal with these disputes, with latent conflicts and manifest outburst of violence and aggression. We see tendencies to prevent and suppress, to increase control and attempts at containment. We also see tendencies to mediate conflict, to bring rivaling groups together, and to build and exploit common ground.

But what strategies work, and when? How do social systems such as families, work groups, and entire societies benefit from conflict, learn from debate and use it to strengthen social bonds? Do different types of conflict require different strategies, and do groups with different cultural backgrounds require being approached differently? What do we know about conflict, about possible ways to manage it, about what happens if we try to suppress it? Do different actors interpret conflict issues differently, and which symbols and rituals are used to give meaning to conflict? Is conflict always bad, or does it have other, more beneficial consequences as well—and to whom? And what causes conflict to escalate, which dynamic and longitudinal characteristics can we identify and use when we need to intervene and call a halt to violence and aggression?

Many of these and related questions have been the focus of research in many different scientific disciplines, yet rarely have they been connected to each other. Not only does this impede scientific development and prohibit creative development, it also means that we continue to design interventions based on incomplete understanding, poor assessment, and loose rather than tight theory. Obviously, inaccurate diagnosis and poorly designed or executed interventions fuel rather than mitigate conflict, and the cure may be worse than the disease.

This volume brings together ten chapters on social conflict within and between groups. The chapters are written by leading scholars from a broad range of scientific disciplines, and they showcase specific theoretical developments and the applied value of concrete interventions. Across chapters, authors engage different levels of analysis, including the interpersonal and small group level, the intergroup level and the societal level, and different types of social conflict are documented and analyzed. Some chapters focus on conflicts of interest and the question of how (groups of) people manage relative deprivation and conflict over resources, others are oriented more towards value conflicts that address (social) identity concerns and elicit deep emotions including feelings of humiliation. Crucially, Harinck and Ellemers document a program of research showing the intricate differences between these types of conflict, and how different conflict issues trigger different motivational, cognitive, and behavioral tendencies that render some possible interventions aimed at conflict reduction less rather than more effective.

In addition to documenting social conflict at various levels of analysis, and in terms of its foci, this volume contains a wealth of information on the (in) effectiveness of conflict regulation. Several chapters deal with bargaining and negotiation as a potentially constructive means of conflict regulation, both in general and within the context of work organizations. Akkerman and colleagues (Chapter 7), for example, provide an insightful analysis of conflict contagion—the idea that conflict and negotiation within one organization or branch spills over to adjacent organizations facing the same issues and debates. In Chapter 6, Postmes and colleagues discuss their own research, and that of others, on how communication within and between groups can channel potentially destructive conflicts into more constructive modes of regulation. Burgoon and colleagues (Chapter 8), and Van der Brug and colleagues (Chapter 9) consider communication processes that occur in the periphery of intergroup and political conflict. Their work highlights that such peripheral communication can both depolarize and fuel conflicts among rivaling ethnic groups as well as among political parties and their allies.

Although migration has been part and parcel of our ancestral past, modern-day migration has become an issue high on the political agenda across the globe. Increasingly, societies are composed of multiple distinguishable groups differing in their ethnic, religious, and political outlook and simultaneously creating their own socio-geographical space while competing for scarce issues such as jobs and access to public goods such as education and health care. These pivotal issues are addressed in Chapters 4 and 5, with a specific focus on the long-term consequences of migration for latent and manifest conflicts among native and newcomer groups. In Chapter 4, Verkuyten and Martinovic consider the consequences of multi-ethnic compositions of society for the emergence and enactment of in-group favoritism and, possibly, intergroup discrimination. Gesthuizen and colleagues (Chapter 5) take issue with the notion that the migration-induced social diversity in society undermines social cohesion and social connectedness, and present solid empirical evidence pointing to other directions than commonly assumed.

Finally, various chapters document and analyze the positive and negative consequences of conflict for individual well-being, group functioning, and societal cohesion. For example, in Chapter 10, Demerouti and colleagues analyze so-called by-stander conflicts and discuss a range of possible interventions to mitigate the stress induced by such by-stander conflicts. However, social conflict can have more beneficial consequences as well. De Dreu and colleagues (Chapter 1), for example, summarize the large literature showing that conflict and competition between groups motivates individuals to self-sacrifice and cooperate with their own group, and that such enhanced cooperative motivation is driven by the desire to strengthen one's own group, rather than to aggress and derogate competing out-groups. Postmes and colleagues (Chapter 6) likewise show that voicing anger about unfair treatments might reduce prejudice and improve intergroup relations. And Burgoon and colleagues (Chapter 8) neatly analyze how media attention for human rights violations in ethnic conflicts motivates conflicting parties to regulate their disputes in more civilized and less violent ways.

The chapters in this volume reflect and summarize a sub-set of programs of research initiated by, and funded through the Netherlands Organization for Scientific Research (NWO). In 2008, NWO launched this Conflict and Security program as a large-scale endeavor to stimulate practically relevant and theoretically rigorous research on social conflict. The result is a unique combination of research from sociology, political sciences, communication sciences, psychology, business and economics. The combined insight that emerges from these various chapters is, accordingly, far more than the sum of its parts, and a springboard for interdisciplinary theory development and for calibrated, evidence-based interventions in social conflict within and across societies.

Louk Hagendoorn
Chair, NWO-Strategic Theme Conflict and Security

1 Intergroup conflict and negotiating settlement

Carsten K.W. De Dreu, Hillie Aaldering, and Ozum Saygi

Introduction

Intergroup competition and conflict create pervasive problems in human society, giving rise to such phenomena as prejudice, terrorism, ethnic cleansing, and interstate war (Choi & Bowles, 2007; Fiske, 2002). At the same time, however, intergroup competition and conflict provide critical impetus for social change and innovations, both within and across groups and the larger societies within which they operate (Alexander, 1990; De Dreu, 2010a; De Dreu, Aaldering, & Saygi, in press). This chapter considers intergroup competition and conflict from two complementary perspectives—social identity theory and interdependence theory—and (representative) negotiation as a strategy for regulating intergroup competition and conflict. Negotiation holds great promise for settling disputes in a constructive and long-lasting manner, so that rivaling groups can co-exist and thrive. We conclude with a summary of the main insights and a description of some avenues for new research.

Origins of intergroup competition and conflict

Conflict between groups includes at least three critical and interrelated components (De Dreu, 2010a): (a) its antecedent conditions (i.e. what triggers conflict?); (b) its core social interaction processes (i.e. how do conflicting parties regulate conflict?); and (c) its main consequences (i.e. what does conflict do to the parties' functioning, well-being, and welfare?). Others before us defined conflict as the clashing of goals and aspirations (e.g. Pruitt & Rubin, 1986), or as situations in which one party's goal pursuit is blocking or impeding another party's goal striving (e.g. Deutsch, 1973). A core ingredient in both definitions is that one party experiences or anticipates outcome deprivation: when one's outcomes—tangible or symbolic—are or will fall below a reasonable standard because of the actions or inactions of another party (De Dreu, 2010a; Pruitt, 1998). Tangible outcomes include the availability of and/or access to desirable resources such as water, territory, or money. Symbolic outcomes include status and recognition, respectful treatment, and basic rights. Tangible and symbolic outcomes are often related (e.g. possessing scarce resources comes with high status), and both types of outcomes matter greatly to people and their groups.

Importantly, for both tangible and symbolic outcomes, deprivation implies a standard against which obtained or anticipated outcomes are evaluated (Kelley & Thibaut, 1978). One such standard is one's level of aspiration (Pruitt & Rubin, 1986): Deprivation is experienced when outcomes fall below the outcome one aspired to, and social conflict emerges when such deprivation is attributed to the (in)actions of some other individual or group. Another standard that is often used is a *comparison level of alternatives*, or the outcome that would have been received in an alternative relation (also see Akkerman et al., this volume). Thus, a social psychology unit may experience outcome deprivation because the status and respect its work receives within its university falls well below the status and respect its work would receive in another university. Finally, outcome deprivation is experienced when one's own group's *outcomes relative to those of a comparison group* are below what one sees as reasonable or justifiable, that is as "unfair."[1]

This scholarly approach on outcome deprivation allows an open view of what happens once parties experience outcome deprivation—how they feel and think, what motivational forces are released, and how they manage the tension with their protagonist. Second, it allows an open view as to what possible consequences social conflict may have—does social conflict always produce destructive outcomes in terms of wasted resources and reduced well-being, or can it also have more constructive outcomes such as enhanced creativity and innovation, better decision making, and improved social relations?

Here we firstly discuss two complementary perspectives on the emergence of outcome deprivation and the function of intergroup competition and conflict. The next section describes how intergroup conflict can be regulated through (representative) negotiations and discusses research in this area.

Social identity theory

Intergroup competition and conflict can be understood from the perspective of *social identity theory* (Tajfel & Turner, 1986; also see Verkuyten and colleagues, this volume). The theory posits that people: (a) quickly and often automatically categorize themselves and others into an in-group and an out-group; (b) base their self-views and evaluations in part on the features and characteristics of the group(s) to which they belong; and (c) strive to develop, maintain, and improve a positive social identity. A positive social identity is achieved by, first of all, in-group favoritism: One emphasizes the positive features and characteristics, and downplays the negative features and characteristics, of one's own group. To some extent, a positive social identity is also achieved through out-group derogation: One downplays the positive features and characteristics, and emphasizes the negative features and characteristics, of relevant comparison groups. Both in-group favoritism and out-group derogation can be explicit, as when individuals allocate resources more to in-group than to out-group members (e.g., Bornstein, Crum, et al., 1983). Both tendencies can also be implicit: For example, people respond more quickly to positive attributes associated with their in-group and to negative attributes associated with a rival out-group (Greenwald, Nosek, & Banaij, 2003; for reviews see Dovidio & Gaertner, 2010; Yzerbyt & Demoulin, 2010).

In-group favoritism alone or in combination with out-group derogation creates intergroup bias—an unfair response that devalues or disadvantages another group and its members while valuing or privileging members of one's own group (Dovidio & Gaertner, 2010). Such unfair responses trigger negative emotions, protests, and possibly even aggression and violence on the part of the disfavored and excluded individuals (Hewstone, Rubin, & Willis, 2002). Put differently, through positive social identity striving, groups and their members indirectly (through in-group favoritism) and directly (through out-group derogation) deprive out-groups of a positive social identity, of respectful and fair treatment, and of (access to) scarce resources. Social identity striving, in short, promotes intergroup conflict.

The primacy of the in-group

There is a wealth of research probing the conditions that stimulate or inhibit in-group favoritism and/or out-group derogation, thus amplifying or reducing intergroup bias and the ensuing deprivation and conflict (for recent reviews, see e.g. Dovidio & Gaertner, 2010; Hewstone et al., 2002; Yzerbyt & Demoulin, 2010). One important insight emerging from these research literatures is that intergroup bias is driven more by in-group favoritism than by out-group derogation (also see Scheepers et al., this volume). Consider, for example, a series of recent studies by Halevy and colleagues (Halevy, Bornstein, & Sagiv, 2008; Halevy, Chou, Cohen, & Bornstein, 2010; Halevy, Weisel, & Bornstein, 2012; also see De Dreu, 2010b; De Dreu, Greer, et al., 2010). These authors developed a team game in which individuals were randomly assigned to in-groups and out-groups and could, at a cost to themselves, contribute to a pool that benefitted their in-group ("in-group favoritism") or to a pool that punished the out-group ("out-group derogation"). Results showed strong in-group favoritism and little out-group derogation; individual group members donated considerable personal resources to the pool benefitting their in-group and much less to the pool that punished the out-group. These results are important because they suggest that intergroup conflicts do not necessarily arise out of a desire among group members to hurt out-groups but, rather, to help their in-group. A similar conclusion derives from an interdependence analysis of intergroup competition and conflict, to which we turn now.

Behavioral game theory and interdependence theory

A complementary perspective on the emergence of intergroup conflict derives from interdependence theory (Kelley & Thibaut, 1978), which builds on and extends the broader theory of games (Colman, 2003; Luce & Raiffa, 1957), and Deutsch's theory of cooperation and competition (Deutsch, 1973). It considers the ways in which parties (individuals or groups) influence each other's outcomes through their individual or coordinated actions. Within this class of theories, it is assumed that outcome interdependencies create a mixture of cooperative and competitive motives (Deutsch, 1973; Komorita & Parks, 1995). Joint cooperation creates better outcomes for each party than mutual competition, yet each party is better off by competing when the other is cooperating. In the words of Harvard economist and Nobel laureate Thomas Schelling:

> These are the "nonzero-sum" games involved in wars and threats of war, strikes, negotiations, criminal deterrence, race war, price war, and blackmail; maneuvering in a bureaucracy or in a traffic jam; the coercion of one's own children ... These are the "games" in which, though an element of conflict provides the dramatic interest, mutual dependence is part of the logical structure and demands some kind of collaboration or mutual accommodation— tacit, if not explicit—even if only in the avoidance of mutual disaster.
>
> (Schelling, 1980, p. 83)

Such mixed-motive interdependencies, both within and between groups, have often been modeled as a prisoner's dilemma (PD). Here, two parties simultaneously and without discussion decide to cooperate or not to cooperate. Both parties are better off when both cooperate than when both fail to cooperate, yet each party is best off when he or she does not cooperate and the other person does (Rapoport & Guyer, 1966; Komorita & Parks, 1995). The PD paradigm models interpersonal and intergroup exchange situations ranging from volunteers in community service to financial traders, from partners sharing a household to soldiers teaming up to fight an enemy, and from colleagues in work organizations to high-ranking consultants preparing a hostile corporate takeover (De Dreu, 2010a; Komorita & Parks, 1995). The PD paradigm can be used to understand, for example, the dilemma during the Cold War, in which the United States and the former Soviet Union continuously had to decide to maintain their level of nuclear arms (the non-cooperative choice) or to reduce it (the cooperative choice). Each country was better off by having a strong army than by unilaterally investing in arms reduction, yet both countries were worse off by continuing to invest money in a level of nuclear arms allowing them to fully destroy their counterpart not only once, but over 60 times, with untold damage to other parts of the world, including their own.

Non-cooperation is driven by fear and greed

Behavioral decision and interdependence theories identify two core motives underlying non-cooperation—greed and fear (Coombs, 1973; Van Lange, Liebrand, & Kuhlman, 1990). Greed refers to the desire to maximize self-interest, or that of one's in-group. For example, the former Soviet Union's decisions to maintain its arsenal of nuclear weapons may have been driven by the desire to dominate the world and to force the United States into subordination. Greed as a motive need not be limited to tangible resources, but can extend to symbolic striving for status and positive (social) identity (De Dreu, 2010a). And although greed can be "absolute," in that an individual or group can strive to maximize its own outcomes while being indifferent about outcomes of others, in intergroup competition and conflict, greed is often focused on relative gain vis-à-vis the out-group.

Whereas greed as a motive for non-cooperation may be difficult to justify and is often deemed immoral in interpersonal and small group settings, in intergroup competition and conflict it can and often is justified as pro-social behavior toward one's in-group (Wildschut, Pinter, Vevea, Insko, & Schopler, 2003). Indeed, non-cooperation with an out-group is often labeled heroic and patriotic and is publicly praised. Acting non-cooperatively toward out-groups causes an individual to be perceived as a loyal, reliable, and committed in-group member who deserves to be included rather than excluded from rewarding within-group exchanges (Arrow, 2007; Brewer, 1999; Choi & Bowles, 2007; Gintis, Bowles, Boyd, & Fehr, 2003). Halevy and colleagues (2012) conducted a series of experiments in which they modeled intergroup competition and varied the extent to which fellow in-group members cooperated with the in-group, and competed against the out-group. Participants were then asked to indicate for each in-group member how prestigious and how dominant they felt this person was. Results showed that individuals ascribe greater prestige to fellow in-group members who cooperate with the in-group, and greater dominance to in-group members who compete against the out-group. Thus, greed-driven non-cooperation is an important explanation for the robust observation that intergroup competition and conflict are often intense and hostile, and easily escalate into increasing levels of intensity.

The second motive underlying non-cooperation, fear, refers to the desire to prevent exploitation by other's non-cooperation (Coombs, 1973) and is inversely related to trust—the positive expectation that one's counterpart will reciprocate cooperation and not abuse or exploit one's vulnerability (Berg, Dickhaut, & McCabe, 1995; Pruitt & Kimmel, 1977). Thus, the former Soviet Union's decisions to maintain its arsenal of nuclear weapons may have been driven by their suspicion that the United States desired to dominate the world and to subordinate the Soviet Union.

Intergroup competition motivates within-group cooperation

In intergroup competition and conflict, greed and fear operate simultaneously at two levels of analysis. Dawes (1980) noted that "soldiers who fight in a large battle can reasonably conclude that no matter what their comrades do, they personally are better off taking no chances; yet if no one takes chances, the result will be rout and slaughter worse for all the soldiers than is taking chances" (p. 170). That is, each individual group member may fear that his or her fellow group members will not join in attacking the rival out-group, thus leaving the individual group member alone and highly vulnerable. Or the other way around, each individual group member has a greedy desire, however weak, to benefit from his or her fellow group members' heroic attack on the rival out-group without personally contributing to the risky attack. On the group level, however, both fear and greed motivate the individuals within the group to attack its rival out-group, thereby increasing the chance to win the conflict. This tension between the collective interest of the group and the interests of its individual members is unavoidable, because the outcomes of the intergroup conflict (e.g. territory, status, pride) are public goods that accrue to all group members regardless of their individual contributions. Thus, although individuals are personally better off by not cooperating when all others cooperate, it is in each group's interest to mobilize within-group cooperation so as to defeat the other group (Bornstein, 2003; Bornstein & Ben-Yossef, 1994; Rapoport, & Bornstein, 1987). This reasoning explains findings by Erev, Bornstein, and Gallili (1993). During the orange harvesting season in Israel, these authors created groups of four workers that were rewarded: (a) for their individual performance—the more oranges they personally picked, the more money they earned; (b) for their in-group's performance—the more oranges their in-group harvested, the more money the group received; or (c) for their group's relative performance—when their in-group harvested more oranges than a competing out-group, they would be rewarded; but if there was a tie or when they harvested less than the competing out-group, no reward would be earned. Results showed that the latter condition led to the most vigorous harvesting behavior—intergroup competition stimulated individuals to work harder and to contribute to their in-group.

Whereas the extra effort mobilized in intergroup competition may be rooted in the greedy desire to outperform rival out-groups, it may also be driven by the fear of being exploited and subordinated by the rival group (Bornstein, 2003; De Dreu et al., 2010; Ten Velden, Beersma, & De Dreu, 2011). Ironically, this fear-driven in-group favoritism creates similar fear-driven in-group favoritism in the rival out-group whose members perceive an increasingly strong rival as threatening, motivating them to invest in their own threat capacity (Bacharach & Lawler, 1981; Jervis, 1976). This so-called security dilemma escalates the competing parties' threat capacity well beyond the capacity needed to fully destroy the other side, and may deteriorate intergroup relations up to a point where intergroup aggression and violence become nearly unavoidable. Consistent with our earlier conclusion that intergroup bias results from in-group favoritism more than from out-group derogation (Brewer, 1999; De Dreu, 2010b; Halevy et al., 2008), the analysis here also suggests that intergroup conflict emerges out of a basic desire to protect oneself and one's in-group (see also Simunovic, Mifune, & Yamagishi, 2013).

Precisely because individual-level incentives for cooperation and non-cooperation (toward the in-group) are at odds with group-level incentives for cooperation and non-cooperation (toward the out-group), groups mobilize individual cooperation through a number of formal and informal strategies (De Dreu, 2010a; Weber, Kopelman, & Messick, 2004). Warring countries impose severe sanctions on individual soldiers who desert the army, and even in times of peace those who avoid military service because of ethical or moral objections are frowned upon, ostracized as traitors and unpatriotic citizens. In addition, others' non-cooperation is often sanctioned through costly punishment—individuals punish, at a cost to themselves, fellow in-group members who fail to cooperate and do not (sufficiently) contribute to the group goal of winning the intergroup conflict (e.g. Fehr & Fishbacher, 2004). Most relevant here is that this tendency appears especially when the non-cooperator is a member of one's in-group (Shinada, Yamagishi, & Ohmura, 2004), and that such costly punishment, or even the mere threat of it, is quite effective in boosting future cooperation among the targets of punishment (Shinada & Yamagishi, 2007). Ironically, then, costly punishment in intergroup competition substantially promotes within-group cooperation, and because within-group cooperation intensifies an intergroup conflict, settings in which individuals can punish fellow in-group members for their non-cooperation escalate the intergroup conflict well beyond the point of mutual destruction (Abbink, Brandts, Hermann, & Orzen, 2010).

Groups not only impose negative sanctions on members who do not contribute; they also reward those who cooperate, for example by decorating them, or by promoting them to senior positions. To our knowledge, systematic research into the effectiveness of rewarding cooperation is missing. Research is needed to examine this general phenomenon, and to discover whether rewarding individual cooperation escalates intergroup conflict more or less than punishing non-cooperation does.

The discussion so far shows that: (a) perceiving out-groups as a threat to the in-group and/or perceiving the out-group as vulnerable and exploitable motivates (b) in-group favoritism and/or out-group derogation, which (c) is subject to within-group sanctioning that strengthens displays of in-group favoritism and/or out-group derogation, and reduces selfishness and free-riding. As a result of these dynamics, (d) the in-group gains strength both in absolute terms and relative to its rival out-group, and (e) may be tempted to aggress against the out-group either to neutralize its threat or to exploit its resources, whereas (f) the out-group may be tempted to aggress against the exceedingly strong in-group to reduce or neutralize its threat.

Regulating intergroup conflict through negotiation

Non-cooperation by out-groups, and ensuing outcome deprivation in the in-group, triggers one of four broad responses in the in-group (Blake & Mouton, 1961; De Dreu, 2010a; Pruitt & Rubin, 1986). First, the in-group may concede and subordinate itself to the dominating out-group, perhaps up to the point where the in-group ceases to exist and is acculturated into the dominating out-group (Berry, 1984). Second, the in-group may "leave the field," flee the scene, and emigrate from their territory. Third, the in-group may respond in kind and approach the out-group in a non-cooperative and aggressive manner. Fourth, and finally, the in-group may invite problem solving and seek solutions that satisfy both in- and out-groups—that is, they may seek a negotiated solution for the perceived intergroup conflict.

Subordination, withdrawal, and especially aggressive responding all contribute to the perpetuation and oftentimes intensification of intergroup conflict (Burton, 1990). Over time, the conflict may even become integrated into socialization processes, thus transmitting conflict-related emotions and cognitions to new generations (Rouhana & Bar-Tal, 1998). This sustains stereotypical beliefs and prejudices, which feed and form collective memories that permeate public discussions and discourse (Bar-Tal, Raviv, & Freund, 1994).

Histories of violence and aggression between groups provide a critical, albeit often implicit, impetus into the fourth strategy identified above, namely dispute resolution initiatives in which groups seek peaceful solutions through collaboration and negotiation (Kelman, 2006; Lindskold & Han, 1988). In fact, several authors have argued that intergroup negotiation and problem solving are often avoided until there is a so-called hurting stalemate—a point where disputants refuse to back down yet also lack the strength to push further (Pruitt & Rubin, 1986; Zartman, 1991). Pruitt (2007) explained that for a hurting stalemate to lead to negotiation and problem solving, parties need to have a sense that victory is unrealistic or carries unacceptable costs or risks or, alternatively, that a victory is unrealistic because of pressure from allies or some powerful third party. Second, parties need to have some optimism about the outcome of negotiation and problem solving. Such optimism may derive from lowered aspirations on one or both sides, from the belief that the other party also wants to escape the conflict, or from the perception that an acceptable agreement is shaping up and that one's adversary is ready to make important concessions.[2]

There are two reasons to consider intergroup negotiation and problem solving. First, and despite the large literature on interpersonal negotiation and bargaining, relatively little is known about negotiation and problem solving between groups (Demoulin & De Dreu, 2010). Second, negotiation as a strategy for regulating intergroup conflict offers a way out of many escalated disputes and seemingly intractable intergroup disputes. Intergroup conflicts often involve multiple issues, some of which are more important to the in-group than to the out-group and vice versa. For example, a typical labor management conflict (e.g. Walton & McKersie, 1965) may involve not only labor law reform, but also salary increases, pension plans, budgets for training and development, vacation days, and so on. Some issues are critical to one side (e.g. labor attaches high importance to blocking labor law reform) and other issues are more important to the other side (e.g. employers attach great importance to restructuring pension plans and reducing vacation). Such asymmetries provide possibilities for creative solutions that benefit all rather than some parties (Lax & Sebenius, 1986). In the labor–management example, both parties would be better off if labor gets its way on law reform and employers get their way on pension plans and vacation, compared to an agreement that splits the difference on each issue. Solutions that integrate both in-group and out-group aspirations create order and stability, foster social harmony, increase feelings of self-efficacy, reduce the probability of future conflict, and stimulate economic prosperity (De Dreu, 2010a; Pruitt & Rubin, 1986).

Integrative solutions are typically reached through constructive negotiation, rather than through continued fighting or leaving the field. Despite its tremendous potential for reducing intergroup conflict, however, negotiation in intergroup conflict poses a number of challenges that are specific to the intergroup context, and may make the task even more difficult than is the case in interpersonal conflicts. First, in intergroup conflicts, negotiators often have greater room for justifying selfishness, as they can privately or publicly frame selfish behavior as patriotic and serving their in-group. Second, negotiators face group pressures and group norms they need to take into account next to the interests of their opponent. The result is that intergroup negotiations are cognitively taxing and time-consuming, and unfortunately, trust and a constructive climate may be rather difficult to establish and remain fragile (e.g. Morgan & Tindale, 2002; O'Connor, 1997; Polzer, 1996).

Representative negotiation

When groups increase in size, intergroup negotiations are commonly delegated to representatives who act on behalf of their group. Representatives are engaged because it is impractical or even impossible to involve all group members, because matters are believed to be better handled by individuals with specific social skills or expertise, or because the group feels a need to shift responsibility and accountability (Mnookin & Susskind, 1999; Pruitt & Carnevale, 1993). The functioning of representatives, in terms of the quality of the agreements they reach and the effectiveness with which they "sell" their negotiated agreements, has a profound impact on the functioning and performance of (sub-units within) groups and organizations (also see Akkerman and colleagues, this volume).

Representatives are vital in assisting groups to communicate, monitor and promote their interests, facilitate change and innovation, and exchange and disseminate information within and across group and societal boundaries (Eisenhardt, 1989; Jensen & Meckling, 1976). Two types of processes operate in representative negotiations: (a) top-down influences in which representatives are influenced by constituent pressures and the broader intergroup conflict within which they operate; and (b) bottom-up influences in which representatives influence constituency dynamics and the broader intergroup relations (De Dreu, Aaldering, & Saygi, in press). The intergroup level delineates the ways groups relate to each other in terms of objective power differentials and history of trust and cooperation vs. hostility, and in terms of intergroup stereotypes, prejudices, fear, and anxiety. The constituency level addresses within-group dynamics, such as whether the constituency is internally divided with regard to the desired negotiation outcome, and how such hawkish versus dovish factions relate to each other (e.g. whether some factions are more powerful than others). Also relevant at this level is how constituencies respond to the negotiation process and outcome— do they buy into a negotiated agreement or not, and why? Finally, the representative level involves the influence of individual-level cognitions (depending on areas of expertise, negotiation skills, expectations, etc.), emotions arising from the conflict, and motives vis-à-vis the counterpart (cooperation vs. competition), the negotiation problem (superficial vs. deep understanding), and the constituency (desire to impress, build a reputation, save face).

Top-down influences: how constituencies affect representative negotiations

There is extant research showing that constituencies have substantial influence over representatives and their negotiation strategies. First and foremost, representatives turn to their constituencies more, and work harder to defend and promote their interests when they need their constituencies' approval of the agreement, or when the constituency has the capacity to reward or punish the representative. Such accountability per se increases representatives' competitiveness toward the out-group protagonist (e.g. O'Connor, 1997; Van Kleef, Steinel, Van Knippenberg, Hogg, & Svensson, 2007). Accountability also amplifies the effects of implicit norms. When the in-group constituency seems to value cooperation with the out-group, accountability increases the representative's cooperativeness (Gelfand & Realo, 1999). As a case in point, Benton and Druckman (1973) compared representative negotiation behavior with cooperative, competitive, or no instructions from the constituency and found that representatives without instructions negotiated as competitively as the ones who received competitive instructions. When the constituency gave cooperative instructions, however, the representative negotiated accordingly and conceded more than those in the competitive and no instructions conditions. Whereas the study by Benton and Druckman involved a single-issue negotiation, it follows that when the negotiation has integrative potential, in-group norms for cooperation are likely to promote constructive negotiation strategies in the representative, who then becomes more likely to craft mutually beneficial and sustainable agreements with the other side.

One problem with the above works is that it proceeded, explicitly or implicitly, on the basis of the assumption that constituents operate as monolithic entities that speak with one voice. Clearly, as the opening examples of some recent and publicly visible negotiations reveal, constituents are rarely homogeneous and quite often deeply divided and organized into factions that have diametrically opposed views on what is, and is not, important in the negotiation with the out-group, or about the strategies to achieve certain goals (Halevy, 2008). To examine the influence of heterogeneous constituencies, Steinel and colleagues (2009) distinguished between hawkish and dovish factions, with hawkish factions promoting competition towards the out-group and dovish factions advocating a lenient and cooperative approach. Their experiment showed that whereas an all-dove constituency led the representative to negotiate more cooperatively than an all-hawk constituency, a hawkish minority in a predominantly dovish constituency drives representatives to negotiate as competitively as they do with an all-hawk constituency. A dovish minority in a predominantly hawkish constituency was, however, largely ignored. Put differently, hawkish factions appeared to have a disproportionate influence on the representatives' negotiation strategy (also see Aaldering & De Dreu, 2013).

Bottom-up influences in representative negotiation

The bottom-up processes outlined above received far less attention in (experimental) research and/or theorizing. This notwithstanding, the possibility of such bottom-up processes in representative negotiation resonates with Kelman's (2006) insight that between-representative contacts and relationships "spread out" in their respective constituencies and may positively influence broader intergroup perceptions and exchanges. His problem-solving workshop approach involves bringing together influential but unofficial representatives of states or groups involved in a destructive conflict who engage in constructive, face-to-face discussions aimed at creating mutual understanding and respect (Burton, 1969; Fisher, 2006). Kelman uncovered (Kelman, 1995, 2005) that these informal exchanges between different target groups led to cognitive changes in the view of the conflict and the other party, and improved relationships between different targets which later spread out to the constituencies and broader intergroup relations (Fisher, 2006; also see Davidson & Montville, 1981; Saunders, 1999).

The possibility of bottom-up influences also fits intergroup contact theory (e.g. Allport, 1954; Tropp & Pettigrew, 2007), which assumes that having contact with an out-group member can influence the perception of the entire out-group. As a case in point, Tam and colleagues (2009) investigated the connection between intergroup contact and intergroup trust in relations between Catholics and Protestants in Northern Ireland. They argued that extended contact would play a particularly important role in establishing out-group trust, and indeed found that trust was a significant mediator of the effects of both direct and extended contact on perceptions and behavioral tendencies toward the out-group. Even among those lacking direct contacts with the out-group, out-group perceptions improved when there was extended contact that built trust with respect to the out-group.

To examine bottom-up influences in representative negotiation, Saygi and colleagues (in press) conducted a series of tightly controlled laboratory experiments. Results showed that competitive (as opposed to cooperative or neutral) communication by the out-group representative decreased satisfaction with the outcome among in-group members, and increased their tendencies to derogate the out-group. In another series of studies, Saygi and colleagues (2013) showed that a cooperative out-group representative elicited more favorable perceptions of the entire out-group only when the representative was seen as a very typical (out-group) member, and one that was not particularly competent. When typicality was low, or competence was high, in-group members became suspicious about the reasons for the out-group representative's cooperativeness, and actually came to see the entire out-group as relatively competitive. These studies suggest that creating favorable intergroup relations through constructive representative negotiation is possible, but fragile and easily backfires.

Summary and main conclusions

Intergroup conflict emerges when individuals feel or expect that the actions or inactions of another group did, or will deprive their own group of reasonable outcomes. Such outcome deprivation triggers a variety of affective, cognitive, motivational, and behavioral responses, including the tendency to cooperate more with fellow in-group members, to compete more against the rival out-group, to reward such behavioral tendencies in fellow in-group members, and to punish its absence. Groups deprive other groups of reasonable outcomes because of two basic motives—the greedy desire to subordinate the rival out-group and to acquire its resources, and the desire to protect and defend oneself and one's in-group from a potentially dangerous competitor (i.e. "attack is the best defense").

The second main section of this chapter focused on the regulation of intergroup competition and conflict through representative negotiation. We approached this from a multilevel perspective, arguing that representatives are both influenced by their respective constituencies as well as the overarching intergroup relations. Past work in this area has focused primarily on (constituency-related) factors driving representative negotiation strategies and outcomes. But almost without exception, researchers in this area have assumed that constituencies are monolithic entities that speak with one voice. Given that most constituencies are divided rather than united, we propose that research needs to be more systematically directed to the influence of different forms and shapes of within-constituency conflicts and disagreements on between-representative negotiations. Furthermore, we noted that exceedingly little work exists on bottom-up influence processes, and we call for more research into the effects of representative negotiation on intergroup relations. Such research would allow a solid integration of currently disconnected theoretical perspectives, including social identity theory, interdependency theory, and negotiation theory.

Intergroup competition and conflict have been critical throughout human evolution, and they constitute one of the key problems facing contemporary societies. Although the costs of intense conflicts are impossible to overestimate, it must be acknowledged that intergroup competition and conflict serve other functions than mere destruction. Uncovering these functions, and the conditions under which they come about, will ultimately provide a basis for sophisticated and effective interventions in destructive intergroup conflicts.

Notes

1 Note that it may be that one's group gains more than its protagonist but still experiences outcome deprivation because it feels that the relative gain is too small in light of what would have been reasonable. Likewise, one's group may receive less than its protagonist but still not experience outcome deprivation because it feels that the relative loss is justifiable and in line with proper standards and principles (e.g. Jost et al., 2001; also see Adams, 1965).

2 Hurting stalemates are not the only reason for parties to a conflict to engage in negotiation and joint problem solving. Sometimes disputants start negotiations because they perceive mutually enticing opportunities or seek to avoid an impending catastrophe

(Carnevale & De Dreu, 2006). These two motives refer to negotiation as "deal making," and not to negotiation as a means of conflict management and dispute resolution—the focus of this chapter.

References

Aaldering, H., & De Dreu, C. K. W. (2013). Why hawks fly higher than doves: Intragroup conflict in representative negotiation. *Group Processes and Intergroup Relations, 15,* 713–724.

Abbink, K., Brandts, J., Hermann, B., & Orzen, H. (2010). Intergroup conflict and intragroup punishment in an experimental contest game. *American Economic Review, 100,* 420–447.

Adams, J. S. (1965). Inequity in social exchange. In L. Berkowitz (Ed.), *Advances in experimental social psychology* (Vol. 2, pp. 267–299). New York: Academic Press.

Alexander, R. D. (1990). How did humans evolve? Reflections on the uniquely unique species. *Museum of Zoology (Special Publication No. 1).* Ann Arbor: The University of Michigan.

Allport, G. W. (1954). *The nature of prejudice.* Cambridge, MA: Addison-Wesley.

Arrow, H. (2007). The sharp end of altruism. *Science, 318,* 581–582.

Bacharach, S. B., & Lawler, E. J. (1981). *Bargaining: Power, tactics and outcomes.* Greenwich, CT: JAI Press.

Baer, M., Leenders, R. T. A. J., Oldham, G. R., & Vadera, A. (2010). Win or lose the battle for creativity: The power and perils of intergroup competition. *Academy of Management Journal, 53,* 827–845.

Bar-Tal, D., Raviv, A., & Freund, T. (1994). An anatomy of political beliefs: A study of their centrality, contents, and epistemic authority. *Journal of Applied Social Psychology, 24,* 849–872.

Benton, A. A., & Druckman, D. (1973). Salient solutions and the bargaining behavior of representatives and non-representatives. *International Journal of Group Tensions, 3,* 28–39.

Berg, J., Dickhaut, J., & McCabe, K. (1995). Trust, reciprocity, and social history. *Games and Economic Behavior, 10,* 122–142.

Berry, J. W. (1984). Cultural relations in plural societies: Alternatives to segregation and their sociopsychological implications. In N. Miller & M. B. Brewer (Eds.), *Groups in contact: The psychology of desegregation* (pp. 11–27). New York: Academic Press.

Blake, R. R., & Mouton, J. S. (1961). Loyalty of representatives to ingroup positions during intergroup competition. *Sociometry, 24,* 177–183.

Bornstein, G. (2003). Intergroup conflict: Individual, group, and collective interests. *Personality and Social Psychology Review, 7,* 129–145.

Bornstein, G., & Ben-Yossef, M. (1994). Cooperation in intergroup and single-group social dilemmas. *Journal of Experimental Social Psychology, 30,* 52–67.

Bornstein, G., Crum, L., Wittenbraker, J., Harring, K., Insko, C. A., & Thibaut, J. (1983). On the measurement of social orientations in the minimal group paradigm. *European Journal of Social Psychology, 13,* 321–350.

Brewer, M. B. (1999). The psychology of prejudice: Ingroup love or outgroup hate? *Journal of Social Issues, 55,* 429–444.

Brown, M. E., & Rosecrance, R. N. (1999). *The costs of conflict.* Boston: Rowman & Littlefield.

Burton, J. W. (1969). *Conflict and communication: The use of controlled communication in international relations.* London: MacMillan.

—— (1990). *Conflict: Resolution and prevention.* New York: St. Martin's.

Carnevale, P. J. D. (2007). Creativity in the outcomes of conflict. In E.C. Marcus, M. Deutsch & P. T. Coleman (Eds.) *The handbook of conflict resolution: Theory and practice* (2nd edn). (pp. 414–435). Hoboken, NJ: Wiley.

Choi, J-K., & Bowles, S. (2007). The coevolution of parochial altruism and war. *Science, 318,* 636–640.

Cohen, T. R., & Insko, C. A. (2008). War and peace: Possible approaches to reducing intergroup conflict. *Perspectives on Psychological Science, 3,* 87–93.

Colman, A. M. (2003). Cooperation, psychological game theory, and limitations of rationality in social interaction. *Behavioral and Brain Sciences, 26,* 139–198.

Coombs, C. H. (1973). A reparameterization of the prisoner's dilemma game. *Behavioral Science, 18,* 424–428.

Coser, L. A. (1956). *The functions of social conflict.* Glencoe, IL: Free Press.

Davidson, W. D., & Montville, J. V. (1981). Foreign policy according to Freud. *Foreign Policy, 45,* 145–157.

Dawes, R. M. (1980). Social dilemmas. *Annual Review of Psychology, 31,* 169–193.

De Dreu, C. K. W. (2006). When too much and too little hurts: Evidence for a curvilinear relationship between task conflict and innovation in teams. *Journal of Management, 32,* 83–107.

—— (2008). The vice and virtue of workplace conflict: Food for (pessimistic) thought. *Journal of Organizational Behavior, 29,* 5–18.

—— (2010a). Social conflict: The emergence and consequences of struggle and negotiation. In: S. T. Fiske, D. T. Gilbert & G. Lindzey (Eds.). *Handbook of Social Psychology* (5th edn, vol. 2, pp. 983–1023). New York: Wiley.

—— (2010b). Social value orientation moderates in-group love but not out-group hate in competitive intergroup conflict. *Group Processes and Intergroup Relations, 13,* 701–713.

De Dreu, C. K. W., Aaldering, H., & Saygi, O. (in press). Conflict and negotiation within and between groups. In: J. Dovidio & J. Simpson (Eds.), *Handbook on interpersonal relations and group processes.*

De Dreu, C. K. W., Greer, L. L., Handgraaf, M. J. J., Shalvi, S., Van Kleef, G. A., Baas, M., Ten Velden, F. S., Van Dijk, E., & Feith, S. W. W. (2010). The neuropeptide oxytocin regulates parochial altruism in intergroup conflict among humans. *Science, 328,* 1408–1411.

De Dreu, C. K. W., & Nijstad, B. A. (2008). Conflict and creativity: Threat-rigidity or motivated focus? *Journal of Personality and Social Psychology, 95,* 648–661.

De Dreu, C. K. W., & Weingart, L. R. (2003). Task versus relationship conflict, team performance and team member satisfaction: A meta-analysis. *Journal of Applied Psychology, 88,* 741–749.

Demoulin, S., & De Dreu, C. K. W. (2010). Introduction: Negotiation in intergroup conflict. *Group Processes and Intergroup Relations, 13,* 675–683.

Deutsch, M. (1973). *The resolution of conflict: Constructive and destructive processes.* New Haven: Yale University Press.

De Wit, F. R. C., Greer, L. L., & Jehn, K. A. (2012). The paradox of intra-group conflict: A meta-analysis. *Journal of Applied Psychology, 97,* 360–390.

Dovidio, J. F., & Gaertner, S. L. (2010). Intergroup bias. In S. T. Fiske, D. T. Gilbert & G. Lindzey (Eds.). *Handbook of Social Psychology* (5th edn, vol. 2, pp. 1084–1123). New York: Wiley.

Eisenhardt, K. M. (1989). Agency theory: An assessment and review. *Academy of Management Review*, *14*, 57–74.

Erev, I., Bornstein, G., & Galili, R. (1993). Constructive intergroup competition as a solution to the free-rider problem: A field experiment. *Journal of Experimental Social Psychology*, *29*, 463–478.

Fehr, E., & Fishbacher, U. (2004). Social norms and human cooperation. *Trends in Cognitive Sciences*, *8*, 187–190.

Fisher, R. J. (2006). The problem solving workshop as a method of research. In P. J. Carnevale & C. K. W. De Dreu (Eds.), *Methods of Negotiation Research* (pp. 49–60). Boston: Martinus Nijhoff.

Fiske, S. T. (2002). What we know about bias and intergroup conflict, the problem of the century. *Current Directions in Psychological Science*, *11*, 123–128.

Gelfand, M. J., & Realo, A. (1999). Individualism-Collectivism and Accountability in Intergroup Negotiations. *Journal of Applied Psychology*, *84*, 721–736.

Gintis, H., Bowles, S., Boyd, R., & Fehr, E. (2003). Explaining altruistic behavior in humans. *Evolution and Human Behavior*, *24*, 153–172.

Greenwald, A. G., Nosek, B. A., & Banaji, M. R. (2003). Understanding and using the implicit association test: I. An improved scoring algorithm. *Journal of Personality and Social Psychology*, *85*, 197–216.

Halevy, N. (2008). Team negotiation: Social, epistemic, economic, and psychological consequences of subgroup conflict. *Personality and Social Psychology Bulletin*, *34*, 1687–1702.

Halevy, N., Bornstein, G., & Sagiv, L. (2008). "In-group love" and "out-group hate" as motives for individual participation in intergroup conflict. *Psychological Science*, *19*, 405–411.

Halevy, N., Chou, E. Y., Cohen, T. R., & Bornstein, G. (2010). Relative deprivation and intergroup competition. *Group Processes and Intergroup Relations*, *13*, 685–700.

Halevy, N., Chou, E. Y., Cohen, T. R., & Livingston, R. W. (2012). Status conferral in intergroup social dilemmas: Behavioral antecedents and consequences of prestige and dominance. *Journal of Personality and Social Psychology*, *102*, 351–366.

Halevy, N., Weisel, O., & Bornstein, G. (2012). In-group love and out-group hate in repeated interaction between groups. *Journal of Behavioral Decision Making*, *25*, 188–195.

Hewstone, M., Rubin, M., & Willis, H. (2002). Intergroup bias. *Annual Review of Psychology*, *53*, 575–604.

Janis, I. L. (1972). *Victims of Groupthink.* Boston: Houghton Mifflin.

Jehn, K., & Bendersky, C. (2003). Intragroup conflict in organizations: A contingency perspective on the conflict-outcome relationship. In R. M. Kramer & B. M. Staw (Eds.), *Research in Organizational Behavior* (vol. 25, pp. 187–242). Amsterdam, The Netherlands: Elsevier.

Jensen, M. C., & Meckling, W. H. (1976). Theory of the firm: Managerial behavior, agency costs and ownership structure. *Journal of Financial Economics*, *3*, 305–360.

Jervis, R. (1976). *Perception and misperception in international relations.* Princeton, NJ: Princeton University Press.

Jost, J. T., Burgess, D., & Mosso, C. O. (2001). Conflicts of legitimation among self, group, and system: The integrative potential of system justification theory. In J. Jost & B.

Major (Eds.), *The psychology of legitimacy* (pp. 363–390). Cambridge, England: Cambridge University Press.

Kelley, H. H., & Thibaut, J. W. (1978). *Interpersonal relations: A theory of interdependence.* New York: Academic Press.

Kelman, H. C. (1995). Contributions of an unofficial conflict resolution effort to the Israeli-Palestinian Breakthrough. *Negotiation Journal, 11,* 19–27.

—— (2005). Interactive problem solving in the Israeli-Palestinian case: Past contributions and present challenges. In R. J. Fisher (Ed.), *Paving the way: Contributions of interactive conflict resolution to peacemaking* (pp. 41–63). Lanham, MD: Lexington Books.

—— (2006). Interests, relationships, identities: Three central issues for individuals and groups in negotiating their social environment. *Annual Review of Psychology, 57,* 1–26.

Komorita, S. S., & Parks, C. D. (1995). Interpersonal relations: Mixed-motive interaction. *Annual Review of Psychology, 46,* 183–207.

Lax, D. A., & Sebenius, J. K. (1986). *The manager as negotiator.* New York: Free Press.

Lindskold, S., & Han, G. (1988). GRIT as a foundation for integrative bargaining. *Personality and Social Psychology Bulletin, 14,* 335–345.

Luce, D. R., & Raiffa, H. (1957). *Games and decisions: Introduction and critical survey.* Oxford, UK: Wiley.

Mnookin, R. H., & Susskind, L. E. (1999). *Negotiating on behalf of others: Advice to lawyers, business executives, sports agents, diplomats, politicians, and everyone else.* Thousand Oaks, CA: Sage.

Morgan, P. M., & Tindale, R. S. (2002). Group versus individual performance in mixed-motive situations: Exploring an inconsistency. *Organizational Behavior and Human Decision Processes, 87,* 44–65.

O'Connor, K. (1997). Groups and solos in context: The effects of accountability on team negotiation. *Organizational Behavior and Human Decision Processes, 72,* 384–407.

Polzer, J. T. (1996). Intergroup negotiations. The effects of negotiating teams. *Journal of Conflict Resolution, 40,* 678–698.

Pruitt, D. G. (1998). Social conflict. In D. Gilbert, S. T. Fiske, & G. Lindzey (Eds.), *Handbook of social psychology* (4th edn, Vol. 2, pp. 89–150). New York: McGraw-Hill.

—— (2007). Readiness theory and the Northern Ireland conflict. *American Behavioral Scientist, 50,* 1520–1541.

Pruitt, D. G., & Carnevale, P. J. (1993). *Negotiation in social conflict.* Buckingham, UK: Open University Press.

Pruitt, D. G., & Kimmel, M. J. (1977). Twenty years of experimental gaming: Critique, synthesis, and suggestions for the future. *Annual Review of Psychology, 28,* 363–392.

Pruitt, D. G., & Rubin, J. Z. (1986). *Social conflict: Escalation, stalemate, and settlement.* New York: McGraw-Hill.

Rapoport, A., & Bornstein, G. (1987). Intergroup competition for the provision of binary public goods. *Psychological review, 94,* 291–299.

Rapoport, A., & Guyer, M. (1966). A taxonomy of 2 X 2 games. *General systems, 11,* 203–214.

Rouhana, N. N., & Bar-Tal, D. (1998). Psychological dynamics of intractable ethnonational conflicts—the Israeli-Palestinian case. *American Psychologist, 53,* 761–770.

Saunders, H. (1999). *A public peace process: Sustained dialogue to transform racial and ethnic conflicts.* New York: St. Martin's Press.

Saygi, O., Greer, L. L., Van Kleef, G. A., & De Dreu, C. K. W. (in press). Competitive representative negotiations worsen intergroup relations. *Group Processes and Intergroup Relations.*

—— (2013). Intergroup relations are endangered when cooperative out-group representatives are seen as a-typical or competent. *Unpublished Manuscript.*

Schelling, T. (1960/1980). *The strategy of conflict.* Cambridge: Harvard University Press.

Schulz-Hardt, S., Brodbeck, F. C., Mojzisch, A., Kerschreiter, R., & Frey, D. (2006). Group decision making in hidden profile situations: Dissent as a facilitator for decision quality. *Journal of Personality and Social Psychology, 91,* 1080–1093.

Sherif, M., & Sherif, C. W. (1953). *Groups in harmony and tension; an integration of studies of intergroup relations.* New York: Harper and Brothers.

Shinada, M., & Yamagishi, T. (2007). Punishing free riders: direct and indirect promotion of cooperation. *Evolution and Human Behavior, 28,* 330–339.

Shinada, M., Yamagishi, T., & Ohmura, Y. (2004). False friends are worse than bitter enemies: "Altruistic" punishment of in-group members. *Evolution and Human Behavior, 25,* 379–393.

Simunovic, D., Mifune, N., & Yamagishi, T. (2013). Preemptive strike: An experimental study of fear-based aggression. *Journal of Experimental Social Psychology, 49,* 1120–1123.

Slaikue, K. A., & Hasson, R. H. (1998). *Controlling the costs of conflict.* San Francisco: Jossey-Bass.

Steinel, W., De Dreu, C. K. W., Ouwehand, E., & Ramírez-Marín, J. Y. (2009). When constituencies speak in multiple tongues: The relative persuasiveness of hawkish minorities in representative negotiation. *Organizational Behavior and Human Decision Processes, 109,* 67–78.

Tajfel, H., & Turner, J. C. (1986). The social identity theory of intergroup behavior. In S. Worchel & W. G. Austin (Eds.), *Psychology of intergroup relations.* Chicago: Nelson- Hall.

Tam, T., Hewstone, M., Kenworthy, J., & Cairns, E. (2009). Intergroup trust in Northern Ireland. *Personality and Social Psychology Bulletin, 35,* 45–59.

Ten Velden, F. S., Beersma, B., & De Dreu, C. K. W. (2011). When competition breeds equality: Effects of appetitive versus aversive competition in negotiation. *Journal of Experimental Social Psychology, 47,* 1127–1133.

Tropp, L. R., & Pettigrew, T. (2007). A meta-analytic test of intergroup contact theory. *Journal of Personality and Social Psychology, 90,* 751–783.

Van Kleef, G. A., Steinel, W., Van Knippenberg, D., Hogg, M. A., & Svensson, A. (2007). Group member prototypicality and intergroup negotiation: How one's standing in the group affects negotiation behavior. *British Journal of Social Psychology, 46,* 129–152.

Van Lange, P. A. M., Liebrand, W. B. G., & Kuhlman, D. M. (1990). Causal attribution of choice behavior in three n-person prisoner's dilemmas. *Journal of Experimental Social Psychology, 26,* 34–48.

Walton, R. E., & McKersie, R. (1965). *A behavioral theory of labor negotiation.* New York: McGraw-Hill.

Weber, J. M., Kopelman, S., & Messick, D. M. (2004). A conceptual review of decision making in social dilemmas: Applying a logic of appropriateness, *Personality and Social Psychology Review, 8,* 281–307.

Wildschut, T., Pinter, B., Vevea, J. L., Insko, C. A., & Schopler, J. (2003). Beyond the group mind: A quantitative review of the interindividual-intergroup discontinuity effect. *Psychological Bulletin, 129,* 698–722.

Yzerbyt, V., & Demoulin, S. (2010). Intergroup relations. In S. T. Fiske. D. T. Gilbert & G. Lindzey (Eds.). *Handbook of Social Psychology* (5th edn, vol.2, pp. 1024–1083). New York: Wiley.

Zartman, W. I. (1991). The Structure of Negotiation. In V. A. Kremenyuk (Ed.). *International Negotiation: Analysis, Approaches, Issues* (pp. 65–77). San Francisco: Jossey-Bass.

2   How values change a conflict

Fieke Harinck and Naomi Ellemers[1]

Introduction

> The issue or issues in conflict between nations, groups, or individuals may be diffuse and generalized, as in ideological conflict, or specific and limited, as in the conflict over possession of a certain property; [...]; it may permit compromise or require the submission of one side to the other.
>
> (Deutsch, 1973, p. 5)

Traditionally, conflict research has primarily addressed conflicts about the allocation of scarce *resources*, such as time, money, or space. This research has generated a vast amount of theory on and insight in how people deal with these conflicts (e.g. De Dreu, 2010; Pruitt & Carnevale, 1993; Thompson, Wang, & Gunia, 2010). However, due to globalization, migration and technological developments such as the internet and social media, we increasingly encounter different groups of people with different norms, values and belief systems (Gesthuizen, Savelkoul & Scheepers, this volume). Differences in core *values* (e.g. justice or religion), which often are embedded in people's socio-cultural identities, have become common sources of conflict. Social psychological theory and research on conflict have not systematically addressed conflict about values as a distinct type of conflict that might require specific insights.

We propose that value conflict nevertheless deserves further attention, as this type of conflict can have profound implications at different levels of society. At an interpersonal level, different work values or work ethics can raise conflict among co-workers (Ellemers & Rink, 2005); at an intergroup level, teachers and parents may have incompatible ideas on how to raise children; and at the societal level, members of different ethnic groups often are unable to appreciate each other's behavioral norms or cultural practices. In all these instances, conflicting values can and will elicit interpersonal and intergroup tensions, while it is not self-evident how these may be addressed with traditional means of conflict resolution, such as negotiation. This is why it is important to examine more specifically how value conflict develops, when it escalates, and how it can be resolved.

In this chapter, we will summarize recent insights gathered in the field of value conflict, to specify when, how, and why value conflict differs from resource conflict. We argue and present evidence that value conflicts are harder to resolve because people take them more personally and because value conflicts seem more (identity) threatening than resource conflicts. We will conclude this chapter by presenting an agenda for future research. Additionally, we will specify how current insights into the characteristics of value conflicts carry practical implications for the resolution of this type of conflict.

Conflict

A conflict is the process that unfolds when one party perceives that another party negatively affects something that he or she cares about (Thomas, 1992; De Dreu et al., this volume). This "something he or she cares about" is the conflict issue— what the conflict is about. In principle, the issue can be anything, ranging from concrete scarce resources such as money, space or time to more abstract values such as principles, ideals or norms about how a person should behave. The different aspects involved in the conflict process are indicated in Figure 2.1 (see De Dreu, Harinck, Van Vianen [1999] for an extensive discussion of this model).

In the present contribution we build on this general model to propose that there is added value in specifying whether the issues relevant to the conflict are dominated by concerns over resources or concerns about values. Specifically, we argue that the domination of resources or values affects the entire conflict process that ensues (Druckman, Rozelle, & Zechmeister, 1977; Druckman, Broome, & Korper, 1988; Harinck, 2004; Harinck, De Dreu, & Van Vianen, 2000; Harinck, & De Dreu, 2004, 2008; Wade-Benzoni, Hoffman, Thompson, Moore, Gillespie, & Bazerman, 2003), as indicated in Figure 2.1. We are aware that real-life conflict may contain several issues, of both types. As such, the clear-cut distinction between resource conflict and value conflict that we make is aimed at understanding and investigating the specific influence of these issues on the conflict process. The processes in actual conflicts, however, will resemble resource and value conflict processes to the extent that resource or value issues are dominant in that specific conflict. In fact, distinguishing between the different issues might help to solve the conflict; either by separating resources from values, or by focusing on or emphasizing those issues that seem to be most successful to resolve. In the remainder of this chapter, we will elaborate on characteristic differences between conflicts depending on whether they are dominated by resources or by values by reviewing empirical evidence that demonstrates these differences for each of the phases in the conflict process.

Conflict issues

Standard approaches define conflict as disagreement about the distribution of resources such as money, time, space, or natural resources (Pruitt & Carnevale, 1993; Thompson et al., 2010). During the past years, we have learned a lot about how resource conflicts develop, and how they can be resolved (De Dreu et al.,

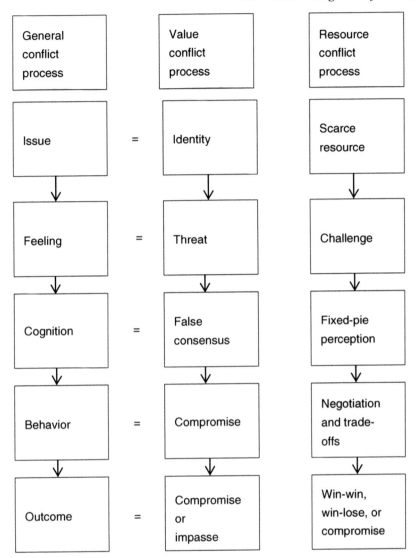

Figure 2.1 The conflict process model for value conflict and resource conflict

1999; De Dreu et al., this volume; Bazerman, Curhan, Moore, & Valley, 2000). These insights primarily elucidate ways towards conflict resolution through *negotiation* about the allocation of resources to different parties (Pruitt & Carnevale, 1993). However, this knowledge does not help us to understand the origins, development, or resolution of *value* conflicts.

A value conflict emerges when parties fail to understand each other's normative convictions and arguments about what is appropriate, reasonable, or just, in a particular situation. Value conflicts that receive prominent coverage in the media indicate instances in which people differ in their endorsement of broad (religious) value systems. A case in point is the discussion of whether or not government employees should be allowed to wear a headscarf to work. However, value conflicts can also emerge due to more domain-specific differences in what people think is the most appropriate course of action in a particular context (Druckman et al., 1977). For instance, two colleagues working together may experience value conflict when they have different views on the moral acceptability of breaking company rules to accommodate customer preferences.

Regardless of whether they are broadly or narrowly defined, values tend to be anchored in our belief systems and socio-cultural identities. Values indicate who we are, what we stand for, and where we belong. The values we endorse convey our beliefs about core aspects of the way we relate to others; values capture our notions of justice, and indicate what we think is morally right or wrong. Values invoke and reveal our identity, and this in itself is a major reason why value conflicts are so hard to resolve. This is the case because value conflicts are likely to be taken personally: someone who disagrees with your norms and ideals implicitly devalues core aspects of your sense of self. As a result, value conflicts can be seen to represent a threat to *identity*. People like to maintain a positive self-view, and being able to think of oneself as a good person with valid norms and values is a major source of well-being. Thus, when someone challenges your norms or disagrees with your values, they convey that they consider your behaviors and judgment to be wrong, implying you are bad person (see De Dreu & Van Knippenberg, 2005, for a similar argument).

We argue that the nature of the conflict issue affects the entire conflict process, from early conflict experiences and interpersonal interactions when the conflict unfolds, to the conflict outcomes. This may have far-reaching implications, as illustrated by recent work on the interpersonal effects of emotions. Evidence from different studies consistently shows that negotiating parties are more likely to give in to an angry counterpart than to a neutral or happy counterpart (e.g. Van Kleef, De Dreu, & Manstead, 2004a, 2004b). However, this may be quite different in the case of values. As value disagreements are taken more personally, it can be expected that people generally are less likely to give in in the case of a value conflict compared to a resource conflict; people usually do not bend their principles when someone is angry with them. Instead, expressions of anger by another party may make them even more determined to hold on to their values and principles.

This possibility was examined in recent research by Harinck and Van Kleef (2012). They investigated people's reactions in a resource or value conflict after having received an angry or neutral negative response to a request they made. Results showed that participants in the resource conflict condition displayed the standard response to anger; they perceived the angry refusal as relatively fair, and took care not to escalate the conflict. Participants in the value conflict condition perceived an angry refusal as more unfair and were more willing to escalate the conflict than participants in the resource conflict condition. When the request had been denied in an emotionally neutral fashion participants' responses took an intermediate position, regardless of the conflict issue. This result suggests that the conflict issue moderates the interpersonal effects of anger expression; compared to resource conflict, in which anger makes the other party more conciliatory, displays of anger backfire in the case of conflicting values, in that these make the other party relatively less conciliatory, rendering escalation more likely.

In Figure 2.1, we specify how the different stages in the conflict process are different for value conflict compared to resource conflict. We will now consider these differences more specifically.

Conflict experience

The conflict experience encompasses the cognitions, feelings and motivations related to the conflict issue and to the other party (De Dreu et al., 1999). People may feel very strongly about the conflict issue or they may be more indifferent. They may view the other party either as a threat—when they fear the other party will defeat them—or as a challenge—when they are confident they can defeat, convince or overrule the other party. The cognitions they form about the conflict are also important because attractive, lasting, conflict solutions cannot be achieved without an accurate understanding of what each party wants and does not want, and preferably also why they want it (Fisher, Ury, & Patton, 1991).

Perceived common ground

We argue that from the very early stages, the experience of a value conflict differs from the experience of a resource conflict. Before the conflict unfolds, parties are likely to expect more common ground and more similarities between their mutual preferences when the issue under debate concerns a value rather than a scarce resource (Harinck et al., 2000; Kouzakova, Ellemers, Harinck, & Scheepers, 2012; Thompson & Gonzalez, 1996). We argue this is the case because of *false consensus*; the phenomenon that people tend to overestimate the extent to which others agree with their opinions and priorities (Gilovich, 1990; Mullen, Atkins, Champion, Edwards, Hardy, & Story, 1985; Ross, Greene, & House, 1977). In their seminal study demonstrating this effect, Ross, Greene, & House (1977) asked participants whether they would be willing to walk around on campus wearing a sandwich board with the text "Repent." Those who agreed estimated that 64 percent of their fellow students would also agree to do so, whereas those who refused estimated that only 23 percent of their fellow students would agree. Similar findings were obtained with a range of different methodologies and measures. Indeed, a meta-analysis by Mullen et al. (1985) showed that the false consensus effect can be reliably found in the domain of personal preferences and expectations, personal problems, personal activities, political preferences and behavioral choices.

While the false consensus effect is now well-established as such, so far it has not been used to inform research on different types of conflict. In the case of a scarce resource, the false consensus effect will elicit perceptions of conflicting interests. That is, when there is one scarce resource (for example, a piece of land) a conflict may arise when two (or more) parties want to have control over it, as they (falsely) assume that the other party wants it as much (or as little) as they do. The nature of the scarce resource invites the conviction that the more one party receives, the less is left for the other party (a so-called zero sum or fixed-pie perception). Thus, assuming that others will have similar preferences and priorities concerning a scarce resource will raise the expectation of conflicting interests and induce the conviction that one party's gains are the other party's losses (Thompson, & Hastie, 1990).

In the case of values, however, false consensus has just the opposite effect, as it initially leads to an overestimation of the extent to which other people *share the same values* or will tend to agree with one's own point of view. For example, false consensus implies that environmentalists overestimate the number of people that would agree saving the environment is more important than economic growth, while false consensus would lead business owners to overestimate the amount of support for policies stimulating economic growth rather than saving the environment. Thus, when it turns out that others disagree with your values, this tends to be unexpected, raising (unpleasant) surprise in finding out that one's own point of view is less generally accepted than anticipated. Violations of prior expectations generally elicit extreme judgments and negative emotions (Biernat, Vescio, & Billings, 1999; Rink & Ellemers, 2007). Thus, as divergent values become apparent, the unexpected nature of these differences may easily lead parties to overestimate the disagreement between them, making it seem more difficult to overcome or resolve the conflict.

Empirical support for this reasoning was obtained in a series of studies conducted by Harinck et al. (2000) and by Kouzakova, Ellemers, Harinck, & Scheepers (2012). Harinck et al. (2000) used a lawyer–district attorney negotiation paradigm, in which participants engaged in a role-play of a lawyer and a district attorney who negotiated about the penalties for several small offenses. The lawyers were instructed to pursue short and light penalties for their clients, whereas the district attorneys were requested to seek longer and heavier penalties. The conflict issue was manipulated by varying the alleged motives of the lawyer and district attorney for having these preferences. In the resource condition, participants were told to view the outcome of the negotiation in terms of personal interests (e.g. arranging a certain penalty will help their career and increase their personal income). In the value condition, participants were told to view the outcome of the negotiations in terms of values (e.g. arranging a certain penalty is fair and just) (Lewicki, Barry, & Saunders, 2010).

The main finding regarding the conflict experience assessed in this study (Harinck et al., 2000) was that people had stronger fixed-pie perceptions when the conflict issue was framed in terms of resources rather than values. This is consistent with the notion that people have a stronger tendency to anticipate conflicting preferences in a resource conflict compared to a value conflict. Indeed, assuming similar preferences when a scarce resource is at stake leads to the perception and expectation of a zero-sum situation in which each party overrates the extent to which the other party wants the same resource. By contrast, especially in the early stages of the conflictual situation—when very little information was available about mutual preferences and priorities—parties in the value conflict assumed similarity between themselves and the other party. This is in line with our analysis based on the false consensus effect.

Kouzakova et al. (2012) extended these findings. One study (Kouzakova et al., 2012, Study 2) followed up on prior evidence examining the impact of emphasizing values versus resources in the same conflict. This study employed a travel paradigm where participants discussed with a counterpart about the acceptability of air travel to reach a holiday destination. All participants were induced to take a stance against air travel. In the value condition, participants defended their resistance to air travel by referring to a value—the importance of environmental protection. In the resource condition, the same position was defended by referring to limited resources, in this case budgetary constraints. Again, before participants knew their counterpart's position or were able to recognize they held conflicting preferences, people anticipated the other party's preferences to be more similar to their own in the value condition compared to the resource condition. Accordingly, in the value conflict condition participants reported being more surprised to learn that the other party held a different position than they had compared to the resource conflict condition, in which the opposing preference of the other party was in line with initial expectations (Kouzakova et al., 2012).

These initial differences in turn explain the diverging responses displayed during later stages of the conflict. That is, because the discovery of opposing viewpoints was more in violation of prior expectations of consensus in the case of a value conflict, once the conflict was recognized and out in the open, parties perceived less common ground and saw less opportunity for reconciliation in the value conflict condition compared to the resource conflict condition. Evidence for this effect was documented in another experiment (Kouzakova et al., 2012; Study 1). In this study, Kouzakova et al. (2012) examined a range of six different situations involving conflict, such as travel preferences, apartment rental or making donations. Each conflict situation was described either in terms of diverging principles (regarding the environment, economic growth, helping or charity) to induce a value conflict, or in terms of scarce resources (budgets, bonuses, time) to induce a resource conflict. Participants read two conflict situations—one resource conflict and one value conflict. Across the range of conflict situations, participants indicated that they felt less sympathy for the other point of view and perceived less potential for reaching a joint solution when they were led to perceive the situation as a value conflict rather than a resource conflict.

In sum, we argue that people generally expect other people to share their views, opinions and priorities. In the case of a scarce resource, the notion of false consensus will lead to fixed-pie perceptions—the conviction that one's own preferences are directly opposed to those of the other party. When values are at stake, false consensus will initially lead parties to anticipate relatively little conflict, as they both expect the other party to mirror their values. However, once they find out that the other party disagrees with them, the expectancy violation decreases the sympathy for the other's point of view and reduces the perceived feasibility of reaching a mutually acceptable solution to the conflict.

Self-involvement and identity threat

A second major difference between value and resource conflict affecting the conflict experience is that people feel more personally involved in a value conflict compared to a resource conflict (Kouzakova et al., 2012; Kouzakova, Harinck, Ellemers, & Scheepers, in press). This was demonstrated in the first experiment conducted by Kouzakova et al. (2012, Study 1, see description above). In this study, participants indicated that they felt more personally involved and felt more personally offended by the disagreement when the issue was described as a value conflict compared to a resource conflict. In the second study, people indicated that they identified more with others who shared their point of view in the value condition rather than the resource condition. Both these findings support our reasoning that one's identity tends to be more involved in the case of a value conflict than in a resource conflict, which in turn helps explain why value conflicts easily escalate and are hard to resolve.

Building upon this finding, we further propose that value conflict is more threatening to people than resource conflict. This was examined in another follow-up study (Kouzakova et al., in press), aiming to obtain psychophysiological evidence for the emergence of threat depending on the nature of the conflict issue, through changes in relevant indicators of heart rate and blood pressure. These indicators allow for a distinction between response patterns characteristic for *negative threat* (indicating a preoccupation with situational demands) versus *positive challenge* (indicating the ability to cope with situational demands) (Blascovich, 2008; Blascovich & Tomaka, 1996).

This study used the same travel paradigm as mentioned above (Kouzakova et al., 2012). However, this time participants took a stance in the conflict by indicating their own personal preference against or in favor of going by plane. They then received (preprogrammed) information always suggesting that their travel partner had opted for the other alternative, to create a conflict. Participants were requested to write down five arguments supporting their position, and give a presentation for a webcam to argue for their position, while assessing changes at the physiological level. This type of "speech task" is commonly used in research studying cardiovascular responses indicating negative threat vs. positive challenge (Blascovich, 2008; Blascovich & Tomaka, 1996; De Wit, Scheepers, & Jehn, 2013).

Results of this study were in line with our reasoning, as people in the value conflict condition showed a physiological response indicating negative threat, whereas people in the resource conflict condition showed positive challenge. Thus, it seems that the greater personal involvement in value conflict is reflected in a physiological threat response when people experience a value conflict, whereas people are more positively challenged in a resource conflict. This elicitation of threat in response to a value conflict is likely to hinder a successful resolution of the conflict, instead leading to escalation or a stalemate resulting in withdrawal.

In sum, evidence from different studies consistently suggests that people feel more personally involved and threatened in a value conflict compared to a resource conflict. This knowledge is important, as it provides a first stepping stone for the development of an intervention targeting the specific implications of a value conflict.

Conflict behavior and outcomes

We will now consider conflict behavior and outcomes, as the final stages in the conflict process. Here we build on the distinction generally made in negotiation research between competitive forcing behavior and cooperative problem solving. Forcing behavior aims at agreements in which one party wins and the other party loses while problem-solving behavior aims at agreements in which both parties are well off. Forcing involves claiming behavior such as making positional commitments, the use of arguments, threats and bluffs, and other attempts at persuading the other party to give in. Problem solving, on the other hand, entails information exchange about preferences and priorities, clarifying underlying principles and concerns to find creative alternative solutions—*why* do you want this?—and trading off less important outcomes for more important ones—so-called logrolling. Problem solving can even lead to win–win agreements—agreements in which both parties are better off compared to a fifty-fifty compromise.

A consistent observation is that trading off less important issues for more important issues—an important problem-solving behavior—is considered less acceptable in value conflicts compared to resource conflicts. As a result, win–win agreements are less likely to emerge in value conflicts compared to resource conflicts (Harinck et al., 2000; Harinck & De Dreu, 2004; Tetlock, Kristel, Elson, Green, & Lerner, 2000; Thompson & Gonzalez, 1996; Wade-Benzoni et al., 2002). Prior research by Tetlock and colleagues (Tetlock, 1999; Tetlock et al., 2000; Tetlock, Peterson, & Lerner, 1996) has shown that people react with moral outrage when they have to consider trading off values against resources (money), especially when this concerns one of their core values—so-called "sacred values" such as love, honor or justice. For example, the possibility of selling babies in an auction or putting a price on human lives is considered as a "taboo trade-off," and proposing or even contemplating this possibility generally instigates indignation and moral outrage.

The—theoretical—notion that people will not make trade-offs on their values has also informed research on negotiation. For example, Wade-Benzoni et al. (2002) argue that in value-based negotiation, parties may be unwilling to cooperate because they fear that "mutually beneficial outcomes require trade-offs and compromises that strike at the core of their moral identity" (Wade-Benzoni et al., 2002, p. 42). Thompson and Gonzalez (1997) have provided an elaborate explanation of how values affect negotiations, and they have given suggestions about how to deal with trade-offs concerning values in negotiations. Importantly, however, these theoretical ideas have not been subjected to systematic empirical testing.

This is why Harinck and colleagues (Harinck et al., 2000; Harinck & De Dreu, 2004) set out to examine whether people in value-based negotiations indeed are unwilling to make trade-offs. In the lawyer–district attorney paradigm described earlier, they revealed (Harinck et al., 2000) that people were less willing to trade off one penalty for another penalty in the value condition—in which the justice value was salient—compared to the resource condition—in which the increase of personal income was salient. Moreover, they showed that parties in the value condition reached lower-quality agreements compared to parties in the resource condition due to the lower level of trade-offs that were made in the value condition.

Finally, because of the different response patterns raised, value and resource conflict also elicit different behavioral patterns. Resource conflicts are known to follow a behavioral pattern of "differentiation-before-integration." This term (Walton & McKersie, 1965) is used to convey that parties tend to display competitive behavior when starting a negotiation, trying to prove their point and getting their way in the conflict. However, when both parties act this way and refuse to give in, they are likely to reach a (temporary) impasse, during which they realize that the current competitive strategy is not very successful, allowing them to switch to more cooperative and integrative problem-solving behavior. Indeed, stepping back and reflecting on the conflict process can facilitate a switch from competitive behavior to more cooperative behavior (Harinck & De Dreu, 2004; Brett, Shapiro, & Lytle, 1998; Pruitt & Carnevale, 1993).

Research comparing value vs. resource conflicts has revealed that this pattern is less likely to ensue in the case of a value conflict. Harinck and De Dreu (2004) used the lawyer–district attorney paradigm and assessed the level of integrative behavior as well as the number of temporary impasses. Although parties involved in a value conflict were equally likely to reach an impasse as those in a resource conflict, these temporary impasses were only followed by higher levels of integrative, problem-solving behavior when the conflict was about resources rather than values. These results suggest that the switch from competitive conflict behavior to more integrative conflict behavior—including problem-solving behavior such as making trade-offs and exchanging information—is easier for conflict parties when the conflict is about a scarce resource rather than a (sacred) value.

In fact, because classic win–win solutions prove less attractive or feasible in the case of a value conflict, a compromise solution might not be that bad. Indeed, recent research (Stoeckli & Tanner, in press) suggests that parties in value conflict are more satisfied with compromises than with win–win solutions that are reached via trade-offs. The opposite is true for resource conflict; parties are more satisfied with win–win solutions that are reached via trade-offs compared to compromises. Traditional negotiation research—mainly focusing on resource conflicts— typically considers win–win agreements to be better and more advisable than compromises. From an objective, resource-based point of view, win–win agreements indeed might be the best solution to reach. From a more subjective, value-based point of view, however, parties may be more satisfied when both give in a little on their values to reach an agreement. In any case, the findings above again show that the standard approach to conflict resolution via negotiation and aiming for win–win solutions is less applicable or even less advisable in value conflicts. This implies that at least two things are needed to identify and understand viable solutions for value conflicts: first we need to broaden our view of potential conflict resolutions beyond standard win–win solutions, second we may need to re-evaluate the notion that a compromise always offers a sub-optimal solution. We will elaborate on these two concerns when discussing future research.

Discussion

Our review of relevant literature above has highlighted some major differences between resource conflict and value conflict. Value conflicts: a) pose a stronger identity threat than resource conflicts; b) might benefit from establishing a shared identity; and c) might be better solved by searching for a compromise rather than a win–win agreement. Now that we have established the differences between the two types of conflict, we will indicate avenues for future research on value conflict. We will conclude by specifying how current insights may inform effective strategies to deal with value conflict.

Future research

Now that we have identified how value conflicts differ from resource conflicts, the next step is to develop and test interventions that cater for the specific properties of value conflict. Conflict management research has studied extensively how we can solve resource conflict via negotiation (Lewicki, Barry, & Saunders, 2010; Pruitt & Carnevale, 1993); however, as argued above, this knowledge is hard to apply in value conflict. Empirical knowledge about how to solve or de-escalate a value conflict is still scarce. Below we will indicate relevant features that should benefit interventions specifically targeting value conflict, based on preliminary evidence pointing to the effectiveness of these measures.

Other-affirmation

Based upon the insights offered by the research reviewed here, we argue that effective interventions in value conflict should include a reduction of the (identity) threat that is incorporated in value conflict. From prior research we know that identity threat can be reduced via *self*-affirmations (Cohen, Sherman, Bastardi, Hsu, McGoey, & Ross, 2007; Correll, Spencer, & Zanna, 2004; McQueen & Klein, 2006; Sherman & Cohen, 2002, 2006). Self-affirmation is the active affirmation of some important aspect of one's self-concept that is unrelated to the self-threat (McQueen & Klein, 2006). Self-affirmations can be used to restore a positive sense of self that is needed to feel well (Steele, 1988; Tesser, 1988). A range of self-affirmation manipulations have been developed, for instance circling a most important value on a list of values and write about why this value is important, identifying and writing about a positive characteristic (of oneself) or a positive experience, or receiving positive bogus feedback from a test. Self-affirmation generally reduces psychological discomfort, enhances feelings of self-efficacy and perceived coping abilities, and makes people more accepting of counter-attitudinal arguments (McQueen & Klein, 2006). Accordingly, it has been argued that self-affirmations might be an effective way to facilitate the solution of value conflict. Indeed, some evidence suggests that affirmation of personal integrity may reduce resistance to yielding, although this was only the case when identity issues were made salient (Cohen et al., 2007).

The specific characteristics of a value conflict, however, suggest that rather than self-affirmation, *other*-affirmation should be particularly beneficial for conflict resolution. That is, although self-affirmation reduces threat, it also makes people more confident about their own judgments and positions. Possibly, this impedes the flexibility and perspective taking that is needed to effectively resolve a value conflict. Instead, other-affirmation, thinking of the other as a reasonable person with valid opinions, is likely to make people more open to their perspective and more willing to consider conflict solutions that satisfy both parties.

This idea was investigated in a study by Rexwinkel, Ellemers and Harinck (2011), in which participants first recalled and wrote about an unresolved value conflict that they had experienced. Then, participants in the self-affirmation condition were instructed to consider and record a positive characteristic of themselves, as in prior affirmation research. Participants in the other-affirmation condition, however, thought and wrote about a positive characteristic of the *other party in the conflict*. Results of this study revealed that people in the other-affirmation condition reported more open-mindedness, a stronger shared identity with the other party, more constructive problem-solving behavior and less destructive forcing behavior than people in the self-affirmation condition. In comparison, self-affirmation was much less effective. Although this first evidence is promising, more empirical research is needed to investigate when and why other-affirmation, rather than self-affirmation, is effective in value conflict.

Conflict outcomes

Traditional negotiation approaches aim for win–win agreements that satisfy both parties' claims to a scarce resource via trading off less important issues for more important ones. Although this type of agreement may *objectively* secure the best joint outcomes, it is often not feasible in value conflict. Moreover, research by Stoeckli and Tanner (in press) showed that people in value conflict prefer a compromise over a win–win agreement that includes logrolling. We therefore argue that *subjective* outcomes, such as satisfaction about the way the conflict was handled (regardless of the final agreement), the reduction of negative feelings and a willingness to cooperate in the future should receive more attention as relevant outcomes of value conflict.

As an illustration of how this might work, Illes, Ellemers and Harinck (in press) showed that the agreements that are often reached in value conflict pertain to reaching consensus about new *behavioral norms* that respect both parties' values. The interesting aspect of this type of agreement is that the values as such are not called into question or modified. Instead, they are detached from the agreement, as parties focus on finding and developing new behavioral norms and regulations that are acceptable to both of them. Aiming for this type of conflict outcome seems very promising as a viable strategy for the resolution of value conflict. Future research might more systematically investigate the effectiveness of agreements that detach the underlying values from the agreement that is made.

Third-party intervention

Nowadays, many conflicts are solved via a mediator—a neutral third party who helps conflict parties to find a solution for their problem. Mediation can be used as an alternative to going to court, for example in divorce mediation or labor dispute mediation. There are clear advantages of mediation compared to going to court, for instance that the parties have more control over the final agreement and that it is usually cheaper to go to a mediator than to seek litigation. While third party intervention—mediation—is a well-known technique for conflict resolution, there are no specific interventions or methodologies for mediators dealing with values, and the effectiveness of this approach in resolving value conflict has not been investigated. Illes et al. (in press) recently set out to explore this possibility by interviewing a sample of mediators, asking how they deal with value conflict. The results from this initial study indicate that mediators do not systematically use a specific approach for value conflict, and that the effect of interventions they use varies widely. This suggests that further investigation is needed to identify and develop tools that can be offered to mediators intervening in value conflicts.

Practical advice: how to solve a value conflict

Although insights into ways to resolve value conflicts are still being developed, the evidence available so far nevertheless allows us to provide some specific pointers on how to effectively deal with the feelings, cognitions and behaviors that characterize a value conflict.

First of all, when dealing with a value conflict, it is important to realize that people tend to be caught off-guard that others don't endorse the same values, as a result of which they experience strong (negative) emotions and take the conflict very personally. It is very likely that people feel threatened, hurt and angry in a value conflict, which makes the conflict hard to solve and easy to escalate.

Do not get angry

Despite these emotional overtones typically raised by disagreements about values, we advise people not to show their anger to the other party in value conflict.

Research has shown that anger has the tendency to fuel the value conflict: in value conflicts an angry response is seen as less appropriate, people are less likely to give in to angry people and more willing to retaliate towards angry people (Harinck & Van Kleef, 2012). Even though it might be very hard to swallow one's anger in a value conflict, it may help to remember that the other party is more likely to consider your argument or position when it is framed in neutral terms. Although anger displays may pay off when negotiating about resources, in value conflict revealing your anger will backfire—a neutrally-framed request is more likely to succeed.

Affirm the other party

Affirming the other party—by thinking about their positive qualities—may help overcome one's own identity threat and cognitive rigidity. Although it might be counterintuitive to think positively about someone you are in conflict with, in our research we discovered that doing so increases the open-mindedness of conflict parties as well as their willingness to search for a conflict solution (Harinck & Druckman, 2013; Rexwinkel et al., 2011).

Compromise

Results of the research by Stoeckli and Tanner (in press), suggests that conflict parties do well to find an agreement in which both give in a little. Agreements with trade-offs requiring people to relinquish their values tend not to be feasible in value conflict. Likewise, win–lose agreements in which one of the parties feels forced to give in to the other tend to be problematic in the long run. A yielding party that does not approve of the agreement or the way it was reached feels less bound to stick to the agreement, or will refuse to collaborate in the future. Agreements in which parties recognize that they both made some concessions, are more suitable in this case, because the pain of yielding is divided equally.

Conclusion

During the past ten years, there has been a sharp increase in the knowledge about value conflicts. We now know that value conflicts are taken more personally and are more threatening than resource conflicts. Importantly, however, this is not just a matter of degree; the resource- or value-based nature of the conflict issue and the further implications this has, fundamentally changes all aspects of the conflict process and is likely to influence conflict outcomes. As a result, whereas resource conflict can be successfully solved by taking a firm stance before making trade-offs to reach a win–win solution, this strategy is often not feasible for those engaged in a value conflict. Unfortunately, despite the recent surge in research on value conflict, the available knowledge on negotiation and conflict resolution mostly pertains to resource conflicts. As a result, we are only beginning to understand the specific strategies and interventions that may be most successful in resolving conflicts about values. This chapter summarizes emerging insights relevant to value conflict, and outlines directions for future research as well as suggests concrete interventions that may help resolve value conflict. Specifically, we have argued for techniques that re-establish ties between the conflict parties, reduce cognitive rigidity and re-evaluate compromises. In doing so, we hope to stimulate future research and to generate knowledge that will help people solve the conflicts they find most problematic and threatening, namely those regarding their values.

Note

1   Part of this research was facilitated by a research grant from the Netherlands Organization for Scientific Research (NWO 432-08-016) in the Conflict and Security Programme, awarded to Naomi Ellemers and Fieke Harinck.

References

Bazerman, M. H., Curhan, J. R., Moore, D. A., & Valley, K. L. (2000). Negotiation. *Annual Review of Psychology, 51,* 279–314.

Biernat, M., Vescio, T. K., & Billings, L.S. (1999). Black sheep and expectancy violation: Integrating two models of social judgment. *European Journal of Social Psychology, 29,* 523–542.

Blascovich, J. (2008). Challenge, threat, and health. In J. Shah and W. Gardner (Eds.), *Handbook of motivation science* (pp. 481–493). New York: Guilford.

Blascovich, J., & Tomaka, J. (1996). The biopsychosocial model of arousal regulation. *Advances in Experimental Social Psychology, 28,* 1–51.

Brett, J. M., Shapiro, D. L., & Lytle, A. L. (1998). Breaking the bonds of reciprocity in negotiations. *Academy of Management Journal, 41,* 410–424.

Cohen, G. L., Sherman, D. K., Bastardi, A., McGoey, M., Hsu, A., & Ross, L. (2007). Bridging the partisan divide: Self-affirmation reduces ideological closed-mindedness and inflexibility in negotiation. *Journal of Personality and Social Psychology, 93,* 415–430.

Correll, J., Spencer, S. J., & Zanna, M. P. (2004). An affirmed self and an open mind: Self-affirmation and sensitivity to argument strength. *Journal of Experimental Social Psychology, 40,* 350–356.

De Dreu, C. K. W. (2010). Social conflict: The emergence and consequences of struggle and negotiation. In S. T. Fiske, D. T. Gilbert, & G. Lindzey (Eds.). *Handbook of Social Psychology* (5th ed, Vol. 2, pp. 983–1023). New York: Wiley.

De Dreu, C. K. W., Harinck, F., & Van Vianen, A. E. M. (1999). Conflict and performance in groups and organizations. In C. Cooper, & I. Robertson (Eds.), *International Review of Industrial and Organizational Psychology, 14* (pp. 396–414). Chichester: John Wiley & Sons.

De Dreu, C. K. W., & Van Knippenberg, D. (2005). The possessive self as a barrier to constructive conflict management: Effects of mere ownership, process accountability, and self-concept clarity on competitive cognitions and behavior. *Journal of Personality and Social Psychology, 89,* 345–357.

De Wit, F. R. C., Scheepers, D., & Jehn, K. E. (2012). Cardiovascular reactivity and resistance to opposing viewpoints during intragroup conflict. *Psychophysiology, 49,* 1523–1531.

Deutsch, M. (1973). *The resolution of conflict: Constructive and destructive processes.* New Haven: Yale University Press.

Druckman, D., Broome, B. J., & Korper, S. H. (1988). Value differences and conflict resolution. *Journal of Conflict Resolution, 32,* 489–510.

Druckman, D., Rozelle, R., & Zechmeister, K. (1977). Conflict of interest and value dissensus: Two perspectives. In D. Druckman (Ed.), *Negotiations: Social-psychological perspectives* (pp. 105–131). Beverley Hills: Sage.

Ellemers, N., & Rink, F. (2005). Identity in work groups: The beneficial and detrimental consequences of multiple identities and group norms for collaboration and group performance. *Advances in Group Processes, 22,* 1–41.

Fisher, R., Ury, W., & Patton, B. (1991). *Getting to yes: Negotiating without giving in.* Penguin Group, New York.

Gilovich, T. (1990). Differential construal and the false consensus effect. *Journal of Personality and Social Psychology, 59,* 623–634.

Harinck, F. (2004). Persuasive arguments and beating around the bush in negotiations. *Group Processes and Intergroup Relations, 7,* 5–17.

Harinck, F., & De Dreu, C. K. W. (2004). Negotiating interests or values and reaching integrative agreements: The importance of time pressure and temporary impasses. *European Journal of Social Psychology, 34,* 595–611.

—— (2008). Take a break! Or not? The influence of mindsets on negotiation processes and outcomes. *Journal of Experimental Social Psychology, 44,* 397–404.

Harinck, F., De Dreu, C. K. W., & Van Vianen, A. E. M. (2000). The impact of conflict issues on fixed-pie perceptions, problem solving, and integrative outcomes in negotiation. *Organizational Behavior and Human Decision Processes, 81,* 329–358.

Harinck, F., & Druckman, D, (2013). Interventions in conflict. *Submitted for publication.*

Harinck, F., & Van Kleef, G. A. (2012). Be hard on the interests and soft on the values: Conflict issue moderates the interpersonal effects of anger in negotiations. *British Journal of Social Psychology, 51,* 741–752.

Illes, R. M., Ellemers, N., & Harinck, F. (*in press*). Mediating value conflict. *Conflict Resolution Quarterly.*

Kouzakova, M., Ellemers, N., Harinck, F., & Scheepers, D. (2012). The implications of value conflict: How disagreement on values affects self-involvement and perceived common ground. *Personality and Social Psychology Bulletin, 38,* 798–807.

Kouzakova, M., Harinck, F., Ellemers, N. & Scheepers, D. (2014). At the heart of a conflict: Cardiovascular and motivational responses to moral conflicts and resource conflicts. *Social Psychology and Personality Science 5,* 35–42.

Lewicki, R. J., Barry, B., Saunders, D. M. (2010). *Negotiation,* 6th Edition. Boston: McGraw-Hill Irwin.

McQueen, A., & Klein, W. M. P. (2006). Experimental manipulations of self-affirmation: A systematic review. *Self and Identity, 5,* 289–354.

Mullen, B., Atkins, J. L., Champion, D. S., Edwards, C., Hardy, D., Story, J. E., & Vanderklok, M. (1985). The false consensus effect; a meta-analysis of 115 hypothesis tests. *Journal of Experimental Social Psychology, 21,* 262–283.

Pruitt, D. G., & Carnevale, P. J. (1993). *Negotiation in social conflict.* Buckingham, England: Open University Press.

Rexwinkel, R., Ellemers, N., & Harinck, F. (2011). Wanneer jij OK bent, ben ik ook OK!: Hoe de bevestiging van een ander het oplossen van een waardenconflict vergemakkelijkt [When you are OK, I am OK. How affirming the other helps to resolve a value conflict]. *ASPO Jaarboek 2011* (pp. 175–178).

Rink, F., & Ellemers, N. (2007). The role of expectancies in accepting task-related diversity: Do disappointment and lack of commitment stem from actual differences or violated expectations? *Personality and Social Psychology Bulletin, 33*, 842–854.

Ross, L., Greene, D., & House, P. (1977). The "false consensus effect": An egocentric bias in social perception and attribution processes. *Journal of Experimental Social Psychology, 13*, 279–301.

Sherman, D. K., & Cohen, G. L. (2002). Accepting threatening information: Self-affirmation and the reduction of defensive biases. *Current Directions in Psychological Science, 11*, 119–123.

—— (2006). The psychology of self-defense: Self-affirmation theory. In M. P. Zanna (Ed.) *Advances in Experimental Social Psychology* (Vol. 38, pp. 183–242). San Diego: Academic Press.

Steele, C. M. (1988). The psychology of self-affirmation: Sustaining the integrity of the self. In L. Berkowitz (Ed.), *Advances in experimental social psychology* (pp. 261–302). New York: Academic Press.

Stoeckli, P. L., & Tanner, C. (*in press*). Are integrative or distributive outcomes more satisfactory? The effects of interest- versus value-based issues on negotiator satisfaction. *European Journal of Social Psychology*.

Tesser, A. (1988). Toward a self-evaluation maintenance model of social behavior. In L. Berkowitz (Ed.), *Advances in experimental social psychology* (pp. 181–227). New York: Academic Press.

Tetlock, P. E. (1999). Coping with trade-offs: Psychological constraints and political implications. In S. Lupia, M. McCubbins, & S. Popkin (Eds.), *Political reasoning and choice*. (pp. 239–263). Berkeley: University of California Press.

Tetlock, P. E., Kristel, O. V., Elson, S. B, Green, M. C., & Lerner, J. S. (2000). The psychology of the unthinkable: Taboo trade-offs, forbidden base rates, and heretical counterfactuals. *Journal of Personality and Social Psychology, 78*, 853–870.

Tetlock, P. E., Peterson, R. S., & Lerner, J. S. (1996). Revising the value pluralism model: Incorporating social content and context postulates. In C. Seligman, J. M. Olson, & M. P. Zanna (Eds.), *The Psychology of values: The Ontario Symposium* (pp. 25–51). Mahwah: Lawrence Erlbaum Associates.

Thomas, K. W. (1992). Conflict and negotiation processes in organizations. In M. D. Dunnette, & L. M. Hough (Eds.), *Handbook of industrial and organizational psychology* (pp. 651–717). Palo Alto: Consulting Psychologists Press.

Thompson, L. L., & Gonzalez, R. (1996). Environmental disputes: Competition for scarce resources and clashing of values. In M. H. Bazerman, D. M. Messick, A. E. Tenbrunsel, & K. A. Wade-Benzoni (Eds.), *Environment, Ethics, and Behavior.* San Francisco: New Lexington Press.

Thompson, L. L., & Hastie, R. (1990). Social perception in negotiation. *Organizational Behavior and Human Decision Processes, 47*, 98–123.

Thompson, L. L., Wang, J., & Gunia, B. C. (2010). Negotiation. *Annual Review of Psychology, 61*, 491–515.

Van Kleef, G. A., De Dreu, C. K. W., & Manstead, A. S. R. (2004a). The interpersonal effects of anger and happiness in negotiations. *Journal of Personality and Social Psychology, 86*, 57–76.

—— (2004b). The interpersonal effects of emotions in negotiations: A motivated information processing approach. *Journal of Personality and Social Psychology. 87.* 510–528.

Wade-Benzoni, K. A., Hoffman, A. J., Thompson, L. L., Moore, D. A., Gillespie, J. J., & Bazerman, M. H. (2002). Barriers to resolution in ideologically based negotiations: The role of values and institutions. *Academy of Management Review. 27.* 41–57.

Walton, R. E., & McKersie, R. (1965). *A behavioral theory of labor negotiations: An analysis of a social interaction system.* New York: McGraw-Hill.

3   Humiliation in conflict

Underlying processes and effects
on human thought and behavior

Kai J. Jonas, Marte Otten, and Bertjan Doosje

Introduction

Conflicts are inextricably linked to humiliation. In the early days of warfare, displaying the heads of the leaders of the opponent on sticks, or capturing military symbols signaled humiliating defeat, even with fighting forces still being formidable. This has not changed much, as evidence from present-day wars show. Corpses of enemy soldiers still get dragged through the dirt (e.g., US special forces after their helicopter got shot down in Mogadishu, Somalia in 1993), or get urinated on (e.g., Taliban insurgents, Afghanistan 2013). But also less violent societal or intergroup conflicts can lead to humiliation. For example, the intentional lower seating of the Turkish ambassador Ahmet Oguz Celikkol in a meeting with Israeli Deputy Foreign Minister Danny Ayalon, and the lack of a Turkish flag next to the Israeli one on the table is just one expression in an ongoing political spiral of negativity, but was nonetheless perceived as humiliating by the Turks (Klein, 2010). In other contexts, humiliation is not the interpretative default: the shoeing of former US President George W. Bush in Baghdad in 2008 was only perceived as humiliating in the West after media reports explained the cultural background in other cultures. Also, humiliation can be experienced indirectly, even if one is not the actual victim: the French perceived the so-called prep walk of the former head of the IMF, Dominique Strauss-Kahn, as a national humiliation:

> There was shock in France after the arrest of Mr. Strauss-Kahn in May and intense criticism of the manner in which he was displayed in handcuffs, pulled unshaven into a televised court session and stuffed into a Rikers Island cell under suicide watch. [… T]here was a sense that it was not just Mr. Strauss-Kahn who was being so jauntily humiliated, but France itself.
>
> (French See Case Against Strauss-Kahn as American Folly,
> *The New York Times*, 3 July 2012)

These examples reveal interesting aspects of humiliation that already define relevant aspects of humiliation: humiliation seems to require the violation of very basic human consensus, or of a shared norm, otherwise humiliation is not experienced, but at the same time cultures can differ greatly in this construal.

Humiliation seems to radiate, in particular, since it does not have to be perceived personally; it seems sufficient that others fall victim to it.

Without doubt humiliation is an emotion often felt, and seems really important for interpersonal and intergroup relationships. However, humiliation is surprisingly under-researched in social psychology and other fields of research. It is an applied aim of the research presented to uncover the processes that underlie humiliation, to understand its consequences and functioning, and to be able to turn the humiliation taboo into an openly discussed topic. Only then will interventions against humiliation, and coping strategies for humiliation, be effective.

In general, humiliation is described as a feeling of being unjustly degraded and put down. In its consequences, humiliation presents as a double-edged sword: victims of humiliation often do not voice their experience, feel ashamed and want to vanish from the surface of the earth, but when victims do respond to their experience, they do so in an utmost violent or excessive form. The reason for this dichotomy lies in the character of humiliation as a complex emotion, with two components. When individuals feel humiliated, they often mention components of shame and anger. The focus of this investigation lies on the victims of humiliation, not on the perpetrators. However, humiliation victims can turn into humiliators themselves as a consequence of their experience.

After presenting a definition of humiliation, we discuss relevant boundary conditions such as chronic discrimination experience and sensitivity, and audience effects. The remainder of the chapter is structured around a discussion of the consequences of humiliation on three levels. First, we summarize effects of humiliation on the individual neuro-cognitive level. Specifically, we explore how the brain processes the humiliation experience, and we consider several specific consequences of humiliation on (neuro-)cognitive functions. Second, we report findings of humiliation in intergroup settings. On this level we investigate effects of vicarious experience of humiliation and the potential of humiliation to fuel group conflicts. Third, we investigate humiliation in intercultural settings, drawing attention to the differential perception based on honor, and on the political stage, for example within the globalized perception of humiliating acts. Finally, we review intervention attempts to alleviate experiences of humiliation.

Definition of humiliation

In the lay conception, humiliation is perceived as an emotion that is experienced in contexts where oneself is the victim of deeply degrading actions. In line with this, scientific scholars have defined humiliation as "the deep dysphoric feeling associated with being, or perceiving oneself as being, unjustly degraded, ridiculed, or put down – in particular, one's identity has been demeaned or devalued" (Hartling & Luchetta, 1999, p. 264). In recent years, there has been a growing interest in the topic (Combs, Campbell, Jackson, & Smith, 2010; Elison & Harter, 2007; Ginges & Atran, 2008; Jasini, Doosje, Jonas, & Fischer, 2012; Leidner, Sheikh, & Ginges, 2012) and the severe consequences of humiliating experiences have been documented. Research from clinical psychological and criminological perspectives list a variety of consequences of humiliation experiences, including health complaints (Giacaman, Abu-Rmeileh, Husseini, Saab, & Boyce, 2006), low self-esteem (Gilbert, 1997; Lindner, 2009; Walker & Knauer, 2011), depression (Brown, Harris, & Hepworth, 1995; Farmer & McGuffin, 2003), anxiety disorders (Kendler, Hettema, Butera, Gardner, & Prescott, 2003), suicidal ideation and intention (Torres & Bergner, 2010; Trumbull, 2008), aggression (Klein, 1991), domestic violence and rape (Proulx, Aubut, McKibben, & Côté, 1994).

Emotion research has contributed also to the understanding of humiliation and pointed to the fact that humiliation is a complex self-conscious emotion. There is an ongoing debate whether humiliation gives rise to a number of other emotions, such as shame or anger, or if humiliation in fact is composed out of these emotions itself. While some authors stressed the self- and other-directed aggression component (e.g., Combs et al., 2010; Elison & Harter, 2007; Fattah & Fierke, 2009; Fontan, 2006; Klein, 1991; Lindner, 2001a, 2001b, 2001c, 2002; D. Smith, 2008; Torres & Bergner, 2010; Trumbull, 2008), others have focused on the shame, guilt and embarrassment component: victims of humiliation have reported that they felt ashamed and embarrassed about what has happened to them, but also that they find themselves guilty for the experience, for example due to previous behavior of themselves, or their group (e.g., Besser & Zeigler-Hill, 2010; Elison & Harter, 2007; Jackson, 1999; Miller, 1993; Tracy & Robins, 2004). This componential structure thus suggests humiliation is a highly complex self-conscious emotion, which in turn triggers a number of research questions. First of all, how do these components pan out to the behavioral level? Is there a sequence of shame-related avoidance and anger-related approach? Secondly, how does humiliation, aside from its structural description and narrative definition, look as a neural correlate? We are going to try to answer these questions shortly.

However, before moving there, it is important to introduce the possibility of indirect, vicarious experiences of humiliation. Based on the intergroup emotions theorizing (Mackie, Devos, & Smith, 2000; E. R. Smith, 1993) it is likely to assume that, through the experiences of another person one shares a common group membership with, humiliation can be felt by other members of the group too. For example, Yzerbyt, Dumont, Wigboldus, and Gordijn (2003), found that self-categorization with members of a discriminated group increases the experience of anger about this discrimination. But when different group memberships were made salient, the emotional experience was weaker. Thus, it is quite likely that a similar effect can be found for humiliation. Some authors have been capitalizing on this notion and posited that it is this experience of vicarious group-based humiliation that fuels current-day intergroup conflicts and terrorism through a spiral of vicarious humiliation and subsequent revenge on the offending out-group as a whole (Ginges & Atran, 2008; Lindner, 2001a; Ricolfi, 2005). While the definition of humiliation is a feasible working basis for further research, triggers or determinants of humiliation have received little research. This facet will be under consideration first.

Triggers and determinants of humiliation experience

The definition of humiliation stresses the situational element, namely being subjected to unjust and degrading treatment in a specific context, but also points to the potential of a subjective interpretation, namely that individuals and group members can perceive to be humiliated, too, without an intentional action from the side of a humiliator. Thus, in this section, we review a number of situational determinants first and then turn to inter-individual differences that can influence the subjective experience of humiliation.

Humiliation can follow from a range of interpersonal experiences, such as degradation, ridicule, being put down and identity devaluation. Another, often overlooked inductor of feeling humiliated is being excluded from a social group which one feels they belong to. Jonas, Doosje and Song (2013) tested this hypothesis in a series of studies. Their results showed that simple exclusion from a group (operationalized with the cyberball paradigm; Williams & Jarvis, 2006) was enough to evoke feelings of humiliation. In the cyberball paradigm, participants play a simple three-person ball throwing game online. In the course of the game, the other two players, who are actually played by the computer, stop throwing the ball to the participant which leads to strong feelings of exclusion. Excluded individuals develop ideas about the reason why the others stopped playing with them. When they linked their exclusion to their own ability, or personality traits (i.e., engaging in internal attributions about the exclusion), their feeling of humiliation was enhanced. Furthermore, revenge tendencies following humiliating exclusion were mediated by the perceived morality of the other players. These results showed that exclusion itself leads to humiliation, but that revenge tendencies (that can fuel a humiliation spiral) are driven by a specific interpretation of the motivation and morality of the perpetrators. Revenge is particularly strong when the experienced humiliation cannot be attributed to inadvertent reasons on the side of the humiliator.

A recent set of studies from our laboratory directly shows that similar acts can evoke different levels of humiliation depending on the broader social situation. Mann and colleagues (Mann, Feddes, Leiser, Doosje, & Fischer, 2013) on a behavioral data level, and Otten and colleagues (Otten, Jonas, Mann, & Van Berkum, 2013) on a neural level found that a laughing audience adds to the intensity of the humiliation. Mann and colleagues exposed individuals from different cultures to humiliating statements in front of an imagined audience. In one condition, the audience responded with laughter, in the other they remained silent. The laughing audience conditions overall enhanced the experience of humiliation. Otten and colleagues adapted the paradigms to an EEG setting and replicated the findings. We are going to discuss their paradigm in more detail later.

In addition to situational humiliation accounts, interview data with minority members (Moroccan immigrants and people with former Dutch colony background; Jonas, Feddes, Mann, & Klok, 2013) revealed subjective differences in humiliation sensitivity and interpretation. The data showed that certain minority members developed a humiliation sensitivity based on a faith-based rejection sensitivity. Rejection sensitivity has been shown to influence race-based discrimination accounts (Mendoza-Denton, Downey, Purdie, Davis, & Pietrzak, 2002), but has not been applied to group membership determined by one's faith. The basic mechanism of rejection sensitivity leads people to attribute ambiguous situations to negative, intentional behavior of the other. In the context of humiliation, this means that individuals or group members suffering from faith-based rejection sensitivity interpret ambiguous situations related to their faith more easily as humiliating than those not inclined to make such attributions. This research was conducted to identify individual difference variables that influence the likelihood of perceiving humiliation. It is of course not the aim of this line of research to withhold subjective humiliation interpretations from individuals or group members and to establish objective criteria, but this approach could pave a way for interventions to create resilience against humiliation.

Based on the outcomes of these interviews, Jonas (2013) conducted a number of studies to test whether motivational mindsets influence the sensitivity for humiliation. We expected that there would be a match between the motivation to avoid negative outcomes (chronic or situational prevention focus as one element of Regulatory Focus Theory; Higgins, 1997, 1998) and humiliation sensitivity within the framework of the regulatory fit hypothesis (Higgins, 2000). First analyses point more to a motivational influence on subsequent responses to humiliation, than on the perception of humiliation itself. In the context of group-based humiliation, prevention focus driven responses are related to individual mobility, namely leaving the group, or loosening the association with the group. Promotion focus based responses are linked to changing the characteristics of the group itself, to make it less prone to humiliation. This impression management response can come at the cost of other group members, too (Jonas, 2013).

The type of response shown to humiliation can cover a broad range of behaviors. Prominent variations range from shame-based withdrawal to anger-based revenge behavior, and can thus fuel a humiliation spiral that turns victims into perpetrators and vice versa. We wanted to shed some light on these behavioral outcomes, particularly when the person responding is not directly affected by the humiliation, but only vicariously. Thus, Otten, Jonas, Doosje and Erbas (2013) tested the influence of the typicality of the in-group humiliation victim on the behavioral tendencies. Participants read vignettes about a humiliating event of an in-group member. Depending on experimental condition, the vignette either described the victim as a typical in-group member (e.g., with text elements such as: "Friends describe X as sober, moderate and tolerant"; for typical Dutch characteristics) or non-typical. Afterwards participants in the study were asked to indicate their response intentions. Their results showed that when the victim was a typical in-group member, humiliation was more likely to be related to withdrawal and revenge. However, the impact of victim typicality was alleviated when the perpetrator had a violent reputation. In those cases, vicarious humiliation was strongly associated with revenge and withdrawal independently of victim typicality. Importantly, to help to disentangle the complex emotion structure, responses to humiliating intergroup incidents are mainly driven by feelings of vicarious humiliation, not by anger or shame.

Taken together, humiliation can be triggered in a situation of unjust degradation, and is enhanced by (laughing) audiences. Individual determinants, such as a heightened sensitivity can lead to an interpretation of ambiguous situations as humiliating. Responses to vicarious humiliation are driven by victim characteristics (typicality), as well as by the violence assessment of the perpetrator. We are aware that this is by far not painting a comprehensive picture of humiliation triggers and behavioral outcomes, but it sketches a roadmap for further research in this area. To inform this research, we now turn to an assessment of humiliation experience on different levels, from neuro-cognitive, over intergroup to intercultural and political levels of analysis.

Levels of humiliation experience

Neuro-cognitive correlates of humiliation

We have argued previously that humiliation is seen as a very intense emotion with powerful implications for the individual, and for society as a whole. Interestingly, there is to our best knowledge no direct empirical test that investigated the assumed intensity of the emotion—all such arguments are indirect evidence. In a line of studies, Otten and Jonas (in press) investigated the neuro-cognitive footprint of humiliation in the human brain. In an initial step we provided the first clear empirical evidence that humiliation is indeed a very intense experience. To do so, we investigated individuals in a laboratory context. Based on the electro-encephalogram recorded from people reading scenarios that evoked either humiliation, anger or happiness, electrophysiological measures of cognitive intensity were derived for each of the emotion types. The analysis of the data showed that late positive potential (LPP), a measure of the level of perceived (negative) affect, was markedly increased in humiliation scenarios compared to happiness and anger scenarios. In addition, event-related desynchronisation (ERD) in the alpha-frequency range, a measure of the overall intensity of cortical activation, was significantly more pronounced for humiliation than for happiness and anger scenarios. Our findings nicely dovetail with more qualitative and self-report data reviewed before, showing that humiliation is a particularly intense experience.

In a second study, we investigated the impact of social context on the processing of humiliating insults (Otten, Jonas, Mann, & Van Berkum, 2013). Humiliating insults (60 short statements about the personality of the participant, vs. 60 complimenting sentences, divided into blocks of 30 each and presented in isolation) evoked a relative increase in N400 and P600 amplitude which points to an initial semantic processing of the insult and a later (if any) emotional impact. The same stimuli presented in the context of a mocking social audience (induced by a statement reading "And they feel the same way" and two seconds of audible laughter from a group presented after the last word of the preceding statement) led to a stronger late positivity, which can be interpreted as a marker of emotional neural processing. When laughter accompanied the insults, the N400 amplitude was absent, further underlining that in such a negative social context insults are perceived as directly personally and emotionally relevant. Taken together, these studies indicate that humiliation is an intense experience, already on a neuro-cognitive level. If experienced in isolation, the humiliation victim, given semantic stimuli, responds with both an increased semantic, as well as an emotional processing. In a social context, the semantic content of the stimulus moves to the background and the emotional processing is dominant. Together, these two studies focus on the cognitive processes and relative intensity of humiliation, but they do not investigate the fine-grained cognitive consequences.

In a third and final study, we tested the cognitive effects of humiliating exclusion (Otten & Jonas, 2013). This is especially relevant, since humiliation, on the behavioral, as well as on the psychological and physiological health level, is linked to severe consequences. The hypothesis that humiliation already negatively hampers very basic cognitive processes such as cognitive control, is thus not far-fetched, but has seen limited evidence so far (see for an exception Jamieson, Harkins, & Williams, 2010). A simple assumption could be that humiliation leads to a broad cognitive impairment. Victims of humiliation would then be simply bad performers on cognitive tasks such as cognitive control, which should filter through broadly in school, or professional performance settings. But a look at existing research on social exclusion quickly reveals that the relationship is not that simple. In this study we investigated whether social exclusion also directly influences cognitive control. In an EEG setting, participants were either excluded or included while playing cyberball (Williams & Jarvis, 2006). To test whether exclusion altered cognitive control, we measured the electrophysiological responses to a Go/No Go task. In this task, participants had to withhold a response (No Go) on a small number of trials, while the predominant tendency was to make an overt (Go) response. Our results showed that compared to Go trials the event-related potential (ERP) evoked by No Go trials elicited an increased N2, reflecting the detection of the response conflict, followed by an increased P3, reflecting the inhibition of the predominant response. The N2 effect was larger for participants who had experienced exclusion, while the P3 effect was smaller. This indicates that exclusion, and concomitant feeling humiliated, leads to an increased ability to detect response conflicts, while at the same time exclusion decreases the neural processes that underlie the inhibition of unwanted behavior.

In sum, our neuro-cognitive line of research showed both the perceived intensity and magnitude of humiliation, especially in social contexts. But our findings also paint a more differentiated picture of the neural response. Victims of humiliation are not generically hampered in their cognitive functioning. Rather, they showed a wide range of cognitive responses, including difficulties to inhibit unwanted behavior, and increased capacity to detect response conflict. Of course these findings address humiliation on a different level than previous research, but are in line with the qualitative description of the experience of humiliation victims.

Intergroup humiliation

While in the previous section we took a micro-analytical view on humiliation, it is also necessary to investigate humiliation on a larger scale, namely on an intergroup level. Most of the previous research on humiliation has been done on the Israeli–Palestine conflict. This is fully understandable, since this conflict produces multiple humiliation instances and re-humiliation cycles. Yet, to understand humiliation processes in other, less conflict-prone societies, such as The Netherlands, such data is only informative to a limited degree. While the humiliation processes, on an abstract level may be similar, the humiliation triggers and humiliation content is vastly different. To this end, we investigated, by means of a series of qualitative interviews, which humiliation contexts are relevant for two large minority groups in The Netherlands: Moroccan immigrants and Dutch with a background in the former colonies of Suriname and the Dutch Antilles. We conducted in-depth interviews with 20 members of both groups in total. Since the topic is a difficult one to address, the interviews commenced with a general section about personal background and life experiences, to build up a connection with the interviewee and then turned to the topic of humiliation. The content analysis of the interviews showed that both minority groups perceive completely different contexts as humiliating (Jonas, Feddes, Mann, & Klok, 2013). For the Moroccan immigrant group, humiliation stemmed from three very different sources. The first context was the disrespect for their Muslim faith. Here also a vicarious element was often pointed to. The identification with the "umma," the perceived worldwide Muslim community, is the reason that disrespectful acts against Muslims or their symbols throughout the world are experienced as humiliating in The Netherlands, too. The second context is the constant distrust and perceived scrutiny of the mainstream society towards members of the Moroccan immigrant group. Expressions of this were found in perceived higher numbers and/or selectiveness of police control, or subtle defense responses by majority members, such as changing seats on public transport, or grabbing one's bags to avoid perceived potential theft. A third and final source of humiliation originated from within the group itself. With honor and family values being strong, humiliation can also be triggered if one's behaviors are in violation of these codes. This puts a younger generation especially into a double bind, when their assimilative behavior into the mainstream is seen as a humiliation reason within their group, and at the same time, their mere group membership triggers humiliating responses by the mainstream.

The pattern looked vastly different for members of the Surinamese and Dutch Antilles group. For them, the main humiliation topic was the slavery past. This topic occurred in different constellations. One rather straightforward aspect is the lack of apology of the Dutch majority and the neglect of the topic in everyday politics. A less clear reason for humiliation is the fact that their forefathers were caught in a life situation, in which they lacked agency and self-determination. This incapacity of their ancestors still overshadowed the self-concept (in a humiliating way) for their current-day descendants. This was especially the case for those with a high achievement motivation. A third topic of perceived humiliation is the annual tradition of Santa Claus and his little helpers ("Sinterklaas" and his "Zwarte Pieten"). In The Netherlands, this Christmas tradition is actually the main festivity of the Christmas season, peaking at December 5 each year with the big entry procession of Sinterklaas (coming from Spain by boat) and street fairs, and shops going on sale afterwards. To understand the humiliating aspect of this tradition, one has to understand that the little helpers, as the name already gives it away in Dutch, are black, while Sinterklaas, as their boss, is white. To make things even worse, members of the white Dutch majority dress up as little helpers by painting their faces black, with thick red lipstick and a curly wig, an eerie reminder of the bigoted "blackface" tradition in other cultures that have dealt with slavery. The inability of the Dutch mainstream to acknowledge this tradition as discriminating can be perceived as humiliation by people from a Surinamese and Dutch Antillean background (Bal, 2004). A final aspect that sets this group apart from the Moroccan immigrants was their meta-knowledge of humiliation context of other minorities. For example, they were aware of the fact that Moroccans suffer from faith-based humiliation, and that a vicarious aspect plays a major role there, too.

In sum, such analyses with the aim to show content and context differences of humiliation among minority groups are novel and necessary to understand the trajectories and to develop made-to-measure roadmaps for interventions. Furthermore, they can uncover often overlooked domains and point to critical issues that otherwise would miss the relevance threshold from a majorities perspective.

By the same token, we investigated the intergroup humiliation perception in The Netherlands also from the perspective of the Dutch majority population. This may be seen as surprising, since a dominant view on humiliation is that only low status groups can fall victim to humiliation. However, we argue that this is clearly not the case. Our neuro-cognitive studies already showed that also high-status members are perfectly able to experience humiliation. While we used individual humiliation context in these studies, we wanted to investigate now whether humiliation is also possible on an intergroup level for high status group members, and if vicarious processes may be at play here, too. In a series of studies Otten and colleagues (Otten, Jonas, Doosje, & Erbas, 2013) tested the responses to vicarious in-group humiliation for the Dutch majority. In these studies, the perpetrator was coming from the Muslim immigrant minority and the humiliating deed always affected an in-group member. We have already elaborated on the relevance of the victim typicality and want to focus on another aspect here instead. The chosen contexts in all cases indicate disrespect for core values of the in-group (freedom of speech, violence free society, norm adherence), which acts as a trigger for intergroup humiliation of high status groups. Opposite to low status minority groups, for whom humiliation is often the prolongation of discriminative behavior taken one step further, high status groups, who are "invincible" on those dimensions, can be affected by attacks on more abstract values. It is not surprising that such behavior quickly entered the political agenda, too. It is this aspect that we investigated in a line of studies as well, and that we now want to turn to.

Humiliation in intercultural settings and as behavior on the political agenda

In our introduction we argued that humiliation is common of the political discourse and is often used as a conscious diplomatic tool. Interestingly, scientific evidence for humiliation to the nation, as much as it is proclaimed by politicians and media, is scarce. To fill this void, we investigated whether evidence of humiliation to the nation can actually be found and what its boundary conditions are. Doosje, Jonas, Jasini, Sveinsdóttir, and Erbas (2013) proposed that the experience of national humiliation depends on the national character, and in particular on differences in honor culture. Honor culture refers to societies in which the evaluation of a person's social status is judged by that individual's community and in which people attach importance to maintaining their honor (e.g., Cohen, 1998; Mosquera, Fischer, Manstead, & Zaalberg, 2008; Mosquera, Fischer, & Manstead, 2000). While humiliation was found to be experienced relatively strongly in countries with strong honor values (e.g., Albania), lower levels of humiliation experience were obtained in low honor value countries (e.g., The Netherlands). A similar difference pattern was found on the level of responses to national humiliation, too. We found that humiliation led to aggressive action tendencies in countries with strong honor values, but in countries with strong harmony values (e.g., Hong Kong), withdrawal was a more likely response to humiliation. Taken together, cultural values play a central role in the perception of humiliation and the associated action tendencies. We have provided evidence for this relation on the national humiliation level, but there is little reason to not believe that the same factor would also filter through on the level of individual or intergroup humiliation. Anecdotal evidence for this was obtained during the data gathering in Albania: during the pre-testing phase of finding relevant situations, many of the interviewees pointed to the potential danger of humiliation simply by asking the question of what is humiliating (thus implying that they do not know).

It has become clear so far that the focus of the analysis of humiliation has to be on the experience, as well as the response to humiliation. To further explore responses to humiliation on the political agenda, we now turn to a different political context, namely the terrorist attack on the World Trade Center, commonly known as 9/11. The reason why this event is relevant for a humiliation analysis is the simple fact that it triggered an array of US political decisions, both relevant inside and outside of the United States, and secondly, since it was often referred to as humiliating for the United States (Saurette, 2006). Furthermore, in our research design, we combined for the first time out-group blame reactions (such as anger and humiliation) with in-group blame reactions (such as shame). In our view, this combination of emotions with different foci is crucial to understand people's reactions in (ongoing) intergroup conflicts. In previous research, people typically have focused either on out-group blame emotions to understand reactions in conflictual intergroup contexts (e.g., anger, Van Zomeren, Spears, Fischer, & Leach, 2004), or on in-group blame emotions (e.g., guilt, Doosje, Branscombe, Spears, & Manstead, 1998). We argue that it is important to consider both types or targets of reactions to fully grasp the complete picture: people can be as emotionally triggered by out-group acts as by in-group acts in conflictual intergroup contexts.

To test our assumptions we conducted a series of surveys in the United States on the topic of experiences of 9/11. Embedded in a number of questions on how they perceived the attacks, where they were at the time, and if close others had been affected, participants were asked to indicate how emotionally affected they were by the attacks, and how they respond to a number of statements regarding US foreign and internal policy. Among other topics, we investigated support for the war in Afghanistan, the Guantanamo prison as such, or the events in Abu Ghraib prison. Furthermore, we assessed how far they could engage in perspective-taking in relation to the Muslim terrorists. Results showed that negative in-group blame emotions (such as shame and guilt) are related to the ability and willingness to acknowledge the mistreatment of an out-group by some members of one's in-group. Negative out-group blame emotions (such as anger and humiliation), on the other hand, were related to harsh treatment of the out-group (Jonas, Doosje, Lobel, & Pysczcynski, 2013). Taken together, our research shows that the anger and humiliation component vs. the shame component contribute differentially to support for political action following a humiliating incident.

Finally, we want to briefly turn to another aspect of humiliation and political behavior that unfolded during our research on humiliation. In Western democratic contexts, there is an almost set agenda of forms and means of political protest that ranges from demonstrations to expression of freedom of speech. In addition, even though they are more rare and often seen as clownish protests, the throwing of objects, such as cream pies and glitter bombs are often used. In addition to these more fun and relatively harmless forms, other objects can be thrown, too. Yet, the use of eggs, tomatoes, or paint are all seen as an attack and as a consequence often trigger prosecution of the thrower.

Interestingly, recent forms of political protest revealed that this list of throwing objects has to be extended. There is a novel humiliating form of political protest that includes the throwing of objects: shoes. Until the moment when former US president George W. Bush fell victim to a shoe thrower in Baghdad in 2008, the act of shoe throwing was virtually unknown in the Western hemisphere, while being a common form of humiliating political protest in countries in which shoes, and the soles of feet are seen as impure (e.g., foot washing rituals and removal of shoes before entering a mosque or Buddhist temple, or pointing of foot soles away from Buddha statues). It is noteworthy that with this incident the Western interpretation of shoe throwing has moved from a random object interpretation to a humiliation interpretation. It is fascinating that Western media constantly refer to the 2008 event as the starting point of this form of protest, overlooking that in many countries shoe throwing happened before, but was not recognized as such. Ever since 2008 more than 40 politicians and representatives worldwide have been shoed, but particularly in the Western hemisphere (Jonas & Doosje, 2013). The humiliating act of shoe throwing apparently filled a political protest vacuum in certain Western democratic countries by fulfilling a need of symbolic humiliation. We have cited the humiliation of Dominique Strauss-Kahn (and the

French nation) during the prep walk after his arrest. In fact, he has also fallen victim to humiliating shoeing during a visit to Turkey before (Reuters, 2009a). One further aspect is quite striking, too. The aforementioned humiliation spiral was also expressed in the context of shoe throwing. Muntadhar al-Zaidi, who threw the "first shoe" at George W. Bush later got shoed himself in 2009 (Reuters, 2009b) by an Iraqi in French exile. The motivation of the pro-US attacker of al-Zaidi was apparently to humiliate him for siding with a dictatorial regime. Clearly, shoeing is a side aspect and also focuses on the perpetrator, but it demonstrates how vivid and adaptable humiliation actually is. Having moved to the political agenda already, it is not a far step to think about interventions, since humiliation, despite all the taboos around it, is obviously quite ubiquitous.

Interventions in the context of humiliation

Given the potential negative consequences of humiliation, it is worthwhile reflecting on possible interventions. Such interventions could serve two goals. First, one would want to raise the awareness of potential humiliating perpetrators for their actions. This group could entail involuntary perpetrators who are not aware of the humiliating potential of their actions, as well as intentional perpetrators who want to use humiliation as a means in a conflict, but are not aware of the severity of their actions, or its escalation spiral. Second, victims of humiliation could benefit from strategies that alleviate experiences of humiliation. In fact, as we have argued before, both goals can be fused into one, since victims of humiliation sometimes can become perpetrators of humiliation, when seeking revenge for their experiences. Thus, we decided to focus on two groups during our intervention pilots. One group was composed of civil servants in the city of Amsterdam, who worked in the social support sector and had client contact. We chose this group since they are potential involuntary perpetrators when dealing with low status clients (sometimes from a different cultural background), but also potential victims of humiliation, given the often harsh responses of their clients. The second group contained immigrant males and females, mostly from a Surinamese and Moroccan background living in The Netherlands. We chose this group for its potential victim status in terms of humiliation.

Designing an intervention requires the reflection on fit of the educational paradigms with the contingencies of the identified training population (e.g., accessibility of the topic, participation motivation, time budgets, etc.). We aimed for a one-day or half-day training, that focuses on opening up the topic, by giving participants the room and time to reflect and report on their own humiliation experiences. The training part was designed to build upon these statements and to develop resilience and coping strategies. It is noteworthy that the operationalization and implementation of the training session, together with an external training company, proved much more difficult than expected. It seemed particularly difficult for institutions and individuals to acknowledge that in their context humiliation, both as a victim or as a perpetrator, was actually possible. Put differently, the need for the intervention trainings was renounced since "officially" no humiliation occurs in their respective contexts. Only the fact of running such training sessions, or extensive pre-training meetings could change this defensive notion.

The one-day trainings were designed as a mix of psycho-education elements, giving participants the opportunity to voice their experiences and informing them about potential strategies to avoid humiliation, or to deal with it. The first two trainings with civil servants could not be evaluated quantitatively due to situational constraints, and we had similar experiences with a group of low-educated immigrant women (although for different reasons, namely difficulties in understanding the questionnaire).

To give an idea of the quantitative results, we report the data from one training session with first or second generation immigrants here. Fourteen females and six males participated in this training session, with a mean age of 20 years (range 16–62). Six participants had completed university, six were in the process of completing university and the rest of the participants had completed mandatory schooling to high school degrees. Fourteen participants were born in The Netherlands, the rest in Suriname or Morocco, while the parent generation was born outside of The Netherlands (Suriname, Morocco). Eleven described themselves as Hindu, five as Muslim, two as Christian and two as undefined. Participants filled out a short questionnaire pre- and post-training. To ensure a 100 percent participation rate, data was gathered on location. In a multiple choice test, we assessed how participants defined humiliation, with all options holding some truth. Furthermore, we assessed how far participants estimated their own likelihood to become a victim, witness, perpetrator and involuntary perpetrator of humiliation. We also asked them how far the training had changed their perception that they can protect themselves in humiliation contexts, de-escalate a humiliation situation, console victims of humiliation and prevent themselves falling victim. All of these items were assessed by marking a spot on a 128mm long line with 1 standing for "do not agree" and 128 for "do fully agree" (actual measure invisible to participant). While the mean differences for the first four questions did not reach conventional levels of significance (all $F < 1$), a clear pattern was obtained for the latter four. The training was experienced as increasing self-protection, de-escalation potential, ability to console a victim, and prevention abilities (for statistical parameters see endnote).[1] In addition, with our multiple choice test for the definition, we recorded a complete reversal of the definition. While in the pre-measure 60 percent of the participants chose the option "Humiliation is denigrating and putting to the ground of people," 25 percent did so in the post-measure. The other main choice, "Humiliation is an emotion that people feel when they are put to the ground based on individual or group characteristic," was chosen in only 25 percent of the cases pre-training, but in 60 percent of the cases post-training, indicating a shift of understanding towards a more affective view of humiliation.

Taken together, we were positively surprised by the effect of a rather short intervention that aimed at making the topic accessible and delivering process information to the participants. As an empowerment strategy for minority members, training such as this seems like an effective way to counteract humiliation experiences. The training conducted in the civil service context revealed that participants also saw themselves more in a victim than in a perpetrator position. While such a self-perception is normal, it raises the question of how to reach potential perpetrators that (want to) use humiliation as a means of intergroup conflict, revenge or as a sign of radicalization.

Summary and concluding comments

In this chapter, we have covered a wide range of results on the topic of humiliation. To start with, we reviewed the definition of humiliation and pointed to the relevant extension of direct humiliation to vicarious experience. Furthermore, we pointed to situational determinants that make humiliation more painful, such as (laughing) audiences and individual differences, such as an increased sensitivity to potentially humiliating experiences. The second step focused on the analysis of humiliation on the neuro-cognitive level with the goal to reveal very basic processes and consequences of humiliation experience. Also on this level, humiliation turned out to be a very intense emotion, with the potential to filter through cognitive control processes. Using different paradigms, in the third step, we investigated the content of group-based humiliation experiences, vicarious humiliation on the intergroup level, and determinants for approach or withdrawal responses. Victim and perpetrator characteristics play a crucial role within the latter. Fourth, we investigated humiliation in intercultural settings pointing to the effect of honor as a trigger for strong effects, compared to individualistic or face-keeping societies. On the political stage, humiliation is an often-used tool, deployed strategically in diplomatic settings, but also as a form of political protest. Finally, we showed that interventions can alleviate humiliation experiences.

We have presented different lines of research on the topic of humiliation in this chapter to inform about the current state of research in this field. Without doubt, humiliation as a research topic needs to attract more scientific attention, since its effects on people and related behavioral outcomes are quite grave and can inflict intractable conflict on society. We have shown that both majority and minority group members, in The Netherlands and elsewhere, can suffer from humiliation and that the related responses have the potential to fuel critical intergroup conflict. The evidence, from both neuro-cognitive and narrative accounts, converge in describing humiliation as an intense emotion with a vast array of responses. From revenge and retaliation to withdrawal from society, many types of response are theoretically possible, and are driven by modulating conditions such as the honor or face-keeping culture, or by a stronger experience of one humiliation emotion subcomponent, such as shame or anger, over the other. It does not take much to imagine that feelings of humiliation of large portions of society can lead to radicalization, but also to hardening of group boundaries and even less integration. But, we have also shown ways out of this dilemma. The results of the pilot interventions are promising, both on a structural level of implementation locations, and on the level of effectiveness. It is now left to actors on the political agenda to employ these results and tools to counter the development into a heartless, humiliating society for many.

Note

1 Participants expect that they know how to protect themselves after the training, and feel that the training met their expectation (M_{pre} = 66.37 SE = 10.58; M_{post} = 93.26 SE = 5.74, $F(1,18)$ = 6.51, p = .02, η^2_p = .266). Also they expected and later estimated an improved de-escalation potential for themselves (M_{pre} = 58.53 SE = 9.92; M_{post} = 74.37 SE = 9.67, $F(1,18)$ = 4.55, p = .048, η^2_p = .2). A marginal effect was found for consolation of a victim (M_{pre} = 62.74 SE = 10.39; M_{post} = 82.21 SE = 8.03, $F(1,18)$ = 4.17, p = .056, η^2_p = .18) and also for prevention (M_{pre} = 57.18 SE = 10.15; M_{post} = 75.41 SE = 8.39, $F(1,16)$ = 2.33, p = .15, η^2_p = .13).

References

Bal, M. (2004). Zwarte Piet's bal masque. In M. S. Phillips & G. Schochet (Eds.), *Questions of tradition* (pp. 110–151). Toronto: University of Toronto Press.

Besser, A., & Zeigler-Hill, V. (2010). The influence of pathological narcissism on emotional and motivational responses to negative events: The roles of visibility and concern about humiliation. *Journal of Research in Personality*, *44*(4), 520–534.

Brown, G. W., Harris, T. O., & Hepworth, C. (1995). Loss, humiliation and entrapment among women developing depression: A patient and non-patient comparison. *Psychological Medicine*, *25*, 7–21.

Cohen, D. (1998). Culture, social organization, and patterns of violence. *Journal of Personality and Social Psychology*, *75*, 408–419.

Combs, D. J. Y., Campbell, G., Jackson, M., & Smith, R. H. (2010). Exploring the consequences of humiliating a moral transgressor. *Basic and Applied Social Psychology*, *32*, 128–143.

Doosje, B., Branscombe, N. R., Spears, R., & Manstead, A. S. R. (1998). Guilty by association: When one's group has a negative history. *Journal of Personality and Social Psychology*, *75*, 872–886.

Doosje, B., Jasini, A., Jonas, K. J., Sveinsdóttir, G., & Erbas, Y. (2013). *When your nation has been dishonored: Group-based humiliation in different cultures.* Manuscript under review.

Elison, J., & Harter, S. (2007). Humiliation: Causes, correlates, and consequences. In J. L. Tracy, R. W. Robins, & J. P. Tangney (Eds.), *The self-conscious emotions: Theory and research* (pp. 310–329). New York: Guilford.

Farmer, A. E., & McGuffin, P. (2003). Humiliation, loss and other types of life events and difficulties: A comparison of depressed subjects, healthy controls and their siblings. *Psychological Medicine*, *33*, 1169–1175.

Fattah, K., & Fierke, K. M. (2009). A clash of emotions: The politics of humiliation and political violence in the Middle East. *European Journal of International Relations*, *15*, 67–93.

Fontan, V. (2006). Polarization between occupier and occupied in post-Saddam Iraq: Colonial humiliation and the formation of political violence. *Terrorism and Political Violence*, *18*, 217–238.

Giacaman, R., Abu-Rmeileh, N. M. E., Husseini, A., Saab, H., & Boyce, W. (2006). Humiliation: The invisible trauma of war for Palestinian youth. *Public Health*, *121*, 563–571.

Gilbert, P. (1997). The evolution of social attractiveness and its role in shame, humiliation, guilt and therapy. *British Journal of Medical Psychology*, *70*, 113–147.

Ginges, J., & Atran, S. (2008). Humiliation and the inertia effect: Implications for understanding violence and compromise in intractable intergroup conflicts. *Journal of Cognition and Culture, 8,* 281–294.

Hartling, L. M., & Luchetta, T. (1999). Humiliation: Assessing the impact of derision, degradation, and debasement. *The Journal of Primary Prevention, 19,* 259–278.

Higgins, E. T. (1997). Beyond pleasure and pain. *American Psychologist, 52,* 1280–1300.

—— (1998). The aboutness principle: A pervasive influence on human inference. *Social Cognition, 16,* 173–198.

—— (2000). Making a good decision: Value from fit. *American Psychologist, 55,* 1217–1229.

Jackson, M. A. (1999). *Distinguishing shame and humiliation.* Lexington, University of Kentucky.

Jamieson, J. P., Harkins, S. G., Williams, K. D. (2010). Need threat can motivate performance after ostracism. *Personality and Social Psychology Bulletin, 36,* 690–702.

Jasini, A. Doosje, B., Jonas, K., & Fischer, A. H. (2012). The role of honor and culture in group-based humiliation, anger and shame. *In Mind, 13,* Retrieved from http://beta. in-mind.org/ (September 13, 2013).

Jonas, K. J. (2013). *Regulatory focus as a determinant for responses to humiliation.* University of Amsterdam: Unpublished dataset.

Jonas, K. J., & Doosje, B. (2013). *Shoe throwing as novel humiliating acts on the political agenda.* Manuscript in preparation.

Jonas, K. J., Doosje, B., Lobel, A., & Pysczcynski, T. (2013). *Humiliation, anger and shame as determinants in intergroup conflict.* Manuscript in preparation.

Jonas, K. J., Doosje, B., & Song, S. (2013). *Being included, ignored, rejected or humiliated? Effects of different forms of social exclusion on pro- and anti-social behavioral tendencies.* Manuscript in preparation.

Jonas, K. J., Feddes, A. R., Mann, L., & Klok, R. (2013). *Differential accounts of humiliation among minority groups in The Netherlands.* Manuscript in preparation.

Kendler, K. S., Hettema, J. M., Butera, F., Gardner, C. O., & Prescott, C. A. (2003). Life event dimensions of loss, humiliation, entrapment, and danger in the prediction of onsets of major depression and generalized anxiety. *Archives of General Psychiatry, 60,* 789–796.

Klein, A. J. (2010). Israel and Turkey: Anatomy of a dissing war. *Time Magazine* http:// content.time.com/time/world/article/0,8599,1953746,00.html (September 13, 2013).

Klein, D. C. (1991). The humiliation dynamic: An overview. *The Journal of Primary Prevention, 12,* 93–121.

Lacey, D. (2011). The role of humiliation in the Palestinian/Israeli conflict in Gaza. *Psychology & Society, 4,* 76–92. Retrieved from www.psychologyandsociety.org/ (September 13, 2013)

Leidner, B., Sheikh, H., & Ginges, J. (2012). Affective dimensions of intergroup humiliation. *PLoS ONE 7*(9): e46375.

Lindner, E. G. (2001a). Humiliation and human rights: Mapping a minefield. *Human Rights Review, 2,* 46–63.

—— (2001b). Humiliation – Trauma that has been overlooked: An analysis based on fieldwork in Germany, Rwanda/Burundi, and Somalia. *Traumatology, 7,* 43–68.

—— (2001c). Humiliation as the source of terrorism: A new paradigm. *Peace Research, 33,* 59–68. Retrieved from www.humiliationstudies.org (September 13, 2013).

—— (2002). Healing the cycles of humiliation: How to attend to the emotional aspects of "unsolvable" conflicts and the use of "humiliation entrepreneurship". *Peace and Conflict: Journal of Peace Psychology*, *8*, 125–138.

—— (2009). Genocide, humiliation, and inferiority. In N. A. Robins, & A. Jones (Eds.), *Genocides by the oppressed: Subaltern genocide in theory and practice.* (p. 138). Indiana University Press.

Mackie, D. M., Devos, T., & Smith, E. R. (2000). Intergroup emotions: Explaining offensive action tendencies in an intergroup context. *Journal of Personality and Social Psychology*, *79*, 602–616.

Mann, L., Feddes, A. R., Leiser, Doosje, B., & Fischer, A. (2013). *When laughing hurts: Antecedents and consequences of humiliation.* Manuscript in preparation.

Mendoza-Denton, R., Downey, G., Purdie, V. J., Davis, A., & Pietrzak, J. (2002). Sensitivity to status based rejection: Implications for African American students' college experience. *Journal of Personality and Social Psychology*, *83*, 896–918.

Miller, W. I. (1993). *Humiliation and other essays on honor, social discomfort, and violence.* Ithaca, New York: Cornell University Press.

Mosquera, P. M. R., Fischer, A., & Manstead, A. S. R. (2002). Honor in the Mediterranean and northern Europe. *Journal of Cross-Cultural Psychology*, *33*, 16–36.

Mosquera, P. M. R., Fischer, A., Manstead, A. S. R., & Zaalberg, R. (2008). Attack, disapproval, or withdrawal? The role of honor in anger and shame responses to being insulted. *Cognition and Emotion*, *22*, 1471–1498.

Otten, M., & Jonas, K. J. (2013). Out of the group, out of control? The brain responds to social exclusion with changes in cognitive control. *Social Cognitive and Affective Neuroscience*, *8*, 789–794.

—— (in press). Humiliation as an intense emotional experience: Evidence from the electro-encephalogram. *Social Neuroscience*.

Otten, M., Jonas, K. J., Doosje, B., & Erbas, Y. (2013). *Feeling through others and acting on it: approach- and avoidance-related response dynamics following vicarious humiliation.* Manuscript under review.

Otten, M., Jonas, K. J., Mann, L., & Van Berkum, J. J. A. (2013). *Laughing matter(s): How the presence of a laughing crowd changes the perception of insults.* Manuscript under review.

Proulx, J., Aubut, J., McKibben, A., & Côté, M. (1994). Penile responses of rapists and nonrapists to rape stimuli involving physical violence or humiliation. *Archives of Sexual Behavior*, *23*, 295–310.

Reuters (2009a). *Student throws shoe at IMF chief in Istanbul protest.* http://uk.reuters.com/article/2009/10/01/uk-imf-protest-sb-idUKTRE59027O20091001 (September 13, 2013)

—— (2009b). *Fellow Iraqi turns tables on Bush shoe-thrower.* www.reuters.com/article/2009/12/02/us-iraq-shoe-idUSTRE5B15F920091202 (September 13, 2013).

Ricolfi, L. (2005). Palestinians, 1981–2003. In D. Gambetta (Ed.), *Making sense of suicide missions* (pp. 77–129). New York: Oxford University Press.

Saurette, P. (2006). You dissin me? Humiliation and post 9/11 global politics. *Review of International Studies*, *32*, 495–522.

Smith, D. (2008). Globalization, degradation and the dynamics of humiliation. *Current Sociology*, *56*, 371–379.

Smith, E. R. (1993). Social identity and social emotions: Toward new conceptualizations of prejudice. In D. M. Mackie & D. L. Hamilton (Eds.), *Affect, cognition and* stereotyping: Interactive processes in group perception* (pp. 297–315). San Diego. CA: Academic Press.

Torres, W. J., & Bergner, R. M. (2010). Humiliation: Its nature and consequences. *The Journal of the American Academy of Psychiatry and the Law. 38.* 195–204.

Tracy, J. L., & Robins, R. W. (2004). Putting the self into self-conscious emotions: A theoretical model. *Psychological Inquiry. 15.* 103–125.

Trumbull, D. (2008). Humiliation: The trauma of disrespect. *The Journal of the American Academy of Psychoanalysis and Dynamic Psychiatry. 36.* 643–660.

Van Zomeren, M., Spears, R., Fischer, A. H., & Leach, C. W. (2004). Put your money where your mouth is!: Explaining collective action tendencies through group-based anger and group efficacy. *Journal of Personality and Social Psychology. 87.* 649–664.

Walker, J., & Knauer, V. (2011). Humiliation, self-esteem and violence. *The Journal of Forensic Psychiatry & Psychology, 22.* 724–741.

Williams, K. D., & Jarvis, B. (2006). Cyberball: A program for use in research on interpersonal ostracism and acceptance. *Behavior Research Methods. 38.* 174–180.

Yzerbyt, V., Dumont, M., Wigboldus, D., & Gordijn. E. (2003). I feel for us: The impact of categorization and identification on emotions and action tendencies. *British Journal of Social Psychology. 42.* 533–549.

4   Minority identity and host national identification among immigrants

Maykel Verkuyten and Borja Martinovic

> When people identify with one another as compatriots, over and above the many more specific gender, ethnic, cultural, or religious identities they may have, they are more likely to display generalized trust, and to show solidarity. This reduces social conflict and increases willingness to cooperate.
>
> (Miller & Ali, 2013, p. 2)

Introduction

Misunderstandings, tensions and conflicts are less likely to occur between people of the same group than of different groups. There is a wealth of social psychological evidence that positive feelings and emotions such as sympathy, trust, commitment and solidarity are spontaneously associated with one's in-group, and that people are more helpful towards someone who belongs to their own group (Brewer, 2007; Dovidio & Gaertner, 2010; also De Dreu, Aaldering, & Saygi, this volume). The distinction between the in-group and a relevant out-group affects people's thoughts, feelings, and actions, especially when meaningful ethnic and religious group differences are involved.

Immigration and cultural diversity can lead to a lack of feelings of belonging together and thereby put a strain on the cohesion of societies. As argued in the quote above, a sense of "we-ness" is beneficial for national solidarity, a unified society and effective democracy. It is argued that diversity in values, religion and ethnic origin make people less willing to sacrifice, trust and share across group boundaries and for the common good (Goodhart, 2013; Scheffer, 2011; also Gesthuizen, Savelkoul, & Scheepers, this volume). Furthermore, politicians and the media often claim that many immigrants have divided loyalties and a lack of attachment to the host society and therefore undermine a cohesive society.

Proponents of multiculturalism argue that a society cannot ignore the demands of diversity because diversity has cultural and economic benefits and because minority groups need and deserve cultural recognition and affirmation (Taylor, 1992). Ignoring these demands would provoke resistance, create suspicions and threaten the very unity and cohesion that politicians, policy makers and citizens seek (Modood, 2007; Parekh, 2000). At the same time these proponents agree that unity and a shared national identity is equally important. They argue that a well-functioning society needs a sense of commitment and common belonging. Without this a society would degenerate into a collection of segregated cultural groups that only trust and feel solidarity towards ethnic or religious in-group members. The lack of a shared sense of national "we" would alienate groups of people and can lead to conflict and fragmentation. National feelings would provide a necessary counter-weight against the call of ethnic and religious group allegiances and loyalties. As the French socialist leader Jean Jaurès put it, "The point is not to destroy patriotism but to enlarge it" (in Goodhart, 2013, p. 286).

This emphasis on a shared national identity is in agreement with social psychological research on the common in-group identity model (CIIM; Dovidio, Gaertner, & Saguy, 2007). An overarching or shared sense of "we" works against intergroup tensions and conflicts because it ensures that the previous out-group is incorporated and becomes one of "us." In this way, the former out-group benefits from the preference that usually exists for the in-group. A shared identity provides a common point of reference and a moral framework with the related sentiments of belonging together, mutual commitments and responsibilities.

A shared sense of "we" requires a widespread notion that immigrants and minorities can be English, German, French or Dutch in the same way as natives. This is far from self-evident, even in an immigrant country like the United States in which white Americans have been found to implicitly associate being American with being White (Devos & Banaji, 2005), and in multicultural Canada "It had to be made clear that one was not closer to the heart of the Canadian identity if one was called Jones than if one's name was Kowalski or Minelli" (Taylor, 2012, p. 417). Defining the national identity of a culturally diverse society is a difficult enterprise leading to heated debates and sometimes triggering ethnic nationalist reactions that have exclusionary consequences for immigrants.

A shared sense of "we" also implies that immigrants and minorities identify with the national category. Cross-national research shows that in almost all countries migrant groups have lower host national identification than the majority group and a relatively weak sense of national belonging to the new country (e.g., Elkins & Sides, 2007; Staerklé, Sidanius, Green, & Molina, 2010). There is also some research evidence for a re-emphasis of ethnic distinctiveness (re-ethnicisation) among minority groups, and some research in Western Europe has found that the majority of Muslim immigrants consider themselves primarily a Muslim rather than a citizen of their host country (e.g., Phalet & Güngör, 2006). On the other hand, there are many immigrants who do develop attachment and commitment to the host society. This raises the question of when and why immigrants develop this sense of national belonging.

Proponents of multiculturalism argue that a dual identity is needed in which ethnic and religious group distinctiveness are affirmed within a context of national connection and common belonging. Similarly, the CIIM has recognized that trying to replace ethnic or religious minority identities with a sense of national belonging implies that minority groups lose their distinctiveness which may arouse strong reactance and result in intergroup tensions and conflicts (Dovidio, Gaertner, & Saguy, 2007). How a sense of national belonging relates to immigrants' ethnic and religious identities is a central question. In this chapter we address this question by discussing some of our research on (host) national identification among first and second generation immigrants in the Netherlands and Germany. After a brief discussion of the role of acculturation, we examine the importance of perceived minority acceptance for immigrants' national identification. Hereby we also discuss research on the "integration paradox" which shows that higher rather than lower educated immigrants can have a less positive orientation towards the host society. Subsequently we discuss the mediating role of ethnic and religious group identification in the relation between perceived acceptance and host national identification. Third, we examine perceived value incompatibility and in-group norms as two factors that can make minority group identification and national identification more contradictory. Finally, we discuss research on the intersection between ethnic and religious identity among Muslim immigrants and the ways in which this can hamper a sense of host national belonging.

Acculturation

To identify with a host society one has to get acquainted with it first. This implies that immigrants have to invest in participating and learning about the culture of the host country if they want to feel that they belong. In the migration literature, immigrants' host nation identification is considered the final stage in the integration process, which only takes place after immigrants have integrated culturally, economically and socially (Esser, 2001; Gordon, 1964). By participating on the labor market, developing contacts with the native population and learning the language of the host country, immigrants become familiar with the norms, values and customs of the receiving culture, which makes it possible for them to develop a stronger sense of belonging to the host nation. In a large-scale study among immigrants in the Netherlands we found that employment, language proficiency and contacts with Dutch natives were all positively related to Dutch identification (De Vroome, Verkuyten, & Martinovic, 2013a). A conclusion would be that immigrants are largely themselves responsible for developing a sense of belonging and that it is up to them whether they want to make the effort. However, the process of national identification is not just an individual endeavor and can be hampered by rejection on the part of the native group in the host country. Importantly, the same study revealed that perceived acceptance is one of the most important determinants of national identification among immigrants in the Netherlands.

Perceived acceptance

In many countries immigrants face discrimination. For example, in a field experimental study in the Netherlands, professional actors who differed in ethnic background were trained to apply in the same way and with the same qualifications for the same jobs. It turned out that immigrants were almost twice as likely to be rejected by temporary employment agencies (Andriessen, Nievers, & Dagevos, 2012). Similar studies in the United States also demonstrate a clear tendency towards ethnic discrimination on the labor market (e.g., Bertrand & Mullainathan, 2004).

Discrimination implies unfair treatment and such treatment tells people that they are not equal members of society and that society itself is less valuable (Tyler, 2001). It is difficult for people to develop a sense of belonging when they have the feeling that they are not really accepted or valued and are treated as second-class citizens. In these cases it is more likely that they feel aggrieved and alienated, and as a result, turn away from the host society. Immigrants are often faced with negative stereotypes and anti-immigrant sentiments in public and political debates, with concomitant ethnic and exclusionary conceptions of host nationhood (Helbling, 2012; Vasta, 2007). Studying immigrant youth in Belgium, Sweden and the Netherlands, Fleischmann (2011) found that perceived discrimination (i.e., experiences of hostility or unfair treatment) was associated with weaker national identification. And in a longitudinal study among Russian immigrants in Finland, it was found that perceived discrimination was causally related to lower national identification (Jasinskaja-Lahti, Liebkind, & Solheim, 2009).

A related stream of research examines subgroup respect, or the extent to which a subgroup is valued and accepted by the receiving society, and has shown that for ethnic minorities lower perceived respect predicts more negative feelings towards the host nation and lower levels of trust in its institutions (Huo & Molina, 2006). For example, in a study among Latino immigrants in the United States perceived rejection from Americans (e.g., "Because I am Latino, I don't think that Americans will ever fully accept me") was associated with lower identification with the United States (Wiley, 2013). Low perceived subgroup respect is negatively related to attitudes towards the nation, because it signifies that the host nation does not recognize and value immigrants as part of the collective.

The integration paradox

Not all immigrants are equally sensitive and reactive to perceived host society acceptance. Politicians and opinion makers often argue that education is the key to integration and the development of a sense of national belonging. This is in agreement with classical immigration theories that suggest that structural integration (improving one's education and economic position) will lead to other forms of integration, such as a more positive attitude towards the host society (Esser, 2001; Gordon, 1964). Yet, the so-called "integration paradox" describes the phenomenon of the economically more integrated and highly educated immigrants turning away from the host society, instead of becoming more oriented towards it (Buijs, Demant, & Hamdy, 2006). The integration paradox suggests that education might form an obstacle for developing positive attitudes towards the majority population and the host society. There are a number of possible reasons for this.

First, the theory of exposure suggests that higher educated immigrants may actually experience more discrimination and lower subgroup respect in everyday life. The higher compared to the lower educated more often use host country media and tend to have more contacts with majority members on the labor market and in associations, and therefore might be more likely exposed to discrimination and derogating messages (Van Doorn, Scheepers, & Dagevos, 2013; also see Gesthuizen, Savelkoul, & Scheepers, this volume).

Second, higher education increases cognitive sophistication which can mean that higher educated immigrants are more aware of, and have a better understanding of processes of exclusion and reduced opportunities in society (Kane & Kyyro, 2001; Wodtke, 2012). Education enables immigrants to become more sophisticated social critics who can seek to challenge derogations and advocate policies that redress group disadvantages.

Third, the theory of rising expectations suggests that immigrants who pursue higher education and try to make a contribution to society, develop higher expectations. Therefore, they are more strongly disappointed about unequal treatment, and feel that the opportunities they are given in the host country do not do justice to their skills. Compared to lower educated immigrants, those who are relatively successful in education might perceive higher levels of relative deprivation with respect to the majority population, which can lead to a lower sense of national belonging (Smith, Pettigrew, Pippin, & Bialosiewicz, 2012).

The integration paradox argues that experiences and perceptions of non-acceptance and disrespect, despite their efforts and achievements, would lead the higher educated to distance themselves from society. Thus, the more successful ones would be more sensitive to ethnic acceptance and equality which in turn would drive their reactions to the host society. We found support for this paradox in one of our studies among large randomly drawn samples of Turkish, Moroccan, Surinamese and Antillean immigrants in the Netherlands (De Vroome, Martinovic, & Verkuyten, 2013b). Using structural equation modeling we investigated the relations between immigrants' education and their perceived acceptance in terms of perceptions of discrimination and of subgroup respect. It was found that the higher educated immigrants perceived more discrimination and less respect for minorities, and these perceptions, in turn, were related to less positive evaluations of the native majority and the host society. This was found for the four immigrant groups and for the first and second generation. Importantly, our findings showed that higher education was associated with lower acceptance among immigrants who were educated in the Netherlands, and not among those educated in the country of origin. The native majority is an especially relevant and meaningful comparison group for those who are educated in the host society. Their sense of relative deprivation stems from perceiving fewer opportunities despite having the same level of education as majority members. The education of majority members is probably a less relevant standard of comparison for immigrants who were educated in the country of origin.

These findings on the integration paradox seem contradictory to the many studies that show that higher educated immigrants tend to have more voluntary and positive contacts with the majority group (e.g., Martinovic, Van Tubergen, & Maas, 2011) and therefore develop a stronger sense of belonging to the host society (De Vroome, Verkuyten, & Martinovic, 2013a). This might mean that there are two pathways involved. On the one hand, higher educated minorities have more frequent contacts with the majority population than lower educated minorities, and more contact is associated with *higher* national identification. On the other hand, higher educated minorities feel less accepted in the country and perceive more discrimination than lower educated minorities, resulting in *lower* national identification. In another large-scale study among randomly drawn samples of Turks, Moroccans, Surinamese and Antilleans in the Netherlands (Ten Teije, Coenders, & Verkuyten, 2013) we found evidence for these two paths (Figure 4.1), and the pattern of associations was quite similar for these four groups.

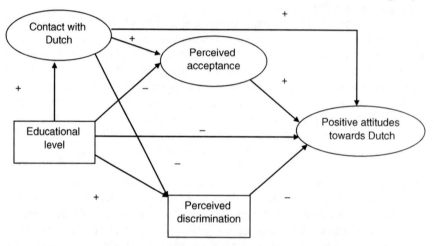

Note 1: Perceived discrimination is distinguished in group discrimination and personal discrimination.
Note 2: Circles indicate latent variables and squares manifest variables.

Figure 4.1 Path diagram model of the direct and indirect effects on the attitude towards the Dutch (based on Ten Teije et al., 2013)

For the first pathway, the findings (Figure 4.1) demonstrated that higher educated migrants indeed had more contact with the native Dutch and that contact was associated with stronger national identification, directly but also through lowered perceptions of discrimination and higher perceived acceptance. Importantly, there was also empirical evidence for the second pathway. Higher educated immigrants perceived lower acceptance of ethnic minority groups in Dutch society and more group discrimination than lower educated migrants. These perceptions were related to weaker national identification. In addition, the unfair treatment of co-ethnics (group discrimination) rather than personal experiences with discrimination, was found to be important for the identification of the higher educated. This supports the idea that the more advantaged members of disadvantaged groups tend to engage in group comparisons and develop more negative attitudes towards the advantaged group (Taylor & Moghaddam, 1994; also see De Dreu et al., this volume). Higher education might increase one's awareness of and concerns about the vulnerable and relatively marginal position of immigrants in society. In addition, when they perceive and experience ethnic discrimination, higher educated minority members might be more assertive (Baumgartner, 1998). Although we did not explicitly test these interpretations, we did find that the higher educated perceived more group discrimination than the lower educated, whereas there was no difference for personal discrimination. In turn, and independently of personal discrimination, higher perceived non-acceptance of migrant groups and of group discrimination were associated with weaker national identification.

Minority group identification

Ethnic discrimination and a lack of subgroup respect implicate one's ethnic group membership. According to social identity theory (Tajfel & Turner, 1979) and the related rejection-identification model (Branscombe, Schmitt, & Harvey, 1999), discrimination is a negative experience that strengthens ethnic identification of minorities. It presents an identity threat that makes people increasingly turn toward the safety and acceptance of their minority group and away from the discriminating majority group. People can cope with threats like discrimination by adopting group-based strategies that increase identification with their minority group and a distancing from the host society. Experimental and longitudinal evidence has shown that perceptions of discrimination, and identity threat more generally, can increase in-group identification or lead to greater emotional attachment to one's group (e.g., Ramos, Cassidy, Reicher, & Haslam, 2012). Furthermore, perceptions of discrimination can also lead to an over-time decrease in immigrants' national identification (Jasinskaja-Lahti et al., 2009, 2012). Thus, perceived social rejection and devaluation might not only result in increased minority group identification but also in decreased national identification. In concrete terms, these perceptions can result in feeling more African as well as less American, more Indian and less British, and more Turkish and less Dutch. Such a combined effect on group identifications gives a more detailed understanding of the implications of perceived acceptance among ethnic minority group members. Furthermore, it has been suggested that ethnic identification (partly) mediates the relationship between perceived social rejection and national identification. For example, a Turkish-Dutch person may have a low Dutch national identification because she emphasizes her Turkish identity, and she emphasizes this identity because she experiences social rejection and devaluation of Turks in the Netherlands. The existence of such a mediating role for in-group identification helps us identify the psychological mechanism by which perceived ethnic group rejection affects national identification.

We found evidence for this mediating role of ethnic identification in three survey studies among Turkish immigrants in the Netherlands (Verkuyten &

Yildiz, 2007). The results of the first study showed that perceived rejection was associated with stronger Turkish identification and, via Turkish identification, with more distancing from the Dutch. Higher ethnic identification thus tended to go together with lower host nation identification. In a second study we examined whether these findings were reliable and could be generalized to another sample of Turkish immigrants, and we additionally looked at the role of religious (Muslim) identification. Debates around issues of immigration and diversity are increasingly revolving around religious diversity. In particular, Islam has taken the central place in diversity debates in Europe (Zolberg & Long, 1999), and is also increasingly discussed in the United States. It is argued that Islam forms a "bright boundary" separating immigrants from host societies (Alba, 2005). An important implication for research is that religious identity should be considered when studying the link between ethnic and national identification. It is possible that Muslim identity clashes more strongly with Dutch national identification than ethnic identity does.

The results of our second study showed a strong positive correlation between Turkish and Muslim identification, indicating that being a Muslim is a centrally important element of what it means to be Turkish in the Netherlands. Furthermore, perceived structural discrimination was associated with stronger Turkish and Muslim identification. However, whereas Muslim identification was a significant negative predictor of Dutch national identification, the independent effect for Turkish identification was not significant. Additionally, the negative effect of perceived discrimination on Dutch identification was partly explained by Muslim identification.

In a third study we focused further on religious identity and examined three aspects of Muslim identity: Muslim identity importance, behavioral involvement and political organization. Furthermore, we made a distinction between host national identification and dis-identification. Low national group identification does not have to be the same as dis-identification which expresses resistance to or active rejection of the host nation and thereby makes it more difficult to create or sustain a sense of solidarity across group lines. Studies among racial and ethnic minority groups have described the development of an oppositional or reactive identity in which people actively separate their identity from the culture and defining aspects of the dominant group (Ogbu, 1993; Portes & Zhou, 1993).

The findings of the third study indicate that an empirical distinction between Dutch identification and Dutch dis-identification can be made. A low sense of belonging and commitment to a group does not appear to be the same as rejecting and distancing oneself from that group. Participants who considered their Muslim identity as a central part of their self, reported again lower commitment to the Netherlands as well as stronger dis-identification. Interestingly, Muslim behavioral involvement and political organization were not independently associated with Dutch identification. They were, however, significant predictors of Dutch dis-identification. Participants who were more strongly involved in actions and practices that directly implicate Muslim identity and participants who more strongly endorsed Muslim political organization tended to dis-identify more. The differential findings for the three dimensions of Muslim identification suggest that it is not so much identity importance but rather the content and meaning of Muslim identity that can make Muslim and host national identity incompatible.

Incompatibility

We set out to examine the role of perceived value incompatibility in a further study among Turkish immigrants in the Netherlands and Germany (Martinovic & Verkuyten, 2012). The Western and Muslim ways of life are often considered to collide. They are perceived to be based on different values that often do not go together (Gijsberts, 2005). Perceived and actual value differences constitute the main boundary between Muslim immigrants and West European majority members (Sniderman & Hagendoorn, 2007).

Values are central to people's judgments and behavior since they present a basic scheme with which people understand each other and a benchmark against which social reality is compared and evaluated. Values define who we are and represent moral guidelines for deciding what is right or wrong, what must be allowed and what must be forbidden. Value incompatibility implies that the content of two cultural identities leads to incommensurable ways of life. This increases the in-group–out-group distinction and makes it "impossible for the different subgroups within a superordinate body to express their identities at the same time" (Sindic & Reicher, 2009, p. 116; see also Harinck & Ellemers, this volume).

It has been suggested that the relationship between Muslim and host national identification depends on perceived value incompatibility. The practical ability to act on the basis of one's group identity is important for most religious groups and for Muslims in particular. In comparison with ethnic identity, the content of religious identity is typically less negotiable and amendable because religion is accompanied by stricter and more clearly delineated rules of conduct related, for example, to eating practices, dress code and rituals. This holds especially for Islam in which orthopraxis is a central defining characteristic of what it means to be a "true" Muslim (Williams, 1994). The five pillars of Islam prescribe the key Islamic practices, like daily prayers and fasting during Ramadan. However, in many European countries these practices, and also the wearing of a headscarf and the building of Mosques, are topics of strong political and legal debates and often defined to be incompatible with the Western way of life. A likely implication is that perceived value incompatibility makes it more difficult to feel a Muslim and a member of the host society at the same time. Thus, religious identification probably relates negatively to national identification only for Turkish Muslims who perceive incompatibility between Western and Islamic values and lifestyles.

Furthermore, Muslim immigrants might respond differently to discrimination depending on the perception of value incompatibility. Discrimination communicates the devaluation of one's group and instigates identity management strategies for achieving a more positive social identity (Tajfel & Turner, 1979). Minority members can react to discrimination with withdrawal from the host society and a stronger emphasis on their minority identity, as predicted by the rejection-identification model. Alternatively, however, they can respond with following an individualistic social mobility path and dissociate themselves from the devalued in-group (Wright, Taylor, & Moghaddam, 1990). This strategy depends on the intergroup structure and presupposes that the group boundaries are seen as relatively permeable, which indicates that membership in the higher status group can be achieved. Those who perceive relatively high value incompatibility are not likely to follow an individualistic mobility path in which they dissociate themselves from their devalued in-group (see also Ramos, Jetten, Zhang, Badea, Iyer, Cui, & Zhang, 2013). Rather, following the rejection-identification model they can be expected to show increased identification with their religious in-group. In contrast, discrimination can be expected not to be related to Muslim identification for those who perceive relatively little value incompatibility and therefore consider the path of individualistic social mobility feasible.

We measured perceived value incompatibility in our research on Muslims in Germany and the Netherlands (e.g., "Dutch/German values and norms are contradictory to Islam," "Islamic and Dutch/German ways of life are irreconcilable") and controlled for demographic factors such as gender, education, age, host country nationality, and length of stay in the host country (Martinovic & Verkuyten, 2012). We found clear evidence for the moderating role of perceived value incompatibility. Figure 4.2 shows the associations from a structural equation model for participants perceiving relatively high incompatibility. For these participants higher perceived discrimination was associated with stronger religious group identification, which in turn was associated with weaker national identification. These associations were not significant for participants perceiving low value incompatibility. Importantly these relationships were found to be similar in Germany and the Netherlands, for first and second generation immigrants and for those with and without host country citizenship.

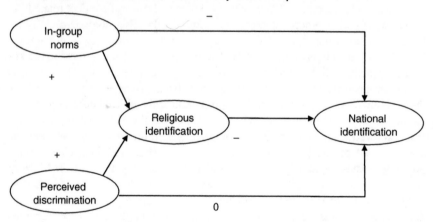

Note: Unstandardized coefficients, with standard errors in the brackets.

Figure 4.2 Results of the structural model for high incompatibility with signs (−, 0, +) indicating significance and directionality; (based on Martinovic & Verkuiten, 2012).

In-group norms

Most of the literature on minority identities focuses on intergroup factors and tends to ignore intragroup processes. However, dynamics within an in-group can also be a source of conflicts and tensions if some in-group members show behavior that deviates from the in-group's norms. Minority groups typically try to maintain their in-group norms and values, and immigrant groups are often engaged in concerted efforts to preserve cultural continuity. Furthermore, group norms influence the behavior of individual group members through processes of social control and group identification (Tajfel & Turner, 1979). Longitudinal research has shown that relationships with others who share the same social identity increase the importance of this identity and the norms attached to it (Ethier & Deaux, 1994). Groups give a notion of collective identity that provides a sense of belonging, place and meaning, and this makes individuals feel grounded, connected and distinctive.

Individuals have a basic need to feel that they belong (Baumeister & Leary, 1995) and they tend to behave in ways that conform to the norms and demands of their in-group in order to secure acceptance as an in-group member. Rejection and not receiving full recognition of one's group membership by in-group members is painful. It makes people uncertain about themselves and their position within their group (Branscombe et al., 1999). According to uncertainty-identity theory (Hogg, 2000), people will be motivated to reduce this self-uncertainty and they can try to do so by identifying more strongly with the groups they belong to, in particular with groups that are highly entitative and distinctive. Religious groups are particularly effective because they provide a source of affiliation as well as clear norms for structuring beliefs and guiding behavior. Furthermore, for most believers, and for Muslim immigrants in particular, religious identity is typically very important (Verkuyten & Yildiz, 2007). When facing uncertainty about acceptance into an important in-group, people will try to present themselves as committed group members (Noel, Wann, & Branscombe, 1995). Therefore, one can expect that in-group norms to maintain one's ethno-religious culture make Muslim immigrants turn to their religion and strengthen their religious group identification.

In addition, distancing from a relevant out-group may be a way of confirming one's in-group membership. In order to gain approval and recognition of one's group membership, immigrants can distance themselves from the host society. This might mean that in the presence of relatively strong in-group norms immigrants identify more strongly with their religious in-group and, via higher religious identification, distance themselves from the host society by showing lower national identification. Thus, a negative relationship between perceived in-group norms and national identification might be explained by Muslim identification. As shown in Figure 4.2, this is exactly what we found in our study in Germany and the Netherlands (Martinovic & Verkuyten, 2012). Over and beyond the effect of discrimination by out-group, the perceived in-group norm to maintain their own ethno-religious culture was associated with religious group identification. The more Muslim immigrants perceived this in-group pressure (e.g., "My group puts pressure on its members to stick to the group's customs and rules," "You have to be careful not to give in-group members reasons to talk bad about you") the more strongly they identified with their religious group. Indirectly, through increased religious identification, in-group norms were related to lower national identification, but only for participants who perceived incompatibility between Islamic and Western values.

This finding is similar to research that shows that within ethnic minority communities there are often normative pressures to maintain one's own culture and not to assimilate. In a study of daily acculturative hassles among Vietnamese-Canadians, Lay and Nguyen (1998), for example, found evidence that not only out-group hassles (e.g., perceptions of prejudice and discrimination by the receiving society) but also in-group hassles (e.g., feeling isolated from the in-group, being perceived as acting too white by in-group members) have a significant negative impact on the acculturation process. These results suggest that in-group norms are an additional important factor in immigrants' group identifications. Additionally, in our study among Turkish immigrants in Germany and the Netherlands we also found that the association between ethnic and host national identification is more negative for those participants who felt a strong psychological commitment to their heritage culture compared to those who had a weak commitment. Identification processes have important intragroup implications and the in-group functions as a key reference group in the everyday life of minority members (Smith & Leach, 2004).

Intersection between ethnic and religious group identification

For Muslim immigrants, ethnicity and religion tend to overlap to a large degree. What it means to be a member of their ethnic minority group intersects with what it means to be a Muslim. The concept of social identity complexity refers to individual differences in the way in which different group memberships are subjectively combined (Roccas & Brewer, 2002). An inclusive or complex identity structure implies that an individual accepts and acknowledges the distinctive memberships of his or her various groups. Alternatively, individuals with a relatively simplified structure perceive a strong overlap and interrelation among their identities. In particular, members of groups holding multiple disadvantaged statuses experience these social categories in close association and simultaneously. For example, one research found lower perceived identity complexity among Asian Australians compared to Anglo Australians, despite the fact that the objective identity overlap was actually greater for the latter than the former group (Brewer, Gonsalkorale, & Van Dommelen, 2013). Roccas and Brewer (2002) argue that perceived threat lowers identity complexity. Evidence for this latter relationship is found in experimental research (Roccas & Brewer, 2002) and in two surveys in the context of Northern Ireland (Schmid, Hewstone, Tausch, Cairns, & Hughes, 2009).

There are cognitive and motivational reasons why lower identity complexity should be associated with less openness and lower out-group tolerance (Roccas &

Brewer, 2002). Low social identity complexity means that multiple identities are embedded in a single in-group representation making an individual who is an out-group member on one dimension also an out-group member on another dimension. This lack of cross-cutting identities increases the in-group vs. out-group distinctions and thereby strengthens the distancing from out-group members and increases the cognitive basis of in-group bias (Crisp & Hewstone, 2006). Additionally, overlapping group memberships strengthen the motivational bases for intergroup differentiation because of the increased self-evaluative significance of social comparisons and the importance of any one social identity for a sense of belonging (Tajfel & Turner, 1979). There is some empirical evidence for the proposition that lower social identity complexity is indeed associated with lower openness, less out-group tolerance and more intergroup bias (e.g., Brewer & Pierce, 2005; Miller, Brewer, & Arbuckle, 2009).

We investigated whether the intersection between ethnic and religious identification is negatively associated with immigrants' attitude towards the host society (Verkuyten & Martinovic, 2012). The main prediction was that the interaction of relatively strong ethnic and strong religious group identifications implies a simplified or exclusive identity that is related to lower national identification and a less positive attitude towards the native majority. We examined this prediction in three survey studies among Muslim immigrants of Turkish and Moroccan origin living in the Netherlands. The first study showed that lower identity complexity (i.e., higher intersection between ethnic and religious identity; "To what extent is it necessary for a person of your own ethnic group to also be a member of your own religious group?") was associated with lower national identification, over and above the effects of measures of perceived incompatibility and perceived subgroup equality. A second study replicated this finding and additionally showed that lower complexity was associated with a more positive evaluative bias towards the in-group compared to the Dutch. In the third study, it was found that lower social identity complexity was associated with lower national identification, lower endorsement of Dutch self-defining liberal practices and less positive stereotypes about the Dutch.

These findings show that there is a relatively high degree of overlap between ethnic and religious belonging among Muslim immigrants in the Netherlands which is also found in other West European countries (Fleischmann, 2011). In these countries, what it means to be a Turk, Moroccan or Pakistani often intersects with what it means to be a Muslim. When these identities are subjectively combined, there is a relatively simplified and exclusive identity structure. As a result, host nationals, who are perceived to be out-group members on one group dimension (ethnicity) are also perceived to be out-group members on the other dimension (religion). This increases the importance of the in-group in intergroup comparisons and the motivation to favor one's own group and to distance oneself from the host society.

Discussion

Questions of immigration and cultural diversity have become inextricably bound up with questions of national identity (Fenton, 2011). There are fierce political, public and academic debates about "rethinking the nation" and "redrawing the national story" in order to be more inclusive for immigrants and minorities but without losing majority public support. Some argue for the importance of a shared historical past and alleged national values, and others claim that equal citizenship rights and duties is sufficient for a shared national identity (Rattansi, 2011). Additionally, there are not only debates about the content of national identity but also about the value we should attach to it. For some, national identity is an outdated notion in our globalized world or it implies ethnic nationalist sentiments that are used to exclude and suppress minority cultures. Others claim that a shared national sense of "we" is necessary for social cohesion and social justice, as illustrated in the quote heading this chapter. National attachment would provide the emotional glue that holds culturally diverse societies together and allows them to function effectively (Goodhart, 2013; Scheffer, 2011), thereby preventing internal conflicts.

There are many difficult aspects and sides to this latter, so-called national identity argument (Miller & Ali, 2013). In this chapter we focused on the question of when and why immigrants develop a sense of host national identification and how this relates to their ethnic or religious identity. This question is relevant because a feeling of home and belonging is very important in itself, but also because politicians, the media and the public often accuse immigrants of having divided loyalties and a lack of attachment to the host society (Sniderman & Hagendoorn, 2007). There are different factors and conditions that stimulate or hamper immigrants' sense of national belonging, and the primary one is familiarity with the host culture that can be achieved through learning the language and making native friends. Additionally, intergroup and intragroup processes are especially influential and we examined perceived acceptance by the native majority, norms dictated by the minority in-group, and the interrelations with ethnic and religious group identifications.

Perceived acceptance appears to be a crucial condition for national identification. When immigrants feel accepted and valued they are more likely to develop host national attachments whereas disrespect and discrimination can lead to stronger ethnic and religious minority identities and a distancing from and dis-identification with the host society. This means, for example, that anti-discrimination policies are critically important because they improve people's opportunities and tell immigrants that they are equal members of society and that society is fair and has trustworthy institutions. As the findings for the integration paradox show, this seems particularly important for the sense of belonging of the more highly educated immigrants who make a strong effort to integrate in society.

In addition to discrimination and subgroup respect, beliefs about value incompatibility make it more difficult for Muslim immigrants to develop a sense of host national belonging. Incompatibility implies moral differences that lead to incommensurable ways of life in which the ability to live by one's religious minority practices is undermined (Sindic & Reicher, 2009). This is particularly problematic for Islam in which orthopraxis is central (Williams, 1994). One societal implication is that the current trend of blaming Muslims for failed integration and depicting Islam as a system of values that undermines the liberal values of the host societies might produce a further distancing from the receiving nation (Helbling, 2012). The perception of incompatibility most likely reflects not only the immigrants' own views but also the views of the majority as perceived by immigrants. By emphasizing a culture clash, politicians and media make the value conflict more salient in immigrants' minds, which can undermine their identity and hamper their feelings of national belonging.

However, beliefs about value incompatibility are also related to in-group norms to maintain their own culture. The more Muslim minorities perceive this in-group pressure, the more strongly they identify with their religious group and the more psychological distance they keep from the host society. Thus, Muslims in Western Europe might display weak national identification because they emphasize their Muslim identity, and they emphasize this identity not only because they experience social rejection and devaluation of Muslims but also due to pressures within the Muslim community to maintain their ethno-religious culture. Furthermore, for many Muslim immigrants there is a strong connection between their ethnic and religious identity. What it means to be a Turk or Moroccan is closely connected to what it means to be a Muslim. A subjectively close connection between these group memberships implies a simplified and exclusive identity structure which is associated with a relatively weak attachment to the host nation. Muslim immigrants who identify strongly with their overlapping ethnic and religious in-groups tend to distance themselves more from the host society than immigrants with a more complex identity structure.

The findings discussed in this chapter contribute to an understanding of the conditions under which immigrants and minority members develop a sense of national belonging, but we were not able to discuss all relevant aspects. In closing this chapter we want to emphasize two additional things. First, we focused on national identification in terms of national attachment but there are various other dimensions of national identification (e.g., sense of interdependence and mutual fate) that can be differently associated to different dimensions of ethnic and religious identities (Ashmore, Deaux, & McLaughlin-Volpe, 2004; Miller & Ali, 2013). It seems particularly important to consider the content of the different identities or the ways in which they are understood. For example, whether immigrants' ethnic identification is compatible with their sense of national belonging is likely to depend on whether the country of settlement has a civic, more pluralistic conception of nationhood, or rather an ethnic one (Phinney et al., 2006). Furthermore, in Germany and the Netherlands, being a Muslim is typically defined as contradictory to being a host national and in contrast to the United States and the United Kingdom, self-identification as German/Dutch Muslim is rather exceptional. These country differences indicate that the ways in which national identities are defined and understood is critical for the question when and why immigrants develop a sense of national belonging and how this relates to their ethnic or religious identity.

Second, there is a possible downside to immigrants' host national identification, particularly in deeply divided and unjust societies. National identification might hamper minority members' involvement in collective action that often is required for redressing structural inequalities and social justice in these societies. In these situations, change is predicated upon actions that aim to improve the rights, power, and influence of disadvantaged groups. This requires not only that people identify with their disadvantaged group but also that they recognize and feel angry about the social inequality and consider change possible. Furthermore, collective action is facilitated when there are clear group boundaries and a generally negative moral characterization of the advantaged majority group (Wright & Baray, 2012). For minority members national identification might imply a lower perception of injustice and less readiness to engage in initiatives to expose inequalities and disadvantages and to demand change. A shared national identity leads to perceiving greater similarity between "us" and "them," a psychological blurring of group boundaries, and a more positive characterization of the advantaged majority group. In research in Turkey, Bilali (2013) showed that for Turks and Kurds a shared national identification was associated with similar official Turkish understandings (e.g., conflict frames, attributions of responsibility, severity of harm) of the Turkish–Kurdish conflict. Thus, national identification among the minority group of Kurds was associated with the state narrative that legitimizes the status quo and hinders efforts to enhance the disadvantaged status of the Kurds. This example shows that national identification can undermine political mobilization and collective action of minority groups. However, this is more likely in deeply divided and unjust societies than in democratic societies in which identification with the society implies feelings of entitlement that stimulate political action. In democratic societies, ethnic minority members would "acknowledge or even stress their identity as a member of that society because only by virtue of their membership in this more inclusive group or community are they entitled to societal support for their claims" (Simon & Klandermans, 2001, p. 326).

References

Alba, R. (2005). Bright vs. blurred boundaries: Second-generation assimilation and exclusion in France, Germany and the United States. *Ethnic and Racial Studies, 28,* 20–49.

Andriessen, I., Nievers, E., & Dagevos, J. (2012). *Op achterstand: Discriminatie van niet-westerse migranten op de arbeidsmarkt.* Den Haag: SCP.

Ashmore, R. D., Deaux, K., & McLaughlin-Volpe, T. (2004). An organizing framework for collective identity: Articulation and significance of multidimensionality. *Psychological Bulletin, 130,* 80–114.

Baumeister, R. F., & Leary, M. R. (1995). The need to belong: Desire for interpersonal attachments as a fundamental human motivation. *Psychological Bulletin, 117,* 497–529.

Baumgartner, M. P. (1998). Moral life on the cultural frontier: Evidence from the experience of immigrants in modern America. *Sociological Focus, 31*, 155–179.

Bertrand, M., & Mullainathan, S. (2004). Are Emily and Greg more employable than Lakisha and Jamal? A field experiment on labor market discrimination. *The American Economic Review, 94*, 991–1013.

Bilali, R. (2013). The downsides of national identification for minority groups in intergroup conflicts in assimilationist societies. *British Journal of Social Psychology* (in press).

Branscombe, N. R., Schmitt, M. T., & Harvey, R. D. (1999). Perceiving pervasive discrimination among African Americans: Implications for group identification and well-being. *Journal of Personality and Social Psychology, 77*, 135–149.

Brewer, M. B. (2007). The social psychology of intergroup relations: Social categorization, ingroup bias, and outgroup prejudice. In A. W. Kruglanski, & E. T. Higgins (Eds.). *Social psychology: Handbook of basic principles* (pp. 695–715). New York, NY: Guilford Press.

Brewer, M. B., Gonsalkorale, K., & Van Dommelen, A. (2013). Social identity complexity: Comparing majority and minority ethnic group members in a multicultural society. *Group Processes and Intergroup Relations, 16*, 529–544.

Brewer, M. B., & Pierce, K. P. (2005). Social identity complexity and outgroup tolerance. *Personality and Social Psychology Bulletin, 31*, 428–437.

Buijs, F. J., Demant, F., & Hamdy, A. (2006). *Strijders van eigen bodem: Radicale en democratische Moslims in Nederland*. Amsterdam, the Netherlands: Amsterdam University Press.

Crisp, R. J., & Hewstone, M. (Eds.) (2006). *Multiple social categorization: Processes, models and applications*. New York: Psychology Press.

De Vroome, T., Verkuyten, M., & Martinovic, B. (2013a). National identification among natives and immigrants in the Netherlands. *International Migration Review* (forthcoming).

De Vroome, T., Martinovic, B., & Verkuyten, M. (2013b). The integration paradox: Education and attitudes towards natives among second generation immigrants in the Netherlands. *Cultural Diversity and Ethnic Minority Psychology* (forthcoming).

Devos, T., & Banaji, M. R. (2005). American = white? *Journal of Personality and Social Psychology, 88*, 447–466.

Dovidio, J. F., & Gaertner, S. L. (2010). Intergroup bias. In S. T. Fiske, D. Gilbert, & G. Lindzey (Eds.), *Handbook of social psychology* (Vol. 2, 5th ed., pp. 1084–1121). New York: Wiley.

Dovidio, J. F., Gaertner, S. L., & Saguy, T. (2007). Another view of "we": Majority and minority group perspectives on a common in-group identity. *European Review of Social Psychology, 18*, 296–330.

Elkins, Z., & Sides, J. (2007). Can institutions build unity in multiethnic states? *American Political Science Review, 101*, 693–708.

Esser, H. (2001). *Integration und Etnische Schichtung*. Mannheim, Germany: Arbeitspapiere – Mannheimer Zentrum für Europäische Sozialforschung.

Ethier, K. A., & Deaux, K. (1994). Negotiating social identity when contexts change— Maintaining identification and responding to threat. *Journal of Personality and Social Psychology, 67*, 243–251.

Fenton, S. (2011). The sociology of ethnicity and national identity. *Ethnicities, 11*, 12–17.

Fleischmann, F. (2011). *Second-generation Muslims in European societies: Comparative perspectives on education and religion*. Utrecht: Ercomer.

Gijsberts, M. (2005). Opvattingen van autochtonen en allochtonen over de multi-etnische samenleving. In *Jaarrapport integratie 2005*. The Hague: SCP/WODC/CBS.

Goodhart, D. (2013). *The British dream: Successes and failures of post-war immigration*. London: Atlantic Books.

Gordon, M. M. (1964). *Assimilation in American life*. London, UK: Oxford University Press.

Helbling, M. (Ed.) (2012). *Islamophobia in the West: Measuring and explaining individual attitudes*. London: Routledge.

Hogg, M. A. (2000). Subjective uncertainty reduction through self-categorization: A motivational theory of social identity processes. *European Review of Social Psychology*, *11*, 223–255.

Huo, Y. J., & Molina, L. E. (2006). Is pluralism a viable model of diversity? The benefits and limits of subgroup respect. *Group Processes and Intergroup Relations*, *9*, 359–376.

Jasinskaja-Lahti, I., Liebkind, K., & Solheim, E. (2009). To identify or not to identify? National disidentification as an alternative reaction to perceived ethnic discrimination. *Applied Psychology*, *59*, 105–128.

Jasinskaja-Lahti, I., Mahonen, T. A., & Liebkind, K. (2012). Identity and attitudinal reactions to perceptions of inter-group interactions among ethnic migrants: A longitudinal study. *British Journal of Social Psychology*, *51*, 312–329. DOI: 10.1111/j.2044-8309.2011.02059.x

Kane, E. W., & Kyyro, E. K. (2001). For whom does education enlighten? Race, gender, education, and beliefs about social inequality. *Gender and Society*, *15*, 710–733.

Lay, C., & Nguyen, T. (1998). The role of acculturation-related and acculturation non-specific daily hassles: Vietnamese-Canadian students and psychological distress. *Canadian Journal of Behavioral Science*, *30*, 172–181.

Martinovic, B., Van Tubergen, F., & Maas, I. (2011). Acquisition of cross ethnic friends by recent immigrants in Canada: A longitudinal approach. *International Migration Review*, *45*, 460–488.

Martinovic, B., & Verkuyten, M. (2012). Host national and religious identification among Turkish Muslims in Western Europe: The role of ingroup norms, perceived discrimination and value incompatibility. *European Journal of Social Psychology*, *42*, 893–903.

Miller, D., & Ali, S. (2013). Testing the national identity argument. *European Political Science Review* (in press).

Miller, K. P., Brewer, M. B., & Arbuckle, N. L. (2009). Social identity complexity: Its correlates and antecedents. *Group Processes and Intergroup Relations*, *12*, 79–94.

Modood, T. (2007). *Multiculturalism*. Cambridge: Polity Press.

Noel, J. G., Wann, D. L., & Branscombe, N. (1995). Peripheral ingroup membership status and public negativity toward outgroups. *Journal of Personality and Social Psychology*, *68*, 127–137.

Ogbu, J. (1993). Differences in cultural frame of reference. *International Journal of Behavioral Development*, *16*, 483–506.

Parekh, B. (2000). *Rethinking multiculturalism: Cultural diversity and political theory*. London: MacMillan.

Phalet, K., & Güngör, D. (2004). *Moslim in Nederland: Religieuze dimensies, etnische relaties en burgerschap: Turken en Marokkanen in Rotterdam*. The Hague: Sociaal Cultureel Planbureau.

Phinney, J. S., Berry, J. W., Vedder, P., & Liebkind, K. (2006). The acculturation experience: Attitudes, identities, and behaviors of immigrant youth. In J. W. Berry, J. S. Phinney, D. L. Sam & P. Vedder (Eds.), *Immigrant youth in cultural transition: Acculturation, identity, and adaptation across national contexts* (pp.71–116). Mahwah, NJ: Lawrence Erlbaum.

Portes, A., & Zhou, M. (1993). The new second generation: Segmented assimilation and its variants. *Annals of the American Academy of Political and Social Science, 53,* 74–97.

Ramos, M. R., Cassidy, C., Reicher, S., & Haslam, S. A. (2012). A longitudinal investigation of the rejection-identification hypothesis. *British Journal of Social Psychology, 51,* 642–661.

Ramos, M. R., Jetten, J., Zhang, A., Badea, C., Iyer, A., Cui, L., & Zhang, Y. (2013). Minority goals for interaction with the majority: Seeking distance from the majority and the effect of rejection on identification. *European Journal of Social Psychology, 43,* 72–83.

Rattansi, A. (2011). *Multiculturalism: A short introduction.* Oxford: Oxford University Press.

Roccas, S., & Brewer, M. (2002). Social identity complexity. *Personality and Social Psychology Review, 6,* 88–109.

Scheffer, P. (2011). *Immigrant nations.* Cambridge: Polity Press.

Schmid, K., Hewstone, M., Tausch, N., Cairns, E., & Hughes, J. (2009). Antecedents and consequences of social identity complexity: Intergroup contact, distinctiveness threat, and outgroup attitudes. *Personality and Social Psychology Bulletin, 35,* 1085–1098.

Simon, B., & Klandermans, B. (2001). Politicized collective identity: A social psychological analysis. *American Psychologist, 56,* 319–331.

Sindic, D., & Reicher, S. D. (2009). 'Our way of life is worth defending': Testing a model of attitudes towards superordinate group membership through a study of Scots' attitudes towards Britain. *European Journal of Social Psychology, 39,* 114–129.

Smith, H. J., & Leach, C. W. (2004). Group membership and everyday social comparison experiences. *European Journal of Social Psychology, 34,* 297–308.

Smith, H. J., Pettigrew, T. F., Pippin, G. M., & Bialosiewicz, S. (2012). Relative deprivation: A theoretical and meta-analytic review. *Personality and Social Psychology Review, 16,* 203–232.

Sniderman, P. M., & Hagendoorn, L. (2007). *When ways of life collide: Multiculturalism and its discontents in the Netherlands.* Princeton, NJ: Princeton University Press.

Staerklé, C., Sidanius, J., Green, E. G. T., & Molina, L. E. (2010). Ethnic minority-majority asymmetry in national attitudes around the world: A multilevel analysis. *Political Psychology, 31,* 491–519.

Tajfel, H., & Turner, J. (1979). An integrative theory of intergroup conflict. In W. G. Austin & S. Worchel (Eds.), *The social psychology of intergroup relations* (pp. 33–47). Monterey, CA: Brooks/Cole.

Taylor, C. (1992). The Politics of Recognition. In A. Gutmann, (Ed.) *Multiculturalism: Examining the politics of recognition.* Princeton: Princeton University Press.

—— (2012). Interculturalism or multiculturalism? *Philosophy and Social Criticism, 38,* 413–423.

Taylor, D. M., & Moghaddam, F. M. (1994). *Theories of intergroup relations.* New York, NY: Praeger.

Ten Teije, I., Coenders, M., & Verkuyten, M. (2013). The paradox of integration: Immigrants and their attitude towards the native population. *Social Psychology 44,* 278–288.

Tyler, T. R. (2001). Public trust and confidence in legal authorities: What do majority and minority group members want from the law and legal authorities? *Behavioral Sciences and the Law, 19,* 215–235.

Van Doorn, M., Scheepers, P., & Dagevos, J. (2013). Explaining the integration paradox among small immigrant groups in the Netherlands. *International Migration and Integration, 14,* 381–400.

Vasta, E. (2007). From ethnic minorities to ethnic majority policy: Multiculturalism and the shift to assimilationism in the Netherlands. *Ethnic and Racial Studies, 30,* 713–740.

Verkuyten, M., & Martinovic, B. (2012). Social identity complexity and immigrants' attitude towards the host nation: The intersection of ethnic and religious group identification. *Personality and Social Psychology Bulletin, 38,* 1165–1177.

Verkuyten, M., & Yildiz, A. (2007). National (dis)identification and ethnic and religious identity: A study among Turkish-Dutch Muslims. *Personality and Social Psychology Bulletin, 33,* 1448–1462.

Wiley, S. (2013). Rejection-identification among Latino immigrants in the United States. *International Journal of Intercultural Relations, 37,* 375–384.

Williams, J. A. (1994). *The world of Islam.* London: Thames and Hudson.

Wodtke, G. T. (2012). The impact of education on intergroup attitudes. A multiracial analysis. *Social Psychology Quarterly, 75,* 80–106.

Wright, S. C., & Baray, G. (2012). Models of social change in social psychology: Collective action or prejudice reduction? Conflict or harmony? In J. Dixon & M. Levine (Eds.), *Beyond prejudice: Extending the social psychology of conflict, inequality and social change* (pp. 225–247). Cambridge, UK: Cambridge University Press.

Wright, S. C., Taylor, D. M., & Moghaddam, F. M. (1990). Responding to membership in a disadvantaged group: From acceptance to collective protest. *Journal of Personality and Social Psychology, 58,* 994–1003.

Zolberg, A. R., & Long, L. W. (1999). Why Islam is like Spanish: Cultural incorporation in Europe and the United States. *Politics and Society, 27,* 5–38.

5 Ethnic diversity and dimensions of in-group solidarity

Overview of insights into empirical relationships in Europe

Maurice Gesthuizen, Michael Savelkoul, and Peer Scheepers

Introduction

Back in the fifties, Allport (1954) produced fundamental theoretical insights that (opportunities for) intergroup contacts would reduce prejudices on the side of the majority against minorities. Over the years, compelling empirical evidence has shown that bringing together people from different ethnic backgrounds comes with positive returns (Pettigrew, 1998; Pettigrew & Tropp, 2006). Living together and sharing a living environment might cause some daily annoyances, but getting to know people from other ethnic minority groups increases knowledge and understanding of the others' habits. Once "we, from one ethnic group" become acquainted with "them, from other ethnic groups" and vice versa, people actually tend to reduce their intergroup prejudices, thereby overall and over time improving intergroup relations, even experiencing each others' company to be enriching in social terms.

Based on these robust empirical insights, many have been convinced that socially or spatially mingling people from various (economic and ethnic) backgrounds is a potentially powerful tool. It may be powerful to increase intergroup social capital, in the form of social contacts and trust among and between different social and ethnic groups and, moreover, to decrease intergroup prejudice and other modes of ethnic exclusionism (Wagner et al., 2003, 2006; Pettigrew et al., 2010; Schlueter & Scheepers, 2010).

The publication "*E Pluribus Unum*: Diversity and Community in the Twenty-first Century" by Putnam (2007) came with a severe challenge to this stream of compelling evidence. His results, based on the Social Capital Community Benchmark Survey, indicated that citizens living in US-regions where many ethnic groups lived together, i.e., with a high level of ethnic diversity and hence, more opportunities for interethnic contacts, distrust citizens belonging to ethnic out-groups more than in regions with lower levels of diversity. This is a finding diametrically at odds with insights from contact theories. However, Putnam's claim is even broader, as he additionally stated that "[...] people living in ethnically diverse settings appear to 'hunker down'" (Putnam, 2007, p. 149), increasing social isolation, even to the extent that people refrain from social contacts with *people from their own ethnic group*, and withdraw from participation in various voluntary associations. Putnam suggested, rather generally, that inhabitants of ethnically diverse communities tend to withdraw from social life, a pattern which encompasses "[...] attitudes and behavior, bridging and bonding social capital, public and private connections" (Putnam, 2007, p. 151). In brief, Putnam claimed that ethnic diversity would decrease bridging, and moreover, bonding social capital, terms that Putnam had already coined in one of his previous insightful contributions (2000).

In terms of insights derived from contact theory, these propositions imply that ethnic diversity would be detrimental rather than beneficial, not only to intergroup relations but, moreover, also to *in-group relations*, and that segregating people from various social and ethnic backgrounds would be most beneficial for maintaining social capital. In this contribution, we will focus on the potential effects of ethnic diversity on deteriorating in-group relations. We will capture these phenomena with an encompassing, short label: *in-group solidarity*, which refers to informal meeting and helping members of one's own group (i.e., informal social capital); and participation in formal voluntary associations (i.e., formal social capital) (cf. Pichler & Wallace, 2007). These voluntary associations can be distinguished by the overall aims they set out to fulfill: providing leisure to their members via sports or hobbies, serving particular economic or consumer interests, or serving general societal goals via charity called activism (van der Meer et al., 2009). In associations serving leisure or consumer interests, the in-groups may be well-circumscribed local or national groups, whereas in the latter type of activist associations, the in-group aimed to serve may often be local or national, however, even at an international level, e.g., helping to combat poverty in the world. According to Putnam, living in ethnically diverse environments would be detrimental for in-group solidarity in terms of both informal *and* formal social capital.

Putnam's publication has generated enormous responses. For one, the media have spent much time and space on the issue, with much emphasis on the negative social consequences of ethnic diversity. Also in the political arena, his general conclusions raised attention. As Putnam mentions in his resumé, his consultancy activities for the White House, British government agencies and the Irish Taoiseach, imply that his findings and views swiftly reached the world's most powerful leaders. Also in the scientific world this wide response was generated, indicated by the well over 500 citations since 2007 in "Web of Science," a scientific database administering how often publications in peer reviewed and officially ranked scientific journals are used as references in other publications. Recently, Portes and Vickstrom (2011) devoted a review article to the stream of scientific literature that emerged from Putnam's contribution to the relationship between ethnic diversity and social capital, followed by a more encompassing review of empirical research in this line (Van der Meer & Tolsma, 2014). Much of the scientific research is rather critical of Putnam's scientific research fueling the debate. Yet within the media and governmental institutions, as well as among policymakers, the general consensus seems to be that Putnam's main conclusion is the way that it works in real life, both in the United States as well as in Europe:

in the short run ethnic diversity would have negative impacts on social cohesion, for intergroup relations, but moreover, also for in-group solidarity.

Many scholars in social and political science have since then published scientific research on the relationship between ethnic diversity and different dimensions of in-group solidarity, which have been published under the heading of (bonding) social capital. Some studies focused on the differences between countries in ethnic diversity and its effect on different dimensions of social capital (e.g., trusting, helping, meeting others but also performing voluntary work for different kinds of voluntary associations (e.g., Gesthuizen et al., 2009; Kesler & Bloemraad, 2010), others on regional ethnic diversity within single countries (e.g., Putnam, 2007; Traunmüller, 2011), others on lower levels like municipalities and neighborhoods (e.g., Tolsma et al., 2009). Previous studies vary extensively in the contextual-level(s) they consider. The high-quality data we had available enabled us to conduct more systematic research at some of the crucial levels that can be distinguished.

Given the wide array of social capital indicators used, ranging from attitudinal measures on trust (foremost: Putnam, 2007) to behavioral measures on participation in different voluntary associations (e.g., Gesthuizen et al., 2009), the picture that arises might seem blurred, due to possible differences in substantial findings as a consequence of different measurements. In this contribution, we will, therefore, employ behavioral measurements on in-group solidarity that are valid and substantially comparable. Unlike some studies that have focused on effects of ethnic diversity among both majority and minority groups (Vervoort et al., 2010; Huijts et al., 2013a/b), we will focus only on consequences among majority groups, for reasons of surveyability.

We will build on and explicate previous theoretical insights, partially complementary, partially contradictory, that have guided a series of rather systematic empirical investigations in the context of Europe and the Netherlands to address these controversial insights proposed by Putnam. Moreover, we describe the robust empirical findings that we obtained for Europe and, more specifically, for the Netherlands, in order to evaluate these theoretical insights against these empirical findings. Building on these empirical findings, we will distill possible policy implications.

Theoretical mechanisms for the relationship between ethnic diversity and in-group solidarity

Constrict theory and crucial hypotheses

In his pivotal contribution, Putnam (2007) introduces "constrict theory," which proposes a general negative impact of ethnic diversity on in-group solidarity and out-group derogation. Although underlying explanations remain implicit, the mechanism explaining why people in ethnically diverse localities would distrust and/or avoid social contacts with people from *other* ethnic minority groups may be derived from the so-called homophily principle (McPherson, Smith-Lovin &

Cook, 2001). People have the tendency to prefer to connect to others who are like themselves in particular characteristics (in terms of, for example, education, income, ethnicity or more generally similar lifestyles), while there seems to be a reluctance—or even an aversion—to connect to people who are different in these respects. This resonates well with social identity theory (Tajfel & Turner, 1979), which is covered in De Dreu et al. (this volume).

This mechanism, however, is located at the level of inter-individual connections and does not directly explain why people in supra-individual ethnically diverse surroundings would distrust and/or avoid people from their *own* ethnic group. Yet, Putnam seems to imply that in such surroundings, there are less people to identify with or to feel familiar with, resulting in overall feelings of discomfort. This supposedly generates a general tendency to retreat from social life and to even refrain from connections with people who share similar characteristics (Gesthuizen et al., 2009).

These insights essentially boil down to hypotheses proposing that ethnic diversity would directly reduce different modes of in-group solidarity, informal meeting and helping members of one's own group (or: informal social capital) or serving their interests via participation in formal voluntary associations (or: formal social capital).

Conflict theory and crucial hypotheses

In another stream of classic theoretical insights, building on conflict theories (Coser, 1956; Blalock, 1967), insights were built that more thoroughly explicate why living in ethnically diverse environments would induce particular social reactions among people living in these surroundings. These classic propositions of conflict theory essentially argue that living in ethnically diverse environments makes people aware of the actual competition taking place between ethnic groups; a competition for scarce material resources, like jobs and houses, but also competition for immaterial, symbolic resources like dominant values and beliefs. Ethnic diversity would hence foster actual competition that would increase perceptions of (ethnic) threat, followed by a series of exclusionary reactions towards out-groups (Scheepers et al., 2002; Coenders et al., 2008, 2009; Schlueter & Scheepers, 2010; Savelkoul et al., 2011a). Moreover, perceptions of (ethnic) threat would also increase in-group favoritism (Coser, 1956; Coenders et al., 2004). The theoretical mechanism would be that those people who perceive to be threatened by out-groups are more likely to seek a safe refuge among the people who are similar to them in crucial respects, like ethnicity, which hence would increase in-group solidarity (also see De Dreu et al., this volume). However, Hooghe et al. (2009) contradictorily argued that perceptions of ethnic threat may generalize into discomfort, even with people from their own ethnic in-group, to such an extent that those who perceive their surroundings as being under threat from different ethnic out-groups may disconnect with members of their in-group. This would imply that perceived ethnic threat would decrease, rather than increase, in-group solidarity.

This theoretical argument was generalized by Savelkoul et al. (2011b, 2013) and Scheepers et al. (2013) proposing that social environments that harbor high levels (or increasing levels) of dissimilar people, i.e., people not sharing similar characteristics (in terms of education, income, ethnicity or lifestyles) may perceive their surroundings to be simply unsafe being surrounded by many dissimilar people, which may increase social discomfort to the extent that it impedes social connections, even with people sharing similar characteristics.

Overall, there is theoretical consensus on the macro-micro-hypothesis for the positive relationship between ethnic diversity and perceived ethnic threat: the higher the level of ethnic diversity, the higher the level of perceived ethnic threat, i.e., the mediating link between ethnic diversity and its consequences. However, there clearly is disagreement on the presumed relationship between perceived ethnic threat and the consequences for in-group solidarity; one classic line proposes the hypothesis that the higher the level of perceived ethnic threat, the higher the in-group solidarity; the contemporary line proposes that the higher the level of perceived ethnic threat, the lower the in-group solidarity.

Contact theory and crucial hypotheses

Classic insights from contact theory (Allport, 1954), as explicated in the introduction, predominantly focus on the relationship between intergroup contact and intergroup attitudes, like prejudice or more general exclusionary reactions towards out-groups. Initial studies proposed that intergroup exclusionary reactions would be reduced under optimal conditions of intergroup contacts (diverse ethnic groups sharing common goals, equal status between groups, intergroup cooperation to reach these goals, and authorities facilitating these common goals). However, compelling meta-analytic evidence shows that even in the absence of these optimal conditions, intergroup contacts reduce exclusionary reactions and, hence, improve interethnic or bridging relationships (Pettigrew & Tropp, 2006).

Extensions of contact theory, building on classic sociological propositions (Blau, 1977, p. 42), stating that "[…] physical propinquity increases the probability of social association…" have received empirical support, showing that a larger proportion of immigrants in people's living environment increases the likelihood of having interethnic contacts (Wagner et al., 2003, 2006; Pettigrew et al., 2010; Schlueter & Scheepers, 2010). Pettigrew (2008, p. 193) refers to this as the "first selection process": people can only (choose to) have actual interethnic contacts if immigrants are present in their living environment.

However, theoretical relationships between intergroup contact and in-group solidarity had been largely unexplored, although Pettigrew (1998) and Wilson (2000) already provided arguments as to why intergroup contacts could also be beneficial for in-group solidarity. Starting from the evidence that ethnic diversity fosters intergroup contacts, these (increased levels of) intergroup contacts, in turn, induce not only quantitatively larger networks (Wilson, 2000), but also qualitatively richer networks that may have a so-called de-provincialization effect (Pettigrew, 1998): intergroup contacts reduce provincial views of the social world and widen people's breadth of perspective, thereby increasing empathy for people of out-groups. Moreover, intergroup contacts might also increase empathy for people belonging to the in-group, as a wider breadth of perspective and a stronger awareness of the social world could also increase one's willingness to invest time and energy in people belonging to one's core social network. Therefore, the general hypotheses, building on these joint insights are straightforwardly that ethnic diversity increases intergroup contacts as a mediating link, which in turn (also) increases in-group solidarity.

High-quality empirical data and advanced methodological analyses

We set out to overview systematic efforts to ascertain (direct and indirect) effects of ethnic diversity, assessed at different levels (countries, regions, municipalities and neighborhoods) on different aspects of in-group solidarity.

We took advantage of high-quality data sources for Europe, i.e., the European Social Survey (2002–2003) and for the Netherlands, i.e., the Netherlands Longitudinal Lifecourse Study (2008–2010) and the Social Statistical Database/ Safety Monitor (2006–2008). These data were enriched with measurements on ethnic diversity (i.e., migrant stock: the percentage of non-native people living in the country, region, municipality or neighborhood). In most instances, analyses were re-run including the Herfindahl-index instead of migrant stock. As both measurements are highly correlated ($r > .95$), we found no substantial differences between these analyses. These data also contain straightforward valid and reliable measurements of in-group solidarity (meeting other people from one's in-group, helping other people from one's [self-defined] in-group, performing voluntary work for voluntary social associations [distinguished by different aims, i.e. leisure, activist, or interest associations]; and moreover, valid measurements of perceived ethnic threat (cf. Coenders et al., 2005, e.g., "do immigrants take away jobs in your country or create new jobs") and having interethnic contacts with immigrants (cf. Wagner et al., 2006, e.g., "do you have friends/colleagues who have come to live in your country from another country?"). In order to ascertain relationships between perceived ethnic threat or intergroup contacts and in-group solidarity, we were restricted to European data as such comparable measurements were not available in the Dutch context. For more elaborate information, we refer to previously published contributions (Savelkoul et al., 2011b; Huijts et al., 2013a/b; Savelkoul et al., 2013; Scheepers et al., 2013).

In all contributions, we relied on multi-level analyses considering individuals to be nested in and affected by characteristics of their social environment (ethnic diversity but also levels of welfare or unemployment), taking into account individual characteristics that of course may, or have been shown to be, related to in-group solidarity (foremost, educational attainment, employment status, religiosity, marital status, age, gender and level of urbanization). These need to be incorporated to assure that the effects of characteristics of the social environment are not confounded by unmeasured individual level characteristics. All determinants in the analyses were checked for possible problems of multi-collinearity and re-run for different samples of the samples to check the robustness of the findings. Overall, these findings have been ascertained to be robust.

Research findings in Europe and the Netherlands

Direct effects of ethnic diversity on dimensions of in-group solidarity

To what extent is the actual and direct impact of ethnic diversity on public and private connections within one's own ethnic group in Europe significantly negative and substantial? To evaluate these effects more systematically than most studies have done before, we present findings from previous studies in Scheme 5.1, presenting the relationships that we have ascertained through rigorous testing of multi-level models, assessing relationships between ethnic diversity at different levels (countries, regions, municipalities and neighborhoods) with valid and substantially comparable measurements of in-group solidarity.

First, considering relationships at the level of *countries* provides us with a very clear picture: we found no significant negative relationships whatsoever between ethnic diversity and dimensions of in-group solidarity (Savelkoul et al., 2011b, 2013). The one significant relationship we found was a positive rather than a negative one: the more migrants there are in societies, the more people tend to help each other. This corresponds with earlier findings from Gesthuizen et al. (2009). Next, we found very consistent relationships between the level of

Scheme 5.1 Direct relationships between ethnic diversity and dimensions of in-group solidarity

	Informal meeting	*Informal helping*	*Leisure association*	*Interest association*	*Activist association*
European countries:					
Migrant stock	0	+	0	0	0
Unemployment	–	–	–	–	(–)
European regions:					
Migrant stock	(–)	0	(–)	–	+
Unemployment	0	(–)	–	(–)	–
	Informal meeting: neighbors	Informal meeting: at work, in school			
Dutch municipalities:					
Migrant stock	(–)	0			
Unemployment	0	0			
Dutch neighborhoods:					
Migrant stock	(–)	0			
unemployment	0	0			

Note: 0 = no statistical relationship, + = positive statistical relationship, - = negative statistical relationship, (-) = negative, non-significant relationship, based on multiple tests on data described in text, including individual level control variables.

unemployment and (nearly) all dimensions of in-group solidarity: the higher the level of unemployment in societies, the lower the level of in-group solidarity, i.e., the less people meet each other, the less people help each other, and the less they are involved in leisure and interest associations. The exception to this rule is the relationship between unemployment and involvement in activist associations, which is negative also but not significant.

Second, considering relationships at the level of *regions* also provides us with a fairly clear picture. We found no significant relationships between ethnic diversity and informal aspects of in-group solidarity, i.e., meeting and helping in European regions (Savelkoul et al., 2011b), nor with meeting neighbors in Dutch regions (Scheepers et al., 2013). Nor did we find a relationship between ethnic diversity in European regions with involvement in leisure associations and a positive rather than a negative relationship between significant ethnic diversity and involvement in activist associations; the exception to the rule is that the higher the regional level of diversity, the lower the involvement in interest associations (Savelkoul et al., 2013). Again, we found some consistent effects of unemployment, now at the regional level: the higher the unemployment, the lower the level of involvement in leisure and activist associations. The relationships between unemployment and informal helping as well as involvement in interest associations are similarly negative but not significant.

Third, considering relationships at the lower level of *municipalities and neighborhoods* in the Netherlands also provides us with a rather clear picture: Here, too, we found no consistent negative and significant relationships between ethnic diversity and meeting neighbors, in-group people at work or in school. However, we found two exceptions to these general findings: in one study, we found a negative relationship at the level of municipalities between ethnic diversity and meeting neighbors, which did, however, not reach statistical significance (at the conventional level of p<.05), as yet, this relationship was significant at a lower level of significance (Huijts et al., 2013a). Moreover, we also found a tendency that the higher the level of ethnic diversity is in neighborhoods, the less people meet their neighbors, which was non-significant in one study based on data derived from the NELLS-survey (Huijts et al., 2013a), but significant in another study using data from the Social Statistical Database/Safety Monitor (Scheepers et al., 2013). In yet another study based on a third data source ("Culturele Veranderingen 2004", i.e., Cultural Changes 2004), Tolsma et al. (2009) did not find a significant relationship between ethnic diversity and contact with neighbors, neither at the level of municipalities, nor at the level of neighborhoods. However, that study did provide empirical evidence showing that a higher level of ethnic diversity at the level of municipalities decreased the rate of voluntary work as an indicator of formal in-group solidarity.

These findings illustrate that the influence of ethnic diversity on in-group solidarity is far from generally negative, as proposed by constrict theory. Rather, ethnic diversity hardly seems to have a direct impact on in-group solidarity. In some exceptional cases, we did find support for a negative influence. However, we also found some positive effects on yet other dimensions of in-group solidarity, raising doubts about the generalizability of Putnam's pessimistic predictions.

Effects of intermediate determinants on dimensions of in-group solidarity

Before we evaluate these findings against the broader theoretical framework, we will also describe the relationships between our explanatory, mediating determinants (perceived ethnic threat and interethnic contacts) with dimensions of in-group solidarity, presented in Scheme 5.2.

We will refrain from describing (again) the relationships between ethnic diversity and dimensions of in-group solidarity, once these intermediate determinants are considered and included in the empirical models. It is, however, worthwhile to mention that we found that ethnic diversity has some negative relationships, reducing the likelihood to be active in voluntary associations.

Focusing on the *indirect* relationship between ethnic diversity and in-group solidarity, three important findings have to be highlighted. First, addressing the relationship between ethnic diversity and both explanatory mechanisms derived from conflict and contact theories (i.e., perceived ethnic threat and interethnic contact), we found no significant relationships between ethnic diversity, at the country nor at the regional level, with perceived ethnic threat (Savelkoul et al., 2011b, 2013). This implies that we found no evidence for one of the core propositions of conflict theory. We did find, however, a consistent positive relationship between ethnic diversity at the regional level and intergroup contact: the higher the level of ethnic diversity, the more interethnic contacts in such regions.

Second, we found very consistent and significant relationships between perceived ethnic threat and (nearly) all dimensions of in-group solidarity: the higher the level of perceived ethnic threat, the lower the level of meeting others and involvement in leisure, interest and activist associations (Savelkoul et al., 2011b, 2013). The only exception is the relationship between perceived ethnic threat and helping others, which did not reach significance (Savelkoul et al., 2011b).

Scheme 5.2 Indirect relationships between ethnic diversity and dimensions of in-group solidarity, via mediating factors

	Informal meeting	*Informal helping*	*Leisure association*	*Interest association*	*Activist association*
European countries:					
Migrant stock	0	+			
Unemployment	–	–			
European regions:					
Migrant stock	(–)	(–)	–	–	+
Unemployment	0	(–)	0	0	(–)
Mediating factors:					
Perceived ethnic threat	–	0	–	–	–
Interethnic contacts	+	+	+	+	+

Note: 0 = no statistical relationship, + = positive statistical relationship, - = negative statistical relationship, (-) = negative, non-significant relationship, based on multiple tests on data described in text, including individual level control variables.

Third, and moreover, we also found very consistent and significant relationships between having interethnic contacts and all dimensions of in-group solidarity, without any exceptions: the more interethnic contacts people have, the higher their level of in-group solidarity, i.e., the more they meet with others, help others and the more they are involved in leisure, interest and activist associations (Savelkoul et al., 2011b, 2013).

Next to these findings directly relevant for our key hypotheses, a number of additional findings consistently emerged. All dimensions of in-group solidarity are much more strongly determined by individual characters (such as people's educational level, gender or age) rather than contextual characteristics, like ethnic diversity or unemployment. Vice versa, in terms of variances to be explained, the variances at the individual level are in most instances more than 10 times as large as at any contextual level, implying that individual-level characteristics are more substantial to explain differences in in-group solidarity (Huijts et al., 2013a/b). Among these individual characteristics, it is particularly educational attainment that is significantly positively related to (nearly) all dimensions of in-group solidarity: the higher the level of educational attainment, the higher the level of in-group solidarity (except for contact with neighbors) (Gesthuizen et al., 2008; Huijts et al., 2013a). Another robust finding is that those who are embedded in institutions (church or marriage) contribute more to in-group solidarity than those who are not embedded. These findings are in line with previous contributions (Wilson & Musick, 1997; Wilson, 2000; Van der Meer et al., 2009).

Evaluation of theoretical insights considering our empirical evidence: conclusions

We found no evidence that ethnic diversity has direct and all-encompassing, substantial impacts on in-group solidarity, as proposed by Putnam (2007), certainly not at higher contextual levels of *countries and regions*, where the economic situation is more important: the higher the level of unemployment, the lower the level of in-group solidarity. However, we did find some evidence for constrict theory, that ethnic diversity at the level of *municipalities* in the Netherlands has a, as yet statistically non-significant, tendency to reduce one dimension of in-group solidarity: meeting in-group neighbors (Huijts et al., 2013a). Other evidence has shown that the level of ethnic diversity of municipalities does also reduce the likelihood to be involved in voluntary work (Tolsma et al., 2009). At the level of *neighborhoods*, we also found a negative relationship between ethnic diversity and meeting neighbors, however, only significant in one study (Scheepers et al., 2013). Overall, this implies that we found some preliminary evidence for Hagendoorn's (2009) proposition that if ethnic diversity would to some extent affect dimensions of in-group solidarity, it may be stronger in smaller geographic contexts like municipalities and neighborhoods, than in larger contexts like countries and regions.

The extent to which ethnic diversity does reduce these social phenomena related to in-group solidarity is rather limited, however. For one, most (94.4

percent) of the variance in meeting with neighbors in the Netherlands is located at the individual level whereas merely 3.7 percent respectively 1.9 percent of the variance is located at the municipality respectively neighborhood level (Huijts et al., 2013a). Second, the effect of ethnic diversity on meeting neighbors is relatively small, implying that with a strong increase of ethnic diversity from 1 percent to 36 percent in a municipality, the frequency of contacts decreases from "almost daily" to "several times a week." Similarly, Scheepers et al. (2013) found that an increase of 10 percentage points in the level of ethnic diversity of the neighborhood was accompanied with an increase of only .1 (on a scale ranging from 0 to 4) of unfavorable evaluations of the neighborhood. These findings therefore contain little substantiality, particularly if compared to the effects of individual level characteristics like educational attainment.

We also did not find convincing empirical evidence for one crucial proposition derived from conflict theory: a nation's, or a region's level of ethnic diversity— objectively measured—was not related with perceived ethnic threat. Schlueter and Scheepers (2010), however, found evidence for the Netherlands that there is a strong relationship between the "objective" demographic level of ethnic diversity and the "subjectively" perceived level of ethnic diversity: the latter was rather strongly related to perceptions of ethnic threat. So, in environments characterized by high levels of objective ethnic diversity, at least part of the population seems to perceive ethnic diversity to be (disproportionally) high, which in turn induces perceptions of ethnic threat. Note that the causal order of the latter relationship is, however, not indisputable, as perceptions of ethnic threat might also induce people to have an unrealistic view of the composition of their social and/or ethnic surroundings.

As yet, we found very strong and consistent evidence for European countries, that perceptions of ethnic threat reduce virtually all dimensions of in-group solidarity: meeting people from one's in-group and involvement in leisure, interest and activist voluntary associations. Only the level of providing informal help appears not to be affected significantly by such perceptions. We suppose that such strong ties are not easily affected by circumstances in people's contexts, nor by perceptions of ethnic threat. This implies overall that we have to reject the classic line (Coser, 1956; Coenders et al., 2004) in favor of the contemporary chain of propositions, derived from Hooghe et al. (2009) and generalized by Savelkoul et al. (2011b, 2013) and Scheepers et al. (2013): perceptions of ethnic threat decrease rather than increase in-group solidarity. Although we have not tested the presumed mechanism underlying these relationships, there is circumstantial evidence that people who perceive ethnic minorities in their surroundings to be a real threat, do feel more unsafe (e.g., afraid to walk alone after dark in this neighborhood), implying social discomfort in their close context (Visser et al., 2013) which is supposed to impede social connections.

We found strong evidence in European countries for the extended version of contact theory. Consistent with classic and contemporary insights (Blau, 1977; Pettigrew et al., 2010), the level of ethnic diversity not only increases opportunities for, but also, actual interethnic contacts. What is more important, however, is that we found very consistent empirical evidence for Europe that the more people have interethnic contacts, the higher their level of in-group solidarity, i.e., the more frequently they meet and help others and the more likely they are to be involved in all kinds of voluntary associations. Unfortunately, we have no data to test underlying mechanisms as proposed by Pettigrew (1998) that interethnic contacts reduce provincial views from one's own ethnic group and increase empathy for others, people belonging to out-groups. This links nicely with earlier research, showing that people with a cosmopolitan orientation are more likely to perform voluntary work (Gesthuizen & Scheepers, 2012).

In sum, the conclusion that needs to be drawn from Putnam's own and the present research is that ethnic diversity, either measured at the country level, or at the regional, municipality or neighborhood level, is not that important for predicting in-group solidarity. The extensive attention for the supposed negative impact of ethnic diversity on so many dimensions of social life, therefore, is unjustified and exaggerated.

Policy implications: discussion

Solutions: policies on ethnic diversity

Increasing levels of social cohesion is an important goal for governments to build better societies in terms of democracy, health, wealth and lower levels of crime (Council of Europe, 2004). The crucial question thus is: what can be done to reach that goal, and what is the role of ethnic diversity in that picture? To answer the question of how people can be motivated to become and continue to be more active in their social networks, in voluntary associations, and to make them more trusting of fellow citizens, it is fruitful to connect well-established scientific knowledge with recent research findings.

We have shown evidence that, first, ethnic diversity (at the level of regions) increases interethnic contacts, as the opportunity to meet people from other groups is simply higher. This is in line with earlier findings at the regional or municipality level (e.g., Wagner et al., 2006; Pettigrew et al., 2010; Savelkoul et al., 2011a). Previous studies have shown compelling evidence that these interethnic contacts reduce exclusionary reactions and improve interethnic relations (Pettigrew & Tropp, 2006). Second, we have now also shown evidence, and this is really the important finding, that these interethnic contacts also increase in-group solidarity, i.e., meeting with and helping friends, and involvement in all types of voluntary associations. Hence, we conclude that ethnic diversity increases (opportunities for) interethnic contact or bridging social capital; and, more importantly, increasing interethnic contacts is also a sound way to develop social capital. Thus, when the policy question is to improve social cohesion in societies, should policies aim *to mingle or to segregate*? To mingle! Our evidence shows clearly that people living in ethnically diverse surroundings have more interethnic contacts, which consistently and substantially contribute to in-group relations, at least among majority groups, next to previous compelling evidence that interethnic contacts contribute to improved inter-group relations (Pettigrew & Tropp, 2006).

Policies designed to decrease ethnic segregation and to increase ethnic mixing have been developed and employed, in the Netherlands as well as elsewhere in Europe: to avoid increases of numbers of ethnic minority groups in particular neighborhoods, to increase numbers of ethnic majorities in neighborhoods with high numbers of ethnic minority groups, or to move ethnic minority groups to neighborhoods with high numbers of ethnic majorities. In most instances, scientific research has not been systematic enough to find significant results (Gijsberts & Dagevos, 2007). As yet, policies developed in the United States, called "Housing Opportunities for People Everywhere (HOPE)" appear to have effects policymakers had hoped for: that more deprived people from minority groups move out of segregated neighborhoods, whereas more privileged people from majority groups simultaneously move into these neighborhoods (ibid., p. 134), overall reducing levels of ethnic concentration.

Solutions: direct merits of investing in educational attainment

Now let's connect these new findings to the well-established knowledge regarding the crucial role of education. To be able to do that, we first need to discuss *why* education, the strongest determinant of in-group solidarity (Gesthuizen et al., 2008), is so important (Wilson, 2000). Scholars of social capital agree that individuals tend to develop social capital more, as they are exposed to the general norm of dedication to the collective good longer and more intensely: citizens develop competences and subsequently internalize norms to participate in public spheres and hence develop and maintain social capital. Parents and teachers play an important role in this process. Particularly that education teaches pupils moral values, that is, "how one should act on behalf of the collective interest," is a long-standing theoretical insight (Durkheim, 1925). Contemporary educational studies show the central position in school curricula of educating pupils to become good citizens (Cogan & Morris, 2001). There is a high level of cross-national consensus that being a good citizen means, among other things, taking part in activities that promote human rights and benefit people in the community (Torney-Purta et al., 2001). These are all activities that show dedication to the collective good, and directly refer to various types of social activities that are generally held to be important for a well-functioning society. Next to parents, teachers are thus important socializing agents. Investing in educating children and adults, but particularly children, is extremely important, because it directly and persistently increases their willingness to act on behalf of the collective interest.

Solutions: indirect effects of promoting education

There are also some very important *indirect* effects of investing in educational attainment of individuals. Here, we can make the connection with the recent research findings discussed above. Education is the most important factor to, firstly, reduce perceptions of ethnic threat and more in general, exclusionary reactions (Scheepers et al., 2002); and, secondly, it is the most important determinant of preferring contacts with ethnic minorities (Hello et al., 2002). Investing in education, therefore, may decrease perceptions of ethnic threat, and vice versa may increase interethnic contacts and, hence, interethnic tolerance and intergroup relations.

There are still some other indirect effects of educational attainment that deserve to be mentioned. When, thirdly, more individuals receive more education and thus attain higher certificates, more people will be successful at the labor market and less people will be unemployed. Integration in the labor market has also been shown to increase social capital (Putnam, 2007). Finally, educational expansion has favorable consequences for the contexts—the nation, the region, the municipality, the neighborhood—that people share. Educational expansion results in contexts suffering less from high poverty and unemployment levels. As the research discussed above shows that particularly these economic and income-related contextual characteristics reduce (the development of) social capital, investing in education also takes the sting out of this process.

There is much room for better educating more children and exposing them to the socializing influence of school for a longer duration, as there are many children who do not reach the level of education that they could be able to attain. Breen and Jonsson (2005) have shown that children from less privileged backgrounds are less likely to continue education as compared to children from more privileged backgrounds, even when their cognitive capacities are similar. These children can—and maybe need to be—stimulated to attend school for a longer duration. This eventually would be stimulating for the generation of social capital, both for the person him/herself and for the community in which he/she lives.

Mingling and educating: no easy task

It would be naïve to believe that a helping hand is unnecessary in generating contact between natives and members of different ethnic groups, and in avoiding high concentrations of ethnic minority groups. In ethnically diverse regions, particularly those that face the toughest problems (such as high levels of crime, unemployment and poverty), a social infrastructure needs to be created where people can actually meet each other. It may also be important to create common collective goals, provide opportunities for intergroup cooperation to reach these goals, facilitated by authorities. Living and working together for jointly shared interests does not only induce results that are favorable for all groups, it also creates a common identity that has been shown to reduce intolerance towards each other.

In these most deprived areas of developed societies, it is also a very difficult task to improve educational attainment of children. From these areas many of the well-off have moved out, and those who were left behind, may often oppose contributing to the collective interests. Here it probably is extremely difficult to change educational institutions in such a way that children from these environments receive better chances to successfully finish school. Rumberger (2011), a leading scientist in Education Studies, reviews a long tradition of research on the causes and consequences of dropping out of high school, and advocates targeting the most vulnerable students, who live in these deprived areas where dropout rates are alarmingly high. In these circumstances, merely investing in education is not enough. Here, thinking of solutions and which role institutions play in them, needs to start with the families in which children grow up. Making sure that more children attend school longer is a way to go. This also holds for stimulating interethnic contact, and reducing perceptions of ethnic threat. Socialization at school is a powerful tool to reach these goals.

Education instead of ethnic diversity

In recent years, considerable attention has been paid to the consequences of living in ethnically diverse environments for community cohesion. Particularly, Putnam's pivotal study attracted much attention, as he claimed that ethnic diversity would have a detrimental impact on intergroup relations as well as in-group solidarity. In this contribution, we provided a systematic overview of a number of recent studies addressing the relationship between ethnic diversity and behavioral indicators of in-group solidarity, i.e., informal meeting and helping and involvement in voluntary organizations. Using high-quality data, these studies considered ethnic diversity at different contextual levels, ranging from neighborhoods to European countries. The overall conclusion is less pessimistic as predicted by Putnam, as we found hardly any direct influence of ethnic diversity on in-group solidarity, neither negative nor positive. In exceptional cases in which ethnic diversity directly affected in-group solidarity, we found both negative *and* positive influences. We did find, however, strong support for contact theory, as ethnic diversity increases actual levels of interethnic contact, which are consistently positively related with in-group solidarity. Conflict theory was only partly corroborated: ethnic diversity did not foster perceptions of ethnic threat. However, such perceptions of ethnic threat consistently reduced in-group solidarity. Moreover, our findings clearly illustrated that individual-level influences have much more impact on in-group solidarity as compared to contextual-level factors like ethnic diversity. Next to the role of individual-level perceived ethnic threat and interethnic contact, in particular educational attainment consistently turned out to have a strong positive effect on in-group solidarity.

Hence, we conclude that, given these findings and the priority given to the improvement of social cohesion (Council of Europe, 2004), policymakers should aim at investing in education: higher levels of educational attainment not only directly increase levels of in-group solidarity, but also indirectly, via increased levels of interethnic contact as well as reduced levels of perceived ethnic threat. As compared to influencing levels of ethnic diversity, this might be a more fruitful solution to reach this policy goal.

References

Allport, Gordon W. ([1954] 1979). *The nature of prejudice*. Boston: Beacon Press.

Blalock, H. M. Jr. (1967). *Toward a theory of minority-group relations*. New York: Capricorn.

Blau, P. M. (1977). A macro-sociological theory of social structure. *American Journal of Sociology, 83*(1), 26–54.

Breen, R., & Jonsson, J. (2005). Inequality of opportunity in comparative perspective: recent research on educational attainment and social mobility. *Annual Review of Sociology, 31*, 223–243.

Coenders, M., Gijsberts, M., & Scheepers, P. (2004). Chauvinism and patriotism in 22 countries. In M. Gijsberts, L. Hagendoorn, & P. Scheepers (Eds.), *Nationalism and exclusion of migrants: Cross-national comparisons* (pp. 29–70). Aldershot: Ashgate.

Coenders, M., Lubbers, M., & Scheepers, P. (2005). Majorities' attitudes towards minorities in Western and Eastern societies: results from the European Social Survey 2002–2003. In M. Coenders, M. Lubbers, & P. Scheepers (Eds.): *Majority's populations attitudes towards migrants and minorities*. Vienna: European Monitoring Centre on Racism and Xenophobia.

—— (2008). Support for repatriation policies for migrants. *International Journal for Comparative Sociology, 49*(2/3), 175–194.

—— (2009). Opposition to civil rights for racial minorities in Central and Eastern Europe. *East European Politics and Societies, 23*(2), 146–164.

Cogan, J., Morris, P. (2001). The development of civic values: An overview. *International Journal of Educational Research, 35:* 1–9.

Coser, L.A. (1956). *The Function of social conflict*. Glencoe, IL: Free Press.

Council of Europe (2004). *A new strategy for social cohesion, revised strategy for social cohesion.* Strassbourg: European Committee for Social Cohesion.

Durkheim, É. 1925. *L'Education morale*. Paris: Alcan/PUF.

Gesthuizen, M., Van der Meer, T., & Scheepers, P. (2008). Education and dimensions of social capital: Do educational effects differ due to educational expansion and social security expenditure? *European Sociological Review, 24:* 617–632.

—— (2009). Ethnic diversity and social capital in Europe: Tests of Putnam's thesis in european countries. *Scandinavian Political Studies, 32,* 121–142.

Gesthuizen, M., & Scheepers, P. (2012). Educational differences in volunteering in cross-national perspective: Individual and contextual explanations. *Non-Profit and Voluntary Sector Quarterly, 41,* 1, 58–81.

Gijsberts, M., & Dagevos, J. (2007). Interventies voor integratie, het tegengaan van etnische concentratie en bevorderen van interetnisch contact. Den Haag: Sociaal en Cultureel Planbureau.

Hagendoorn, L. (2009). Ethnic diversity and the erosion of social capital? *APSA Newsletter, 20*(1), 12–14.

Hello, E., Gijsberts, M., & Scheepers, P. (2002). Education and ethnic exclusionism in European countries, explanations for differential effects of education tested. *Scandinavian Journal of Educational Research, 46*(1), 5–24.

Hooghe, M., Reeskens, T., Stolle, D., & Trappers, A. (2009). Ethnic diversity and generalized trust in Europe: A cross-national multilevel study. *Comparative Political Studies, 42*(2), 198–223.

Huijts, T., Sluiter, R., Kraaykamp, G., & Scheepers, P. (2013a). Ethnic diversity and informal intra- and inter-ethnic contacts with neighbors in the Netherlands, (accepted) *Acta Sociologica*.

—— (2013b). Ethnic diversity and personal contacts at work and at school in the Netherlands, *Journal of International Migration and Integration*, DOI 10.1007/ s12134-013-0286-4.

Kesler, Ch., & Bloemraad, I. (2010). Does immigration erode social capital? The conditional effects of immigration-generated diversity on trust, membership and participation across 19 countries, 1981-2000. *Canadian Journal of Political Science*, *43*, 319–347.

Letki, N. (2008). Does diversity erode social cohesion? Social capital and race in British neighbourhoods. *Political Studies*, *56*, 99–126.

McPherson, M., Smith-Lovin, L., & Cook, J. (2001). Birds of a feather: Homophily in social networks. *Annual Review of Sociology*, *27*, 415–444.

Pettigrew, Th. (1998). Intergroup Contact Theory. *Annual Review of Psychology*, *49*, 65–85.

—— (2008). Future directions for intergroup contact theory and research. *International Journal of Intercultural Relations*, *32*, 187–199.

Pettigrew, Th., & Tropp, L. (2006). A meta-analytic test of intergroup contact theory. *Journal of Personality and Social Psychology*, *90*, 751–783.

Pettigrew, Th., Wagner, U., & Christ, O. (2010). Population ratios and prejudice: Modelling both contact and threat effects. *Journal of Ethnic and Migration Studies*, *36*, 635–650.

Pichler, F., & Wallace, C. (2007). Patterns of formal and informal social capital. *European Sociological Review*, 23(4), 423–435.

Portes, A., & Vickstrom, E. (2011). Diversity, social capital and cohesion. *Annual Review of Sociology*, *37*, 461–479.

Putnam, R. (2000). *Bowling alone: The collapse and revival of american community*. New York: Simon & Schuster.

—— (2007). E Pluribus Unum: Diversity and Community in the twenty-first century. The 2006 Johan Skytte Prize Lecture. *Scandinavian Political Studies*, *30*, 137–174.

Rumberger, R. W. (2011). *Dropping out: Why students drop out of high school and what can be done about it.* Cambridge: Harvard University Press.

Savelkoul, M., Scheepers, P., Tolsma, J., & Hagendoorn, L. (2011a). Anti-Muslim attitudes in the Netherlands, tests of contradictory hypotheses derived from ethnic competition theory and intergroup contact theory. *European Sociological Review*, *27*, 6, 741–758.

Savelkoul, M., Gesthuizen, M., & Scheepers, P. (2011b). Explaining relationships between ethnic diversity and informal social capital across European countries and regions: Tests of constrict, conflict and contact theory. *Social Science Research*, *40*, 1091–1107.

—— (2013). Ethnic diversity and formal social capital in European countries and regions: Tests of constrict, conflict and contact theory. *Non-Profit and Voluntary Sector Quarterly*, DOI: 10.1177/0899764013498652.

Scheepers, P., Gijsberts, M., & Coenders, M. (2002). Ethnic exclusionism in European countries, public opposition to grant civil rights to legal migrants as a response to perceived ethnic threat. *European Sociological Review*, *18*(1), 17–34.

Scheepers, P., Schmeets, H., & Pelzer, B. (2013). Hunkering down and other dimensions of community cohesion, regional-, municipal-, neighborhood- and individual-level effects. *Procedia, Social and Behavioural Sciences*, *72*, 91–106.

Schlueter, E., & Scheepers, P. (2010). The relationship between outgroup size and anti-outgroup attitudes: A theoretical synthesis and empirical test of group threat and intergroup contact theory. *Social Science Research, 39*(2), 285–295.

Tajfel, H., & Turner, J. (1979). An integrative theory of intergroup conflict. W. Austin & S. Worchel (Eds.), *The social psychology of intergroup relations* (pp. 33–47). Montery: Brooks/Cole.

Tolsma, J., Van der Meer, T., & Gesthuizen, M. (2009). The impact of neighbourhood and municipality characteristics on social cohesion in the Netherlands. *Acta Politica* 44, 286–313.

Torney-Purta, J., Lehmann, R., Oswald, H., & Schulz, W. (2001). *Citizenship and education in twenty-eight countries: Civic knowledge and engagement at age fourteen.* Amsterdam: IEA.

Traunmüller, R. (2011). Moral communities? Religion as a source of social trust in a multilevel analysis of 97 German regions. *European Sociological Review, 27,* 346–363.

Van der Meer, T., Te Grotenhuis, M., & Scheepers, P. (2009). Three Types of Voluntary Associations in Comparative Perspective: The Importance of Studying Associational Involvement Through a Typology of Associations in 21 European Countries. *Journal of Civil Society, 5*(3), 227–241.

Van der Meer, T., & Tolsma, J. (2014). Ethnic diversity and its supposed detrimental effects on social cohesion. *Annual Review of Sociology,* conditionally accepted.

Vervoort, M., Flap, H., & Dagevos, J. (2010). The ethnic composition of the neighbourhood and ethnic minorities' social contacts: Three unresolved issues. *European Sociological Review, 27*(5), 586–605.

Visser, M., Scholte, M., & Scheepers, P. (2013). Fear of crime and feeling of unsafety in European countries, macro and micro explanations in cross-national perspective. *The Sociological Quarterly, 54,* 278–301.

Wagner, U., Christ, O., Pettigrew, T. F., Stellmacher, J., & Wolf, C. (2006). Prejudice and minority proportion: Contact instead of threat effects. *Social Psychology Quarterly, 69,* 370–380.

Wagner, U., van Dick, R., Pettigrew, T. F., & Christ, O. (2003). Ethnic prejudice in East- and West-Germany: The Explanatory power of intergroup contact. *Group Processes and Intergroup Relations, 6,* 22–36.

Wilson, J. (2000). Volunteering. *Annual Review of Sociology, 26,* 215–240.

Wilson, J., & Musick, M. (1997). Who cares? Toward an integrated theory of volunteer work. *American Sociological Review, 62*(5), 694–713.

6 Escalation and de-escalation of intergroup conflict

The role of communication within and between groups

Tom Postmes, Ernestine H. Gordijn, Martijn van Zomeren, Hedy Greijdanus, Bart de Vos, Susanne Täuber, and Elanor Kamans

Introduction

Few would dispute that over the course of the first decade of the twenty-first century, Western countries have become increasingly hostile towards ethnic minorities and immigrants. Although this development has affected many countries, it has been particularly striking to witness the transformation of countries that traditionally prided themselves on traditions of tolerance or equality, such as the Netherlands, Sweden, Denmark, Norway and Australia. Understanding this transformation has been a long-term preoccupation of our research unit. Our primary focus in this research has been communication, often in small groups and in relatively innocuous settings, sometimes via mass media and leadership figures. It is our belief that changes in mass communication and small-scale conversations have played a key role in changing intergroup relations. Understanding the workings of communication is of key importance for the development of interventions for those who aim to reverse this trend. In this chapter we present an overview of our research that examined how communication influences perceptions and action in intergroup conflict. By means of this research we aim to explain how hostility between (ethnic) groups can emerge, and also, how interventions in communication within and between groups may lead to de-escalation of conflict.

Why study communication?

One might wonder why communication should occupy such a central role in our research, when there are so many other ("bigger" and more dramatic) factors that could play a role. Indeed, the major theories of intergroup relations tend to assume that psychological process follows from social structural strains. One particularly pervasive idea is that intergroup hostility flows quite naturally from some form of competition between groups (cf. Sherif, 1966; also see De Dreu, Aaldering, & Saygi, this volume). Indeed, different waves of immigrants have changed the ethnic composition of many Western countries, thereby changing labor relations and the division of resources within a society—these might be grounds for feelings of threat and subsequent strife with members of certain out-groups. Economic circumstances, too, may contribute to increasing competition, creating threats of joblessness and a sense of conflict (Bonacich, 1972) and perhaps fuelling a sense of aggrieved entitlement from those who feel threatened with displacement (Blumer, 1958). And further, there is an apparently natural tendency to favor one's own group (Tajfel & Turner, 1979), and to therefore harbor suspicions against newcomers who might threaten our established societal practices (and identity) with change or corruption (Branscombe, Ellemers, Spears, & Doosje, 1999). In sum, existing theories emphasize that social structure creates the conditions under which individual men and women may experience feelings of realistic or symbolic threat from an out-group, and this fuels conflictual and discriminatory behavior.

If we consider what this means in practice, in late twentieth-century Western societies, then we should look for signs indicating that ethnocentrism and xenophobia flared up when there were large numbers of immigrants and when economies were down. Numerous sociological studies examined these hypotheses, but they provided few firm answers. Probably the most consistent effect is that if the population contains a substantial proportion of immigrants, there tends to be somewhat higher support for extreme right-wing parties and feelings of threat are higher (e.g., Lubbers, Gijsberts, & Scheepers, 2002). But the research is quite contradictory and inconclusive in other respects: competition and hardship are not related to hostility towards minorities and immigrants in a straightforward and direct manner at all (Coenders, Lubbers, Scheepers, & Verkuyten, 2008; Coenders & Scheepers, 2008; Savelkoul, Scheepers, Tolsma, & Hagendoorn, 2011; Gesthuizen, Savelkoul, & Scheepers, this volume). Furthermore, because economic factors are largely unrelated to strife, conflict and the overt suppression of minorities, it appears that competition is probably not an immediate or crucial cause (Green, Glaser, & Rich, 1998; Knigge, 1998). This discrepancy between theory and empirical data offers scope for new interpretations.

The tenuous relationship between these variables and intergroup hostility does not mean that the theoretical concepts themselves are entirely irrelevant, however: It is clear that populist right-wing politicians in countries such as Austria, Belgium, France, Australia and the Netherlands have found a willing audience with their rhetoric of threats due to competition, hardship and loss of identity. Indeed, it appears that the strongest predictor of support for extreme right-wing parties is "public opinion" on issues such as democracy and immigration (Lubbers et al., 2002). Thus, the theoretical concepts identified by theories of competition and identity may be important and influential within the *social climate* surrounding specific current affairs. Immigrant numbers may go up and down, but this only becomes relevant when "immigration" becomes problematic in public awareness. Our reasoning is that this can happen if, in public debate, one can refer to a certain category of "immigrants" as if they were one single entity, and one can (jointly with others) form a stereotyped understanding of who these people are and that they form a problem for "us," our way of life, our livelihood, and so on (Koopmans

& Muis, 2009; Postmes, 2009; Täuber, Gordijn, Postmes, & van Zomeren, 2013). In sum, in order to understand when and how *feelings* of competition, hardship and identity threat become activated and consequential for intergroup behavior, we need to study public discourse in which these concepts are mobilized.

Beyond the classical theories of intergroup relations, other factors may also explain political developments in Western society around the millennium. Various factors may have contributed to a growing sense of international insecurity or unpredictability. The optimism after the West's apparent "victory" in the cold war, following the fall of the Berlin wall on "11/9" 1989, was gradually eroded by a string of conflicts in regions including the Balkans, Rwanda, Afghanistan, Iraq and many other states, undermining perceptions of power and moral authority. Moreover, the hegemony of Western society was called into doubt by the successes of emergent economies such as China, Brazil, India and Russia, and the evident failures in regulating the financial sector. But although these events may all have fuelled a sense of anxiety, again there is no clear correspondence between key events and the rise of anti-immigrant hostilities (Mols & Jetten, 2013). Together this suggests that there is scope to enrich our understanding of how conflict between groups escalates and how it can be de-escalated by looking beyond the factors that are traditionally considered key predictors of intergroup conflict. For reasons that will be explained shortly, we believe that it would be beneficial to consider processes of communication between and within groups.

The workings of communication

Before explaining more about our research program, it would be beneficial to make a few general observations. All have implications for the role that communication plays in intergroup conflict. Putting them together, we can provide a theoretically grounded overview of the approach to communication contained in our research.

The first observation is that intergroup conflict is effortful, time-consuming and rather rare. If we look around us, the possibilities of dividing up the world into neat categories of "them" and "us" are near-endless. We may distinguish social groups on the basis of gender, social class, ethnicity or religion. Or we may attribute meaning to geographical differences that we associate with nationality, regional identity, or even city neighborhood. Within a society we find further possibilities to group people according to their language, accents, age group, astrological sign, political views, sports activities, friendships, families and clan-like social networks, or even their preference for a cat or a dog as a pet. In order to signify belonging to groups people are willing to change their physical appearance through clothing, piercings, tattoos, physical modifications such as circumcision, stretching of nostrils, earlobes and lips, hairdo, and various fashions of beards and mustache. Although some of these groupings are more frivolous and light-hearted, individual humans are capable of attaching strong value and meaning to all of them, at times (Cannadine, 2013; Postmes, Baray, Haslam, Morton, & Swaab, 2006). Given these seemingly endless opportunities for making distinctions between different kinds of people, we find it remarkable not just that categorization is central to intergroup relations and conflict (e.g., Turner et al., 1987), but also that such a lot of categorization happens around us all day, without there being any apparent social conflict whatsoever. The most common consequence of distinguishing between "us" and "them" is probably a very mild tendency to value one's in-group positively (Brewer, 1999). The implication is that in order for intergroup conflict to arise, categorization alone is not enough: a lot of work goes into making those categories meaningful. This implies that a particular out-group does not emerge naturally as the consequence of particular events or conflicts: "The enemy" is a social construction that we work hard at defining through communicating among ourselves about how we think about them (i.e., intragroup communication) and toward them directly (e.g., intergroup communication).

Indeed, one reason for intergroup conflict to arise is that, especially in cases where there is some degree of (budding) intergroup tension, social interaction takes place mainly *within* the in-group. The consequence is that we only *rarely* talk with members of out-groups (Marsden, 1987), even in settings that would outwardly appear to be integrated and thereby encouraging intergroup contact (Haualani, Chitgopekar, Morrison, & Dodge, 2004). So if we seek to understand more about the role that communicative processes such as conversation and talk play in intergroup conflict between "us" and "them," we probably need to take a close look at the conversations that happen within groups of like-minded people. Accordingly, we believe that intergroup tensions are probably going to be played out not so much in social interactions between groups, but rather in one group discussing the other—in intragroup communication about "them," in other words. This is somewhat ironic, for the vast majority of research on communication and intergroup conflict has focused on the contact hypothesis, which assumes that intergroup contact will reduce prejudice (see Dixon, Durrheim, & Tredoux, 2005, for a critical review). At the same time, this is also encouraging: to engineer intergroup interactions on a sufficiently large scale is time-consuming, complex and costly, particularly if its effects on producing social change are debatable (Maoz, 2011). In comparison, interventions to change intragroup dialogue may be somewhat easier to develop and implement: this is where most social interaction takes place, after all.

The second observation is that communication with out-groups often takes place through mass media. We rarely, if ever, interact with members of an out-group in real life as we do with our own kin and kind. Instead, we hear of them and their views through newspapers, television, radio, and internet. The implication is that our views about out-groups are shaped disproportionally by visible manifestations of the out-group (iconic events and figures). This selective exposure to recognizable out-group individuals is another key way, we believe, in which stereotypes can be created, maintained and undermined. Extending this, the portrayal of out-group characters in mass media may offer one way of (de) escalating conflict.

The final observation concerns the reasons why people have conversations (often with in-group others, but occasionally involving members of out-groups) in the first place. The many reasons for talking to other people include, sometimes, a genuine desire to share or seek information or to understand. But often, the passing of information is not the main goal of an interaction. Communication helps individuals to get things done. These things may be very concrete: when trading goods we need to agree on a price and when cooking a meal together we need to coordinate our actions. But very often, having the interaction itself is the goal. If we meet with friends or with people we would like to be friendly with, the topic we discuss tends to be chosen because it enables us to establish or maintain a social relationship (or so we hope). We may choose to talk or gossip about "them," but if we do so and we come to agree about certain values and judgments in the process, the out-group that we are talking about is in some sense merely the instrument that helps us bond. It follows from this that intergroup conflict may be a side effect of social processes occurring within a certain in-group. Moreover, not all conflicts between groups are about actual competition, power differences or some other form of rivalry. The out-group may be merely an instrument for an ambitious individual to get ahead within the in-group, or it may prove useful to shore up solidarity within the group (Postmes & Smith, 2006). All these observations about the workings of communication are important to keep in mind when studying the social effects of intragroup and intergroup communication in intergroup conflict.

Outline of the research program

Putting these elements together, we can see the outlines of our approach. We make use of the familiar distinction between interpersonal communication and mass communication. It is our belief that both of these can shape perceptions that people have about themselves and other groups within society, and can thereby produce constructive and destructive intergroup behaviors. But the processes we are interested in differ considerably. In line with the theoretical considerations mentioned above, we propose that interpersonal communications that occur within the informal context of small groups with relatively casual and unstructured social interaction are a forum at which individuals can socially validate abstract thoughts about social relations between groups. In that context, we have mainly explored what happens when people are talking about an out-group among themselves (e.g., what are the consequences of intragroup gossip for intergroup relations and for intragroup levels of solidarity)? And how does such intragroup communication influence the expected interaction with the out-group (e.g., does gossip have implications for how we approach them and expect them to treat us)?

In mass communication, by contrast, we have focused mainly on the consequences of portrayals of the out-group and in particular personal and individuated communications from individual out-group members: for most in-group members, these would be the most vivid interactions with "them." Here, we have mainly been interested in the question of how an out-group should be portrayed (or should portray itself) in order to achieve improved intergroup relations. In particular, we have focused on the impact of the emotional expressions that group members make on the subsequent perceptions of intergroup relations, both among the affected in-group and among third parties. How do people deal with emotive communications from an out-group about their situation and about possible injustices or wrongs? When are out-group members attended to as human beings with legitimate needs and concerns? Below, we provide an overview of our key findings in these two domains.

Intragroup communication

Words such as "us" and "them" are easily used in conversations with like-minded others, and perhaps it is because of this that we tend to overlook how much effort goes into defining them. Let us begin with an example. It is often assumed that skin color is a powerful cue to group membership. This cue, in combination with the socio-structural relations between the social groups they denote, has often been considered sufficient for conflict to emerge. In other words, everyone can see the difference between Black and White, everyone can notice that Whites have higher status and thus conflict must necessarily ensue. The reasoning here is essentially no different to that suggested by Philip Zimbardo for the outcomes of the "Stanford Prison experiment:" the wearing of uniforms is the first step to violent tyranny (see Haslam & Reicher, 2006, for a critical review). But on closer inspection, this is a very problematic assumption. In countries such as the Netherlands, the blackest minority group are from Suriname, who tend to have quite positive relations to the indigenous majority, despite the fact that their numbers have increased steeply over the years. Another relatively dark-skinned minority are Moluccans who used to be considered a very problematic group in the 1970s, but are now considered fully integrated Dutch. Instead, Dutch anxieties about minorities have become focused since about 2000 on Moroccans and Turks, many of whom are fair-skinned and pretty indistinguishable from some indigenous Dutch. Simplistic assumptions about color being a sufficient cue simply cannot account for such dynamics. What we have to look into therefore is the process by which out-groups are transformed into a problem, or a blessing, for the in-group.

Intragroup communication is of central importance here, because it is *within* groups that perceptions and meta-perceptions of the out-group and of intergroup relations are validated and become normative. In other words, all the theoretical constructs that are central to social identity theory, realistic group conflict theory, and so on (competition, stereotypes, categories, status relations) are not given but socially constructed. It is this process of opinion formation that determines the emotions towards out-groups (e.g., Noelle-Neumann, 1984) and it is the normative validation of them by in-group members that co-determines whether people are willing to act on them (van Zomeren, Spears, Fischer, & Leach, 2004).

Consensus and validation

Normative validation is not something that requires an awful lot of effort: it appears to happen quite spontaneously. Small-scale conversations within groups that expect to get along, but have not had much prior contact, will generally trigger a process of norm formation in which group members are keen to discover and adopt new conventions (Postmes, Baray, Haslam, Morton, & Swaab, 2006; Postmes, Spears, & Lea, 2000). In groups interacting via CMC or email, for example, we find that imitation processes occur that subtly change message style (how we type). If some people in a group use many exclamation marks, this is likely to become a convention for the group. But interestingly, group members do not use this style when they email someone outside their group. These are not mere habits: these are group-specific and therefore normative patterns of behavior (Postmes et al., 2000). The same processes affect message content (what we type about), but here effects are a lot stronger. In some groups, elaborate humor becomes the norm. Others are dominated by complaints. Thus, spontaneous processes such as imitation provide a platform for norm development.

In small-scale conversations about out-groups, similar processes occur: these lead to the formation of stereotypes, they fuel emotional responses and give rise to norms for intergroup behavior (Amiot & Bourhis, 2005). We have examined this process in a line of research examining the emergence of anti-immigrant stereotypes and its consequences. What we did in our experiments was to give small groups of schoolchildren of 16 to 17 years old the opportunity to discuss the abstract concept of "immigrants" for five minutes. In effect, we provided them with a safe environment to exchange their views about "them." We compared group discussions to a control group who did not discuss the issue, but thought about it alone. In order to focus the discussion on the stereotype, we asked them to write down the top five characteristics of immigrants (Smith & Postmes, 2011a, Study 1).

Results showed that a discussion brings up different opinions than individual thinking does (see also Haslam, Turner, Oakes, McGarty, & Reynolds, 1998). Even though the stereotypes that surface in private thought and in group discussion appear to be similar content-wise, the group discussion is more focused on determining the *social relationship* between "us" and "them." Intergroup relations are described as conflictual or tense, and the thought that "they" have come here to benefit from "us" crops up in nearly all conversations. While these are not unexpected or unusual themes per se, what is striking is that individuals on their own rarely mention them spontaneously. As a result, the group discussions tend to result in portrayals of the immigrant out-group that reveal fear and contempt, and only little empathy. The immediate consequence of such a conversation is that afterwards, people express more hostile intentions towards immigrants. They are more likely, for example, to say that immigrants should not get free healthcare or unemployment benefits—things that everyone in Britain is entitled to. And they are more willing to take action against immigration.

One might think that this is simply due to group polarization (Myers & Lamm, 1976; Turner, 1991). But the results provide clear pointers that something else is going on. In none of the studies we conducted did we ever find that group discussion changed participants' *attitudes* (or prejudice) towards immigrants. But discussion does bring feelings of certainty coupled with consensus: a sense that we all agree and that my personal views about immigrants are valid. The implication is that these discussions empower prejudiced people to openly display and enact their prejudices.

We carried out several other studies to find out more about the processes involved in these effects, in particular to establish the limits of these effects. Importantly, group discussion only has these effects if there is *strong* consensus. In one carefully controlled study, we took the statements by participants in the earlier research, and asked actors to stage a scripted discussion. We rearranged the order of what these actors said in such a way that they appeared to first mildly disagree and then agree fully, or conversely we had them first agree fully and then mildly disagree. In other words, all the statements about immigrants were exactly the same, but the group appeared to agree over time, or it appeared to agree somewhat less over time. Participants showed more hostility when they had listened to discussions that moved towards agreement. These results show that hostility does *not* increase because of the arguments we hear, but because there is social consensus among people "like us" about the stereotype of immigrants. This is an important finding, we believe, for it points to a way of preventing the negative effects of stereotypes: simply undermining the assumed consensus should work (see also Smith & Postmes, 2011b).

There is some indication that these processes can influence meaningful and consequential social behavior. In one study, we let youngsters cast votes for the British Youth Parliament. We presented participants with statements from three candidates: a Conservative party candidate, a candidate for Labour and one for the UK Independence Party. The first two are mainstream parties whose policy on immigration is virtually indistinguishable. UKIP is different: it is more right wing with an anti-immigrant agenda. We gave participants the real party statements on these issues. The results showed that when participants had debated about the characteristics of immigrants, they were 83 percent more likely to vote UKIP as when they had thought about the issue on their own. However, when group consensus was undermined by asking groups to also consider policy implications, they were 77 percent less likely to vote UKIP (Smith & Postmes, 2011a). A further line of research suggests that these intragroup processes may even legitimate *hostile* actions towards an out-group. Notably, the administration of harm to an out-group is extremely rare (Mummendey & Otten, 1998). But after consensual intragroup discussion, punishments to an out-group are meted out more readily (Smith & Postmes, 2009).

The anticipation of interactions

So far we have discussed research that was concerned with the abstract category of immigrants. Such abstract categories did not "exist" as material realities for the participants in our studies: immigrants were rare in the part of the country that we conducted the research in and they would not necessarily be recognized in the street as such. The impact of conversation might be quite different in contexts in which one interacts about a group that one is in some form of conflict with but that also lives close by and whom one has day-to-day interactions with. We conducted studies to examine what would happen when one talked about such an out-group behind their backs (i.e., gossip). The particular issue we were interested in was to examine the turn that such conversations would take in anticipation of direct interaction with "them."

We studied these processes in a setting in which intergroup conflict was already a live issue (Greijdanus, Postmes, Gordijn, & van Zomeren, 2013a). The issue was the "town and gown" conflicts between students and city dwellers in the University City of Groningen. This conflict has a long pedigree, but in recent years various neighborhoods had undertaken actions against student inhabitants and the city council had attempted to assuage city dwellers' concerns by "capping" student residency numbers in particular areas of the city (a policy which in practice meant that students were banned from living in certain areas of the town: a policy perceived as unjust and later proven not legally sustainable). The animosity between the groups is sustained by negative and hostile stereotypes along the lines that students cause disturbances, are noisy and arrogant, whereas city dwellers are uncivilized and ignorant. Both groups tend to dehumanize the other: city dwellers are brainless and students a pest.

In this context, we wondered firstly whether intragroup communication would exacerbate the perceived conflict: we thus compared conditions in which group members talked with one another about the out-group with conditions in which participants wrote down their thoughts about the out-group on their own. More importantly, we wanted to know how the anticipation of direct contact with the out-group would affect the discussion. One could reason that anticipated contact would reduce tension (for example because it increases interdependence with the out-group; see also Crisp & Turner, 2009). But it might also be that anticipation of contact in a conflict situation raises anxiety and makes groups more defensive.

This study showed support for the second prediction of increased defensiveness. Group members who anticipate interacting with an antagonistic out-group brace themselves for anticipated hostility, but only when they talked about this within their group and not when anticipating on their own. Content analyses of intragroup discussions revealed that when intergroup contact is anticipated, individuals share anecdotes about intergroup hostility rather than about positive intergroup contact. Thus, the content of *spontaneous* intragroup communication, in a context in which intergroup relations are tense to begin with, is predominated by negative concerns—although the context is very different this resonates with the findings of Smith and Postmes (2011a) that conflict and threats are a central theme in in-group discourse about "them." These discussions had various consequences. One was that it boosted group identification—this provides a clear pointer to the functionality of such conversations for the *in-group* itself. In addition, there was evidence that this led to the devaluation of the out-group: participants became convinced that their in-group was negative about city dwellers. Finally there was an interesting effect of anticipated contact on meta-stereotypes (the stereotypes that one believes "they" have about "us"). Here we found that people began to recast negative in-group traits (lazy, slovenly) as positive traits. Taken together, we interpret this package of findings as evidence of "steeling": a hardening of attitudes in anticipation of a clash or unpleasant encounter.

We reasoned that this effect of steeling was due to a latent anxiety about encountering the out-group. But unfortunately, the study did not contain any variables that measured this process directly. Therefore we conducted a follow-up study in which we played back these group discussions to a new set of participants who were completely unaware of the details of the first experiment. We showed that the group discussions in which the group braced itself for (hostile) intergroup interactions induced more intergroup anxiety than the discussions in which intergroup interaction was not anticipated.

Zooming in on processes: shared cognition and abstraction

Considering the lines of research discussed thus far, we see that if an in-group has a brief conversation about an out-group, a range of responses indicates that intergroup conflict is likely to increase: expression and validation of negative stereotypes, the emergence of hostile norms that condone harmful actions, a stronger identification with the in-group and an elevated level of intergroup anxiety. What is it about intragroup discussions that encourages these kinds of effects? Is this kind of outcome inescapable and always harmful for intergroup relations?

Part of the process, we believe, revolves around the maintenance of some form of consensus within the in-group (see Haslam et al., 1998; Postmes, 2003). At the level of the *individual group members*, this desire for agreement manifests itself in two ways: in intragroup communication people expect to agree with one another on topics that are commonly valued. For example, if one expresses an opinion about an out-group, one would normally expect this opinion to be echoed or corroborated by others within the group. If this is not the case, the individual experiences this as unpleasant. Asch (1956) described the mental state of deviants from a majority as one of "paradox and conflict." Neuroscientific research suggests that a majority group opinion other than one's own activates brain areas associated with cognitive conflict and pain (Berns et al., 2005). It is not surprising then that even before such clashes of opinion occur, group members are motivated to achieve consensus within the in-group: they organize their actions (the topics they discuss and avoid, the responses they give to others) in such a way that agreement is preserved, for example by ensuring that conversations revolve around commonly held knowledge or *shared cognitions* (Gigone & Hastie, 1993). But consensus does not appear to be the end goal here: when the group has norms that promote pluralism and dissent, individual group members are more likely to deviate and they value unique individual inputs and deviance more positively (Haslam, Adarves-Yorno, Postmes, & Jans, 2013; Hornsey & Jetten, 2004; Postmes, Spears, & Cihangir, 2001). Thus, group members strive to respect and reproduce that which is normative within the group. This is directly relevant for stereotypes, which may also acquire normative properties (Sherif, 1936).

The most general phenomenon thus seems to be that group members strive to preserve and reproduce normative beliefs and shared knowledge. This means that it would be functional for group members to center conversations around knowledge that we assume would be shared by "people like us": stereotypes, prejudices and perceptions of intergroup relations are all concepts which one assumes to be socially shared knowledge within the in-group (Postmes, Haslam, & Swaab, 2005; Swaab, Postmes, van Beest, & Spears, 2007). And so we tend to talk about "them" in generic terms, using more simplistic abstract references to entire categories (immigrants) rather than to subgroups (Polish migrant workers, Somali refugees). The use of such abstract categories is not just easier: it will probably also increase the likelihood of agreement. The chance that another person is knowledgeable about "the French" is much larger than the chance that this person will have specific views on people living in the Provence, let alone the inhabitants of Nice. Moreover, abstract categories tend to be less clearly defined, making the chance of disagreement smaller.

The immediate consequence of this is that existing stereotypes are reproduced. But the use of abstract category references is also likely to have *negative* consequences for intergroup relations (Verkuyten, 1997). In general, abstract language tends to undermine the ability for pluralism. Yet minorities differ greatly in how culturally distinct they are from the host society: some minorities are strongly accepted, although others may be less so. In a country such as the Netherlands, most minority groups are completely accepted and positively valued, but some are not. What happens when all these different groups are referred to as "immigrants"? We examined this question in two experiments (Täuber et al., 2013). In line with research on social categorization and exemplar-category relationships, we reasoned that categorizing different minority groups under a shared label (i.e., "immigrants") vs. as distinct groups negatively affects majority members' acceptance of these minorities. We further anticipated that assimilation will occur at the expense of a moderately different minority rather than to the benefit of an extremely different minority, because people have a general tendency to maximize differences between categories. Based on this so-called category-accentuation effect (Eiser & Stroebe, 1972; Krueger, Rothbart, & Sriram, 1989) we predicted that majority members are more likely to assimilate members of a moderately different minority to members of an extremely different minority than vice-versa. This is because assimilating two ethnic minority groups such that both groups become moderately distinct from the majority contradicts the tendency to maximize the differences between the categories "us" and "them."

Two studies examined this idea, one using natural groups in the Netherlands (specifically Moroccans and Surinamese) and the second study using fictitious minorities that allowed more experimental control. Both studies showed that categorization had strong effects on majority members' acceptance of minorities. Specifically, categorization as a single group (i.e., "immigrants") leads to assimilation effects. But this assimilation was not beneficial for the extremely different groups: the use of a common category did not make the perceptions of the extremely different minority (Moroccans) any more positive, but it did make perceptions of the moderately different minority (Surinamese) substantially more negative. In other words, the prototype of the superordinate group of "immigrants" is disproportionately influenced by the more negatively perceived (and salient) minority. The implication of these findings is that discourse that lacks nuance and that categorizes different minorities as a single group of "immigrants" (or by extension as "aliens" or "foreigners") can inadvertently exacerbate the perception of societal conflict, both from the majority and the minority group perspective. Such language lumps various out-groups together, accentuating the differences between "us" and "them," thereby magnifying any tensions or disagreements that may exist. By implication, in conflict de-escalation attempts one should strive to avoid generic terms and avoid generic "us–them" language.

The shift towards abstraction may also occur for more subtle, cognitive, reasons. In a recent line of research we examined the hypothesis that even the *anticipation* of communication puts people in a more abstract mindset (Greijdanus, Postmes, Gordijn, & van Zomeren, 2013b). Our reasoning was simply that conversations by definition rely on abstract concepts and language as contained in shared perceptions of reality. Thus if one anticipates having a conversation with another person or with a group, one would expect to find that cognition shifts towards a more abstract level of thinking—after all, this is the level at which consensus and common ground can be found. In two studies we therefore manipulated whether participants encountered stereotype confirming or stereotype disconfirming information about an out-group. We reasoned that, in general, stereotype disconfirming information is processed concretely, whereas stereotype confirming information is processed abstractly. But the studies also showed that when participants anticipated interacting with other people about this information, the stereotype inconsistent information was processed much more abstractly. Thus, the mere anticipation of group discussion cognitively prepares group members for the use of abstract-level concepts (such as "us" and "them") which tend to be associated with stereotypes and generic beliefs.

In sum, in addition to "objective" conflict with an out-group over (say) limited resources, we see that there is a combination of within-group processes which have the capacity to highlight (or downplay) awareness and perceived relevance of such conflicts. The implication is that even objective conflicts need to become subjectively relevant before they can have any real implications for intergroup behavior. We believe that this knowledge can be used beneficially, to de-escalate conflict. Because ideas about the out-group are *used* as a vehicle for achieving things among "us" (e.g., maintaining harmonious relationships, achieving prominence or power), conflict can be avoided or reduced if group outcomes can be achieved in a different way.

Developing intragroup interventions to de-escalate conflict

All the findings mentioned thus far have implications for how to de-escalate conflict. It may be useful to sum up the main lessons learned, before considering some of the ongoing research in which the effectiveness of these interventions is being put to the test. The central finding is that conflict exacerbates when groups consensualize (or converge) on negative stereotypes. Preventing consensus from emerging is quite easy: Janis (1982), for example, recommends appointing devil's advocates or "mindguards" to every decision-making group. But there are more subtle and more effective means of preserving pluralism. One simple way of achieving this is by asking complex rather than simple questions. Indeed, several studies have shown that validation breaks down the moment there is some (slight) disagreement within the in-group. For instance, hostile norms towards immigrants are undermined as soon as a discussion contains some limited dissent, or even if there is uncertainty (e.g., when groups are asked to think about the implications of their discussion for immigration policy, Smith & Postmes, 2011a).

The challenge, however, is that consensus and stereotypes give the group something which is valued in its own right: individuals acquire a sense of belonging and the group a sense of shared identity. The process of consensualization, in other words, is valuable for the in-group in its own right. An alternative strategy for undermining hostile stereotypes is to ask groups to consensualize on counterfactuals: can they think of reasons why the prevailing stereotype is erroneous? Research indirectly suggests that such interventions might have the power to undermine or even reverse the negative impact of stereotypes. For example, Smith and Postmes conducted two studies in which groups of women (and men) were asked to consensualize on the generic stereotype that "women" would be bad at mathematics. The consequence of disputing a negative stereotype within the in-group was that traditional stereotype threat effects on women's math performance were undermined and to some extent even reversed compared with male performance (Smith & Postmes, 2011b). The implication of this is that as long as we can agree that the traditional stereotype does not apply, this should both preserve within-group consensus and reduce hostility towards "them."

But the previous research also suggests that it might be beneficial to undermine the tendency to think in abstract terms about "them" in the first place. In a pair of studies (Greijdanus et al., in preparation) we began to develop interventions that followed this combined approach of having groups discuss stereotype-inconsistent topics (versus stereotype consistent) and having them discuss concrete cases of individual out-group members (versus abstractly considering the out-group as an entity). Again, we manipulated the nature of group discussion simply by giving groups direct instructions. In the concrete-inconsistent condition, instructions would be to come up with concrete examples that are inconsistent with the prevailing stereotype of Moroccans. In the abstract-stereotype consistent condition groups consensualized on general statements such as "Moroccans are dangerous." In the concrete-inconsistent condition, they gave examples such as "I have a Moroccan friend who is very kind." Importantly, we found that in all conditions groups manage to reach consensus and they appear to be satisfied with the group outcome. As one can see, a very simple shift in instructions leads to quite different conversation topics. But does this then translate into reduced prejudice? Our initial results suggest that such an intervention does indeed have the intended consequences for particular forms of prejudice. Specifically, the combination of *abstract* and stereotype *inconsistent* content reduced prejudice, in particular its cognitive and behavioral components (but less so its affective dimension).

Considering all findings together, we may conclude that intragroup processes can be targeted in interventions designed to reduce prejudice or to de-escalate intergroup conflict. We emphasize, however, that the laboratory-based research conducted so far needs to be supplemented by field trials before we can draw any definitive conclusions about the effectiveness and viability of these intragroup interventions.

Intergroup communication and conflict (de)escalation

Our research also sought to understand processes in intergroup communication. Again we focused in particular on the factors that offer the potential for conflict de-escalation. The traditional approach to this issue in social psychology has been to focus on the boundary conditions which need to be met for intergroup contact to be productive. To broadly summarize the key findings, interpersonal contact and friendships have often been demonstrated to have positive consequences (Pettigrew & Tropp, 2000). But at the same time, research documents these interpersonal contacts to be very rare. Attempts to promote person-to-person encounters in protracted conflict situations also note the practical obstacles to organizing such encounters and note that the evidence for their success is limited (Maoz, 2011).

In all, it appears that a lot of our contact with out-group members and out-group actions is likely to be mediated by mass media. A quite extensive literature documents effects of television and other media portrayals of ethnic and gender groups on a range of socio-psychological outcomes (Hargrave & Livingstone, 2009). There is some evidence that mass media portrayals may "prime" and perpetuate prejudices (e.g., Gilliam Jr & Iyengar, 2000), but overall the effects are quite small and there are some interesting moderators (Hargrave & Livingstone, 2009). For example, news portrayals of African Americans as offenders may influence those who have limited direct contact with that group more strongly (i.e., because they live in segregated white neighborhoods, Gilliam, Valentino, & Beckmann, 2002) and may influence those who watch little news more strongly (i.e., because there is more scope to influence their views, Dixon, 2006). But although there are abundant studies that document how media portrayals can (sometimes) encourage stereotyping (Hargrave & Livingstone, 2009), there appears to be little research that focuses on the concrete question of *how* a certain group should be portrayed in order for it to be perceived more positively.

An emotions-based approach

Our approach to this issue was informed by the literature on (intergroup) emotions. In intergroup conflict, it is well documented that the out-group is depersonalized (Turner, Hogg, Oakes, Reicher, & Wetherell, 1987) and ceases to be perceived as human with distinctly human characteristics such as secondary emotions and pro-social values (Haslam, 2006; Leyens et al., 2003). This suggests that a more humanized portrayal of an out-group is likely to affect intergroup relations. The straightforward implication is that our understanding of an out-group increases to the extent that we recognize their emotions and motives as valid and legitimate. But given that we are concerned here with communication in conflict situations, there are some complications, both with the kind of emotions that the out-group might communicate and with the kind of legitimacy one evokes. Concretely, if one communicates anger or contempt at an out-group, would this really have positive consequences? And if observers witness these emotions and recognize their legitimacy, would they not end up legitimizing the use of violence? Our approach was that one would need to consider not just what emotions are communicated, but also the context. It may be most instructive to illustrate first when the communication of emotions would appear to be *counter-productive.*

We sought to illustrate the kind of contextual factors that play a role here in a set of studies examining third-party (independent) responses to violence in intractable conflict (Kamans, van Zomeren, Gordijn, & Postmes, 2013). In intractable intergroup conflicts, groups often try to frame intergroup violence as legitimate through the use of emotional appeals. The studies we set up portrayed a violent conflict cycle between African tribes (a topic that participants would be unaware of, we expected) but with characteristics which are generalizable to many intractable conflict situations with violence. The core question was to what extent these outsiders would condone or condemn violent retribution from one target tribe. We kept the description of the conflict cycle constant, but varied two things: whether the perpetrator of the violence was powerful or not and whether they expressed anger or fear. The reason for focusing on these two emotions in particular is that they are so prevalent in conflict situations characterized by power imbalance.

The results of the study show that although outsiders generally have very little sympathy with the use of violence, they nevertheless have somewhat more sympathy for powerless groups' use of violent retribution, presumably because of their "underdog" status. But interestingly, the communication of emotions changes this sympathy as revealed by shifts in the level of perceived legitimacy. If the emotions are congruent with the power-relations, observers express more understanding for the use of violence. Thus, third party observers legitimize the use of intergroup violence most when a *powerless* group communicates *fear* and when a *powerful* group communicates *anger*. In short, it does appear to be the case that the expression of understandable emotions enhances the likelihood that one's actions will be recognized as justifiable. Fear communicates that the group is a victim and evokes a response in the audience suggesting that these powerless people cannot be blamed for their violence. Anger, by contrast, communicates that the group feels wronged, and to an audience this has the potentially troubling consequence that their violence may seem righteous and morally justifiable.

These results illustrate that among third party observers, the expression of emotions that are considered authentic can function as a direct appeal for understanding. As a result, violence can be condoned. One might conclude from this that the expression of emotions has negative consequences, for example third parties might be less likely to intervene or to remain independent in the conflict.

But we also interpret the finding as a signal that it is possible to have understanding for an aggrieved party notwithstanding their objectionable actions, as long as we begin to comprehend their motives and consider these to be valid. Indirectly, the findings speak to our starting assumption: emotions may signal that there is a problem, but they also remind us of our common humanity. Indeed, different emotions such as anger and fear have different *relational* themes (Lazarus, 1991) that turn their communication into appeals for relating, understanding, and perspective taking. What we take from this is that the overt expression of emotions is a way of changing intergroup dialogue from an interaction about abstract entities, to a dialogue among people. And although such a dialogue between people may be negative because of a troubled intergroup relationship, it is exactly this relationship that the dialogue maintains (rather than destroys). In this sense, it is often better to communicate than it is to stop communicating altogether.

Witnessing an out-group's emotional response

Mass media portrayals of intergroup conflict are perhaps more interesting and relevant to people when they concern an out-group that is directly relevant to oneself. What do emotions expressed by such an out-group achieve? Building on the reasoning in the previous section, we argued that during between-group interaction negative emotions can have a powerful communicative function in sending signals between groups about how "we" feel about "them" (Klein, Spears, & Reicher, 2007), but also, and importantly, what we wish the future relationship between "us" and "them" to be (de Vos, van Zomeren, Gordijn, & Postmes, 2013c; Fischer & Roseman, 2007). In this context, the expression of conflict-related emotions such as anger can signal an intention to engage in destructive conflict behavior such as aggression, but anger can also serve as an overture to constructive conflict behavior such as negotiation and discussion (De Dreu & Van de Vliert, 1997; Van Zomeren et al., 2004; Yzerbyt, Dumont, Wigboldus, & Gordijn, 2003; Yzerbyt, Dumont, Mathieu, Gordijn, & Wigboldus, 2006). The key reason for the latter possibility is that the communication of anger has a relational function (see Fischer & Roseman, 2007)—it has the potential to invite empathy and understanding from others by sending the dual signal that: (a) there is conflict; but (b) there is a desire to resolve it while maintaining—or even strengthening—the relationship (de Vos et al., 2013c).

Our research explored these relational effects of the communication of anger and a second prevalent conflict emotion, contempt, in the context of intergroup conflict. Anger is often accompanied by the experience of other negative emotions and some of these combinations may motivate destructive conflict behavior (Cottrell & Neuberg, 2005; Kamans, Otten & Gordijn; 2011). For example, anger about unfair treatment may be accompanied by contempt. Contempt *signals* to both oneself and the out-group that the out-group is an unworthy negotiation partner (Fischer & Roseman, 2007) and implies that one should terminate the relationship (De Vos et al., 2013a). In contrast, the expression of "pure" anger (i.e. devoid of other emotional content) has somewhat paradoxically positive consequences. In interpersonal relations, saying to someone that one feels angry about something is, in effect, an invitation to the other person to resolve this negative emotion together (Fischer & Roseman, 2007). It is thus an expression of a desire for the relationship between "me" and "him/her" to continue and improve. It is also a powerful cue that one wants the other party to attend to one's plight—an invitation for empathy, in other words.

We examined these ideas in three sets of studies. In the first set of studies (De Vos et al., 2013), we aimed to show that communicating group-based anger towards the out-group can evoke empathy and thus reduce intergroup conflict. This is because it stresses the value of maintaining a positive long-term intergroup relationship, thereby increasing understanding for the situation (in contrast to the communication of contempt). Three experiments were designed in which participants read a news report of an angered out-group. The news report contained a generic description of a situation in which the out-group was discriminated against. The article then zoomed in on one particular representative member of the out-group. This person either expressed group-based anger at the situation, group-based contempt, a combination of both group-based anger and contempt or no emotion.

Across three studies the communication of group-based anger was found to *reduce* destructive conflict intentions compared to control conditions in which only unfairness was communicated (devoid of emotion) (Experiments 1 and 2), compared to the communication of group-based contempt (Experiment 2) and compared to the combination of group-based anger and contempt (Experiments 2 and 3). In addition, all three studies revealed direct evidence for the role of out-group empathy as a mediator of these effects. The communication of "pure" group-based anger thus raised empathy levels in all studies, which in turn predicted conflict intentions in all studies.

Follow-up research extended these findings and sought to identify boundary conditions of the empathy-inducing effects of the communication of group-based anger (de Vos, van Zomeren, Gordijn, & Postmes, 2013b). As is implied in the previous studies, one important precondition for anger to have these (positive) effects is that it must be perceived to be a legitimate emotion. We wanted to isolate this factor in a follow-up study. We found, as predicted, that the communication of group-based anger only evoked empathy and only reduced destructive conflict intentions when it was expressed in a context in which the target group perceived it to be a legitimate emotion. In other words, for anger to have any benefits it must center on a legitimate grievance (e.g., inequity or a violation of basic rights). Moreover, the first set of studies zoomed in on one particular individual representative of the out-group that expressed an emotion on behalf of the group. In the follow-up research we wanted to establish whether these emotions had to be grounded in *group consensus* (i.e., we varied the "sharedness" of the anger communication). The experiment showed that anger communication only had empathy-inducing effects if there was high out-group consensus concerning the anger. These findings were replicated in a third study which mentioned both variables jointly. Results revealed that either antecedent is sufficient to cause anger's positive effects, suggesting that: (a) even a lone group member with a legitimate claim can evoke empathy for his or her group's cause through the communication of anger; and that (b) even a doubtful claim can be similarly influential as long as the group expresses its anger collectively.

The third set of studies, finally, applied the notion of the relational function of the communication of anger to long-term conflicts in which the core of group grievances may lie in past events (de Vos, van Zomeren, Gordijn, & Postmes, 2013a). As stated above, we believe that anger has positive effects because it signals an intention to continue and improve the relationship. By contrast, contempt signals that the relationship has no value and, by implication, that it can be terminated. To find direct evidence of these relational underpinnings of expressed emotions, we systematically varied the communication of emotions within the context of a long-term conflict (between Moluccans in the Netherlands and the Dutch society, consisting of the government and its people). We used similar materials as in previous research, but now varied whether emotions of anger and contempt were communicated in relation to *past* conflictual events or whether emotions were communicated as if they were still felt to this day.

The results of two experiments showed that the communication of present-day anger (compared with the communication of present-day contempt) has the effects described above of enhancing empathy and making conflict intentions more positive. But for the communication of these emotions in the past (e.g., we were angry then), this pattern shifted around. The communication of anger in the past did little to improve empathy and conflict intentions in the present. However, when past anger was communicated as still being felt today, its empathy-inducing effects returned. In line with the disparate relational function of contempt, we found the opposite pattern for this emotion. We interpret these findings as a strong confirmation of the relational underpinnings of emotion expression (at least when it comes to anger and contempt; Fischer & Roseman, 2007; see also Lazarus, 1991). The communication of past anger is a signal that the anger may have now been resolved—as such there is no longer a problem and the relationship requires no immediate attention. By contrast, an admission of past contempt is a signal that the relationship may have been restored—we were no longer on speaking terms but this seems to have been improved, and the conflict situations appears to offer a renewed opportunity to be resolved.

All these findings enrich our understanding for how to intervene in intergroup conflict. For example, it appears to be important to advise group members that expressing anger does not necessarily escalate conflict: it may be beneficial to express anger at unfair treatment, especially if the out-group can be made to see the legitimacy of these claims and can be convinced that these emotions are consensually held. The underlying reason for this advice is important: even groups in conflict engage in relationship regulation and, thus, a focus on the future maintenance of intergroup relations may open up new ways toward restoring empathy, understanding, good intentions, and, hopefully, an end to intergroup conflict.

In sum, our findings offer a range of pointers to the efficacy of portrayals of out-group members. There already is a broad literature suggesting that intergroup conflict is exacerbated when we cease to see the out-group as real human beings with emotions. Our research adds to this that it helps to portray them as beings with *understandable* emotions, with emotions that are *socially shared* by their group, and with (negative) emotions that signal a desire for future *relations* to become more *positive*.

Conclusion

The sprawling literature on intergroup conflict devotes a lot of its attention to structural arrangements in society, competition between groups or (status) inequalities between groups. In studies of conflicts between genders, nations and ethnicities, abstract social categories can become reified as concrete entities which can somehow relate to one another. In the research reviewed in this chapter, we recognize this approach to intergroup relations as quite characteristic of the way in which small in-groups talk about "them" among each other. But as our research also shows: in conversations these categories are as easily contested and complicated. What matters most, to those in the conversation, may not be what is being said about "them." Other things may be more important, such as what the conversation means for one's personal relationship to other concrete individuals that one is talking with. From that perspective, it makes sense to maintain a sharp distinction in our theorizing from what is being *said* about minorities and what is generally believed to be true about "us" and "them," and what the relations between concrete people from both groups actually are. This approach may, to some extent, resolve the paradox that the sharp discontent with immigration in many Western countries can coexist with peaceful and harmonious relations between ethnic communities. The discontent centers on the abstract *idea* of immigration. The day-to-day interaction takes into account the various individuals that have immigrated. One thus needs to divorce one's approach to solving ideological intergroup conflict (e.g., xenophobia) from solving material intergroup conflict (e.g., hate crime).

Our research has offered various solutions for ideological intergroup conflict. Our first location for finding solutions was within the in-group: it is here that most of our interaction takes place and it is here that we are socialized from our earliest age. What we learned is that for various reasons that appear to be intrinsic to the maintenance of good social relationships within one's in-group, it is likely that the group members will talk about out-groups in ways that encourage hostility. Intragroup conversations about "them" are likely to take the existing consensus about "them" as their starting point, and aim to develop and maintain such consensus. Thus, stereotyping *appears* inevitable. But on closer inspection, what group members are trying to achieve is not to mechanically reproduce negative stereotypes in the dogged pursuit of consensus: they are seeking to maintain harmonious interpersonal relationships. If we offer them the means of consensualizing on positive stereotypes, they readily do so.

Intragroup conversations are also to debate "them" at a level of abstraction which no longer is relevant to any one particular out-group member (or, for that matter, in-group member). To illustrate: gender differences are often discussed in mixed company but they are preferably discussed as if they are not about the present company. The category is invoked as an abstract entity, not as a concrete reality residing within ourselves. As a result, men and women may end up talking about masculinity and femininity with a curious degree of personal detachment: when discussing to what extent men are from Mars and women from Venus, the people in the conversation tend to dissociate from what they personally do on planet Earth. Our research offers several suggestions for how to re-connect conversations so that the abstract idea of "them" is located in the situated context of actual people.

Our research on intergroup communication adds that at that level of having conflict with actual people, it may not be such a terrible thing to disagree and fight. We can express our anger without it exacerbating conflict. What matters, again, is the establishment of a concrete relationship, coupled with an implicit or explicit desire for its continuation.

Turning finally towards future research on this topic, we note the need to integrate these insights about intragroup and intergroup communication. Thus far, the conceptual links between them are clear enough—pointing to the need to re-connect intergroup hostility to its relational foundations. But the pragmatic difficulty of this should also be clear: whatever solutions we devise for making social interactions more positive, self-segregation will tend to prevent us from establishing productive relations to an out-group. Ultimately, this means that however powerful the solutions that communication offers, they will be no more than one (powerful) component of a successful resolution of intergroup conflict.

References

Amiot, C. E., & Bourhis, R. Y. (2005). Discrimination between dominant and subordinate groups: The positive-negative asymmetry effect and normative processes. *British Journal of Social Psychology, 44*, 289–308.

Asch, S. E. (1956). Studies of independence and conformity: I. A minority of one against a unanimous majority. *Psychological Monographs: General and Applied, 70*(9), 1–70.

Berns, G. S., Chappelow, J., Zink, C. F., Pagnoni, G., Martin-Skurski, M. E., & Richards, J. (2005). Neurobiological correlates of social conformity and independence during mental rotation. *Biological Psychiatry, 58*(3), 245–253.

Blumer, H. (1958). Race prejudice as a sense of group position. *Pacific Sociological Review, 1*, 3–7.

Bonacich, E. (1972). A theory of ethnic antagonism. *American Sociological Review, 77*, 547–559.

Branscombe, N. R., Ellemers, N., Spears, R., & Doosje, B. (1999). The context and content of social identity threat. In N. Ellemers, & R. Spears (Eds.), *Social identity: Context, commitment, content* (pp. 35–58). Oxford, England: Blackwell Science Ltd.

Brewer, M. B. (1999). The psychology of prejudice: In-group love and out-group hate? *Journal of Social Issues, 55*(3), 429–444.

Cannadine, D. (2013). *The undivided past: History beyond our differences*. London: Penguin.

Coenders, M., Lubbers, M., Scheepers, P., & Verkuyten, M. (2008). More than two decades of changing ethnic attitudes in the Netherlands. *Journal of Social Issues, 64*(2), 269–285. doi:10.1111/j.1540-4560.2008.00561.x

Coenders, M., & Scheepers, P. (2008). Changes in resistance to the social integration of foreigners in Germany 1980–2000: Individual and contextual determinants. *Journal of Ethnic and Migration Studies, 34*(1), 1–26. doi:10.1080/13691830701708809.

Cottrell, C. A., & Neuberg, S. L. (2005). Different emotional reactions to different groups: A sociofunctional threat-based approach to "prejudice". *Journal of Personality and Social Psychology, 88*(5), 770.

Crisp, R. J., & Turner, R. N. (2009). Can imagined interactions produce positive perceptions?: Reducing prejudice through simulated social contact. *American Psychologist, 64*(4), 231.

De Dreu, C. K. W., & Van de Vliert, E. (1997). *Using conflict in organizations*. London: Sage.

de Vos, B., van Zomeren, M., Gordijn, E. H., & Postmes, T. (2013a). *Don't look back in anger*. Manuscript in preparation.

—— (2013b). *Explaining why group-based anger induces empathy: The power of consensus and perceived illegitimacy*. Manuscript submitted for publication.

—— (2013c). The communication of "Pure" group-based anger reduces tendencies toward intergroup conflict because it increases out-group empathy. *Personality and Social Psychology Bulletin 39*, 1043–1052.

Dixon, J., Durrheim, K., & Tredoux, C. (2005). Beyond the optimal contact strategy: A reality check for the contact hypothesis. *American Psychologist, 60*(7), 697.

Dixon, T. L. (2006). Psychological reactions to crime news portrayals of black criminals: Understanding the moderating roles of prior news viewing and stereotype endorsement. *Communication Monographs, 73*(2), 162–187.

Eiser, J. R., & Stroebe, W. (1972). Categorization and social judgment. Oxford: Academic press.

Fischer, A. H., & Roseman, I. J. (2007). Beat them or ban them: The characteristics and social functions of anger and contempt. *Journal of Personality and Social Psychology, 93*(1), 103.

Gigone, D., & Hastie, R. (1993). The common knowledge effect – information sharing and group judgment. *Journal of Personality and Social Psychology, 65*(5), 959–974.

Gilliam Jr, F. D., & Iyengar, S. (2000). Prime suspects: The influence of local television news on the viewing public. *American Journal of Political Science*, 560–573.

Gilliam, F. D., Valentino, N. A., & Beckmann, M. N. (2002). Where you live and what you watch: The impact of racial proximity and local television news on attitudes about race and crime. *Political Research Quarterly, 55*(4), 755–780.

Green, D. P., Glaser, J., & Rich, A. (1998). From lynching to gay bashing: The elusive connection between economic conditions and hate crime. *Journal of Personality and Social Psychology, 75*(1), 82–92.

Greijdanus, H., Postmes, T., Gordijn, E. H., & van Zomeren, M. (2013a). *Steeling ourselves: Intragroup communication while anticipating intergroup contact evokes defensive intergroup perceptions*. Manuscript submitted for publication.

—— (2013b). *When abstraction does not increase stereotyping: Preparing for intragroup communication enables abstract construal of stereotype-inconsistent information*. Manuscript submitted for publication.

Halualani, R. T., Chitgopekar, A. S., Morrison, J. H. T. A., & Dodge, P. S. (2004). Diverse in name only? Intercultural interaction at a multicultural university. *Journal of Communication, 54*(2), 270–286. doi:10.1111/j.1460-2466.2004.tb02628.x.

Hargrave, A. M., & Livingstone, S. M. (2009). *Harm and offence in media content: A review of the evidence.* Intellect Books.

Haslam, N. (2006). Dehumanization: An integrative review. *Personality and Social Psychology Review, 10*(3), 252–264.

Haslam, S. A., Adarves-Yorno, I., Postmes, T., & Jans, L. (2013). The collective origins of valued originality: A social identity approach to creativity. *Personality and Social Psychology Review 17,* 384–401.

Haslam, S. A., & Reicher, S. D. (2006). Rethinking the psychology of tyranny: The BBC prison study. *British Journal of Social Psychology, 45*(1), 1–40.

Haslam, S. A., Turner, J. C., Oakes, P. J., McGarty, C., & Reynolds, K. J. (1998). The group as a basis for emergent stereotype consensus. In W. Stroebe, & M. Hewstone (Eds.), *European review of social psychology* (pp. 203–239). Chichester, England: Wiley.

Hornsey, M. J., & Jetten, J. (2004). The individual within the group: Balancing the need to belong with the need to be different. *Personality and Social Psychology Review, 8*(3), 248–264.

Janis, I. L. (1982). *Groupthink: Psychological studies of policy decisions and fiascoes* (2nd ed.). Boston, MA: Houghton Mifflin.

Kamans, E., Otten, S., & Gordijn, E. H. (2011). Power and threat in intergroup conflict: How emotional and behavioral responses depend on amount and content of threat. *Group Processes and Intergroup Relations, 14,* 293–310.

Kamans, E., van Zomeren, M., Gordijn, E. H., & Postmes, T. (2013). Communicating the right emotion makes violence seem less wrong: Power-congruent emotions lead outsiders to legitimize violence of powerless and powerful groups in intractable conflict. *Group Processes & Intergroup Relations,* 1368430213502562.

Klein, O., Spears, R., & Reicher, S. (2007). Social identity performance: Extending the strategic side of SIDE. *Personality and Social Psychology Review, 11*(1), 28–45.

Knigge, P. (1998). The ecological correlates of right-wing extremism in western Europe. *European Journal of Political Research, 34*(2), 249–279.

Koopmans, R., & Muis, J. (2009). The rise of right-wing populist Pim Fortuyn in the Netherlands: A discursive opportunity approach. *European Journal of Political Research, 48*(5), 642–664. doi:10.1111/j.1475-6765.2009.00846.x.

Krueger, J., Rothbart, M., & Sriram, N. (1989). Category learning and change: Differences in sensitivity to information that enhances or reduces intercategory distinctions. *Journal of Personality and Social Psychology, 56*(6), 866.

Lazarus, R. S. (1991). *Emotion and adaptation.* New York: Oxford University Press.

Leyens, J., Cortes, B., Demoulin, S., Dovidio, J. F., Fiske, S. T., Gaunt, R., Vaes, J. (2003). Emotional prejudice, essentialism, and nationalism, the 2002 tajfel lecture. *European Journal of Social Psychology, 33*(6), 703–717.

Lubbers, M., Gijsberts, M., & Scheepers, P. (2002). Extreme right-wing voting in Western Europe. *European Journal of Political Research, 41*(3), 345–378.

Maoz, I. (2011). Does contact work in protracted asymmetrical conflict? Appraising 20 years of reconciliation-aimed encounters between Israeli Jews and Palestinians. *Journal of Peace Research, 48*(1), 115-125. doi:10.1177/0022343310389506.

Marsden, P. V. (1987). Core discussion networks of Americans. *American Sociological Review, 52*(1), 122–131.

Mols, F., & Jetten, J. (2013). *Explaining the appeal of populist radical right parties in times of economic prosperity.* Manuscript submitted for publication.

Mummendey, A., & Otten, S. (1998). Positive-negative asymmetry in social discrimination. In W. Stroebe, & M. Hewstone (Eds.), *European review of social psychology* (pp. 107–143). Chichester, England: Wiley.

Myers, D. G., & Lamm, H. (1976). The group polarization phenomenon. *Psychological Bulletin, 83*(4), 602–627.

Noelle-Neumann, E. (1984). *The spiral of silence.* Chicago: University of Chicago Press.

Pettigrew, T. F., & Tropp, L. R. (2000). Does intergroup contact reduce prejudice: Recent meta-analytic findings. In S. Oskamp (Ed.), *Reducing prejudice and discrimination: 'the claremont symposium on applied social psychology'* (pp. 93–114). Mahwah, NJ: Erlbaum.

Postmes, T. (2003). A social identity approach to communication in organizations. In S. A. Haslam, D. van Knippenberg, M. J. Platow, & N. Ellemers (Eds.), *Social identity at work: Developing theory for organizational practice* (pp. 81–98). Philadelphia, PA: Psychology Press.

—— (2009). Understanding how groups form and societies transform: Communication, identity and social reality. *Inaugural Lecture*, University of Groningen.

Postmes, T., Baray, G., Haslam, S. A., Morton, T., & Swaab, R. I. (2006). The dynamics of personal and social identity formation. In T. Postmes, & J. Jetten (Eds.), *Individuality and the group: Advances in social identity* (pp. 215–236). London: Sage.

Postmes, T., Haslam, S. A., & Swaab, R. I. (2005). Social influence in small groups: An interactive model of social identity formation. *European Review of Social Psychology, 16,* 1–42.

Postmes, T., & Smith, L. G. E. (2006). *Why do the privileged resort to oppression? A look at some intragroup factors.* Unpublished manuscript.

Postmes, T., Spears, R., & Cihangir, S. (2001). Quality of decision making and group norms. *Journal of Personality and Social Psychology, 80*(6), 918–930.

Postmes, T., Spears, R., & Lea, M. (2000). The formation of group norms in computer-mediated communication. *Human Communication Research, 26,* 341–371.

Savelkoul, M., Scheepers, P., Tolsma, J., & Hagendoorn, L. (2011). Anti-muslim attitudes in the Netherlands: Tests of contradictory hypotheses derived from ethnic competition theory and intergroup contact theory. *European Sociological Review, 27*(6), 741–758. doi:10.1093/esr/jcq035.

Sherif, M. (1936). *The psychology of social norms.* New York: Harper.

—— (1966). *In common predicament: Social psychology of intergroup conflict and cooperation.* Boston: Houghton Mifflin.

Smith, L. G. E., & Postmes, T. (2009). Intragroup interaction and the development of norms which promote intergroup hostility. *European Journal of Social Psychology, 39*(1), 130–144.

—— (2011a). The power of talk: Developing discriminatory group norms through discussion. *British Journal of Social Psychology, 50*(2), 193–215. doi:10.1348/014466610X504805.

—— (2011b). Shaping stereotypical behaviour through the discussion of social stereotypes. *British Journal of Social Psychology, 50*(1), 74–98. doi:10.1348/014466610X500340.

Swaab, R. I., Postmes, T., van Beest, I., & Spears, R. (2007). Shared cognition as a product of, and precursor to, shared identity in negotiations. *Personality and Social Psychology Bulletin, 33*(2), 187–199.

Tajfel, H., & Turner, J. C. (1979). An integrative theory of intergroup conflict. In S. Worchel, & W. G. Austin (Eds.), *The psychology of intergroup relations* (pp. 33–47). Monterey, CA: Brooks-Cole.

Täuber, S., Gordijn, E., Postmes, T., & van Zomeren, M. (2013). *When 'they' are all alike: How categorization affects the majority's acceptance of different ethnic minorities.* Manuscript submitted for publication.

Turner, J. C. (1991). *Social influence.* Milton Keynes, UK: Open University Press.

Turner, J. C., Hogg, M. A., Oakes, P. J., Reicher, S., & Wetherell, M. S. (1987). *Rediscovering the social group: A self-categorization theory.* Oxford, England: Basil Blackwell.

Van Zomeren, M., Spears, R., Fischer, A. H., & Leach, C. W. (2004). Put your money where your mouth is! Explaining collective action tendencies through group-based anger and group efficacy. *Journal of Personality and Social Psychology, 87*(5), 649.

Verkuyten, M. (1997). Discourses of ethnic minority identity. *British Journal of Social Psychology, 36*(4), 565–586.

Yzerbyt, V., Dumont, M., Mathieu, B., Gordijn, E., & Wigboldus, D. (2006). Social comparison and group-based emotions. *Social Comparison Processes and Levels of Analysis: Understanding Cognition, Intergroup Relations, and Culture,* 174–205.

Yzerbyt, V., Dumont, M., Wigboldus, D., & Gordijn, E. (2003). I feel for us: The impact of categorization and identification on emotions and action tendencies. *British Journal of Social Psychology, 42*(4), 533–549.

7 Contagious conflict

Spill-over effects of labor conflict between and within organizations

Agnes Akkerman, René Torenvlied, Alex Lehr, and Kirsten Thommes

Introduction

The current field of industrial relations is characterized by scholars' attempts to explain the prevalence of industrial conflict both in sectors and in countries. A prominent question in the field is: "why do some countries exhibit more strikes than other countries?" The actual effects of strikes—although widely recognized in the literature—have received much less systematic scholarly attention and theoretical-empirical study. Yet, if a strike occurs, this event may have profound effects beyond the instance of actual industrial conflict, and beyond the immediate stakes of the participants in the bargaining process, which is restricted in time and place. The aim of this chapter is to move the study of industrial conflict forwards by looking at the *effects* of strikes in two distinct areas: (1) collective bargaining that takes place *outside* the immediate scope of the focal bargaining organizations; and (2) work relations among employees *within* organizations affected by a strike.

Most explanations of industrial conflict consider strikes to be independent and rather isolated events (for an overview, see Franzosi, 1995). The bargaining process between negotiation partners is assumed to be unaffected by conflict elsewhere, and conflict in the bargaining process is not assumed to affect other bargaining events. Micro-economic models developed in bargaining theory explain the occurrence of a strike from its information-providing function: a strike provides negotiators with information about their relative strength, which is necessary information to obtain an equilibrium outcome (Hicks, 1932; Mauro, 1982; McConnell, 1989; Reder & Neumann, 1980). By exclusively focusing on the strike during the focal negotiations as an information device, micro-economic models ignore the possibility that negotiators may reduce their uncertainty also, or perhaps primarily, by looking *sidewards*; informing themselves about what other negotiators do (or have done) in comparable circumstances (Heckathorn, 1996).

The assumption of independence and isolation of strike events is not very plausible for two reasons. First, from this assumption it would follow that strike-waves and sudden rises of industrial conflict can only be understood as coincidental phenomena that may arise from a conjunction macro (socio)-economic and political factors. However, these factors are insufficient to fully explain macro level strike activity (Franzosi, 1995). Second, the assumption that bargaining parties are uninformed about what happens in the rest of the world is not very plausible. Modern collective bargaining practices make use of well-trained and highly professionalized negotiators, often responsible for multiple collective bargaining negotiations. Moreover, these negotiators partake in an extensive network of peers and other professional contacts. It would be rather naive to assume that negotiators ignore information from other bargaining events, such as claims made by parties, or employers' resistance and workers' willingness to strike in those events. Such information is shared among negotiators and used in other bargaining events. In this chapter we study how the use of strategic information from other bargaining events affects the negotiations and the probability of conflict between employers and unions.

Industrial conflicts, in particular strikes, do not only have an effect outside the realms of the organization involved in the strike. The aftermath of a strike is often a long-lasting process and involves personal and relational costs that may have profound effects on production in the long run. During strikes, several fault-lines may arise, not only between management and employees but also between groups of employees. It is well-documented that during strikes emotional confrontations occur between employees "on strike" and employees who "break" the strike and remain at work (Francis, 1985; Getman, 1998). The case studies' findings suggest that social relations between management and employees—as well as among those employees who joined the strike and those who did not—can become severely damaged by the process of the strike. However, systematic empirical research into the effects of strikes for social relations among employees within organizations lacks to date. To fill this gap, we present the results of our studies that aim to reveal the conditions under which social relations on the shop floor are affected by strikes.

Information spill-over between organizations and conflict

A remarkable feature of industrial conflict, such as strikes, is that it sometimes "spreads all over the country like a forest fire" while at other times it is confined to a single sector or a single firm. Standard *bargaining models* in economics and industrial relations studies offer little explanation for these strikingly different patterns (Hicks, 1932; Mauro, 1982; Reder & Neumann, 1980). Bargaining models attribute the occurrence of a strike to the information problem of bargaining partners, who must assess each other's bargaining power, as well as the employer's willingness and ability to pay. Under the condition of full information all bargaining partners can perfectly calculate their capacity to endure conflict, and therefore will always reach an outcome peacefully. Under conditions of imperfect or asymmetric information, however, miscalculations will lead to mistakes and mismatches in the strategic behavior of bargaining partners, which result in conflict. In other words, traditional bargaining models view strikes as dysfunctional incidents. In a world of static bargaining power, industrial conflict would never recur. However, in reality we observe that industrial conflict continues to occur, even in well-established bargaining relations.

Both bargaining theory and theories on protest mobilization have a fairly restricted view on actors' retrieval and use of strategic information (Andrews & Biggs, 2006; Biggs 2002, 2005; Meyers, 2000; Soule, 2004). "Example strikes" show that workers learn from strategic information about the *outcomes* of industrial conflict: learning about successes in one firm or industry may drive workers in another firm or industry to engage in a strike. Connell and Cohn (1995) found that even lost strikes inspired other workers to engage in a subsequent strike. However, when focusing on professional negotiators it would be quite unrealistic to assume that they base their bargaining strategy exclusively on the *outcomes* of other conflicts. Negotiators need much broader strategic information, for example about the resistance of unions/employers to engage in a conflict: the judicial, social or political acceptability of specific means of protest; the potential for a mobilization of workers; or the specific costs and benefits associated with conflict. The first question of this chapter is how strategic information spreads between bargaining events in negotiations between employers and unions. *How and under which conditions does information about other bargaining events influence the probability of negotiators experiencing conflicts in collective bargaining?*

Theoretically, there are two mechanisms that relate strikes—or other events of industrial conflict—to each other: *rational learning* and *social comparison*. For both mechanisms it is assumed that negotiations take place under uncertainty. The union and its members are uncertain about the economic situation of the employer, while the employer is not fully informed about his employees' willingness to strike. During a strike both parties learn about each other's resistance, and a strike can thus be seen as a source of information (see, for instance, Hicks, 1932; McConnell, 1989). Several economic bargaining models studied the effect of past negotiations on later negotiations and found indications that negotiators learn from bargaining in the past, thus referring to *backward looking* learning (Heckathorn, 1996). As proposed by Mauro (1982) and Gramm and colleagues (1987), negotiators use previous conflicts as a source of information and adapt their strategies to avoid costly strikes. In Lehr, Akkerman and Torenvlied (2013) we argue that what holds for backward looking learning, also holds for information spill-over across negotiations for different organizations, thus proposing *sideward looking* learning (Heckathorn, 1996).

Bargaining outcomes of, and conflict in other organizations, reveal information that serves to limit uncertainty (Kuhn & Gu, 1999), thus creating a conflict-decreasing effect of information spill-over across organizations. While these economic bargaining models assume pure rational behavior of negotiators—maximizing their utility and thus avoiding costly strikes when possible—more sociological approaches of bargaining point at social comparison as an alternative mechanism (Babcock, Wang, & Loewenstein, 1996; Babcock, Engberg, & Greenbaum, 2005; Fehr & Falk, 2002; McCarthy, O'Brien, & Dowd, 1975; also see De Dreu et al., this volume). Ideas of equity and fairness affect the point of reference negotiators (and employees) take in judging information as relevant. For instance, workers will use the wages in other organizations as a point of reference for "fair wage increase" in their own organization (cf. Akerloft & Yellen, 1990; Frank, 1984; Rees, 1993). Therefore, information about other negotiations, in other organizations, especially those that are settled favorably for the employees, would increase conflict across negotiations in other organizations (Babcock, Wang, & Loewenstein, 1996; Connel & Cohn, 1995).

The first empirical study we present on the question of whether conflict leads to less or to more conflict, is a survey among employer and union negotiators. This survey study shows that information about nearby conflict has a clear conflict-increasing effect. The second empirical study is an experiment with which we investigated the effect of social comparison versus learning on conflict more systematically.

Rational learning versus social comparison: a negotiators' survey[1]

During Fall 2011 and Winter 2012, survey data was collected about the kind of information negotiators use for collective bargaining among a total of 128 professional negotiators from both the employer and the union side, the response rate being 28 percent of the 451 negotiators we invited to fill in the questionnaire. Each respondent was invited to complete the questionnaire for a specific collective bargaining process, predetermined by the researcher. The semi-structured web-based survey gathered data on:

- *the occurrence of conflict* during the bargaining;
- the *information source* the respondent uses (being: prior bargaining with/for the same organization; bargaining events in other organizations in the same sector; and bargaining events in other sectors); and
- *the content of the information* used in preparation of or during the negotiation (being: the outcomes of the bargaining; employees readiness for action; and success of industrial action).

Forty-four respondents reported that no conflict happened during the specified negotiations, 72 respondents reported an impasse, while 12 reported industrial conflict (for instance, a strike or a work stoppage).

Information about prior bargaining in the same organizations and information about "nearby" bargaining, that is bargaining events in different organizations in the same sector, appears to be most influential. Information about bargaining in other sectors is not considered to be relevant for the negotiators' own bargaining event. This holds for all three information contents we distinguished.

In general, the negotiators reported that information about outcomes was more important to them than information about employees' readiness for industrial action and the success of industrial action. Indeed, information about the outcomes of prior bargaining and nearby bargaining events is not statistically related to the probability of conflict in their own bargaining. The statistical analysis, however, showed that information about conflict ("employees' readiness for action" and "the success of industrial action") *is* related to a higher probability of industrial conflict.

It is difficult to determine the causal direction of this relation. It could mean that negotiators who are exposed to information about prior and nearby conflict, are more likely to engage in conflict. Or, it could signify that negotiators in a situation of a looming conflict make more use of information about employees' readiness for action, and the success of industrial action in prior or nearby collective bargaining events.

Rational learning versus social comparison: experimental evidence[2]

The negotiator survey indicates that especially "nearby" negotiations, that is in the same sector, are used as sources of information by negotiators. Moreover, the more information spill-over from other bargaining events is used by negotiators, the more likely it is that they will experience conflict in their own collective bargaining. Whether this means that the exposure to nearby conflict increases the probability of conflict or whether a looming conflict in one's own bargaining makes negotiators more aware of, or urges them to actively scan the environment for information about conflict, is not clear yet. To investigate the use of information that spills over from other bargaining events more systematically, we studied the rational learning and social comparison explanations in an experimental study.

We designed an experimental study in which one firm and one union negotiator negotiate about the distribution of the firm's profit (for a discussion of such representative negotiations, also see De Dreu et al., this volume). In this experiment the union negotiator makes the first move ("a demand" or "opening proposal") after which the firm negotiator responds by either accepting this proposal or by making a counter offer, after which the union negotiator can make another counter offer etc. After 60 seconds the negotiation stops. When one of the bargaining parties accepts an offer of the other party within these 60 seconds, an agreement is reached. When neither of the parties accepts an offer of the other party within these 60 seconds no agreement is reached, and the final offer is automatically rejected, a situation which reflects a conflict.

The treatments in this game concern the information the negotiators were given about other negotiations. The first treatment consists of information about the bargaining outcome in another organization for which the profits equal those of the organization with whom the union negotiates (correlated information). The other treatment consisted of information about the bargaining outcome in another organization with an unknown profit (uncorrelated information). The subjects were presented two types of information: (1) whether the information given is correlated or uncorrelated; and (2) whether the outcome of the negotiation for this correlated or uncorrelated organization was high, low or a rejection, from the trade *union negotiator's perspective*. In the first treatment both mechanisms, rational learning as well as social comparison may operate, while in the uncorrelated information treatment, there is nothing to learn rationally. In this treatment any influence of spill-over must be attributed to social comparison.

The computerized experiments were held in October 2012, in the Nijmegen Decision Lab at the Radboud University of Nijmegen. In total 70 students participated in the experiments. They were randomly assigned to one of the two treatments and to the role of union or employer. The reward for participating in the experiments included a fixed show-up fee and a variable part depending on what they earned in the negotiations. In total, we obtained data from 490 valid negotiations.

The experiments allowed us to investigate the effect of information spill-overs on:

- the opening proposal of the union;
- the accepted proposal; and
- conflict (the rejection).

A first important finding is that information about conflict in other negotiations did *not* affect either of the three dependent variables. Information about the outcome of other negotiations did affect the opening proposals (the demands) of the union, both in the correlated and the uncorrelated treatment. As the effect in the correlated treatment was linear—meaning that lower outcomes elsewhere lead to lower opening proposals and higher outcomes to higher opening proposals—in the uncorrelated treatment another effect was found. In the uncorrelated treatments only the higher outcomes were used as a point of reference, while the lower outcomes were ignored. This shows that negotiators exhibit self-serving biases in choosing their reference point. Especially union negotiators, who are at an informational disadvantage, not only ignore unfavorable information but even counter it with escalating demands. At the same time both sides anchor on information that is favorable to them. This leads to divergence between the negotiators and increases conflict. The process of bargaining itself reduces this conflict greatly, a finding that serves as an important caveat to previous experimental findings based on one-shot games. Whether or not self-serving biases lead to conflict is dependent on context. If there is clear information and common knowledge that reference points actually reveal private information, the conflict-increasing effects of social comparisons are prevented.

Taken together, the results of the experiments offer support for the learning mechanism as well as for the social comparison mechanism, albeit only with regard to the demands and outcomes of negotiation and not with regard to the probability of conflict. This seems to contradict the results of our first survey study, and brings us back to the causality question we posed for the positive relation found in the survey study between negotiators' use of nearby conflict information and the probability of conflict in their own negotiations. Does exposure to conflict information ignite conflict or does looming conflict lead to seeking information about nearby conflict? The results of the experiments indicate that the first direction, information leads to conflict, is less plausible. Bearing in mind that the "conflict" in the experiment was in fact "only" reflecting an impasse and not a manifest conflict such as a strike, the second proposed causal direction (looming conflict leads to observe nearby conflicts), seems plausible: information about conflict elsewhere becomes important only in conflict situations.

Contagious conflict within organizations

The second main question of this chapter is how social relations on the shop floor are affected by strikes. We are particularly interested in the question why and when strikes cause segregation in working teams and when this affects production.

Theoretically we depart from the working hypothesis that fault-lines, which develop during a strike, can have long-lasting effects for work relations, and may play out even long after a strike has been settled. The deteriorated work relations affect long-run productivity through associated problems of cooperation, a lack of motivation combined with socially detrimental behavior—such as harassment and even bullying. There is evidence supporting this hypothesis from economic, psychological and sociological literature. A small branch of economic literature in the past already tried to analyze the economic consequences of strikes (Addison & Teixeira, 2009; Krueger & Mas, 2003; Mas, 2006; Gruber & Kleiner, 2010). All these case studies confirm that productivity is hampered not only during, but also for some time after, the strike.

Although these studies consider the possibility that obstruction and cooperation problems are causing sub-optimal production after strikes, economic research fails to specify the causal mechanisms that link strikes to economic performance. Psychological research reports prolonged effects of strikes on workers' psychological health and job satisfaction (Barling & Milligan, 1987; De Dreu & Weingart, 2003; Fowler, Gudmundsson, & Whicker, 2009; Kelloway, Barling, & Shah, 1993). Although these studies verify that strikes have strong effects on occupational health, they cannot explain why employees experience stress still long after the dispute—the stressor—was settled. Fowler and colleagues (2009) suggest that social factors are responsible for a continuation of stress. Indeed, sociological case studies indicate that social factors are responsible for a prolonged experience of stress and frustration. Case studies of severe strikes reveal strong and destructive cleavage groups within the organization (MacDowell, 1993). These studies show that overt hostilities persist after dispute settlement between the former strikers and strike-breakers and even report instances of physical and verbal harassment (Brunsden & Hill, 2009; Francis, 1985; Waddington, Dicks, & Critcher, 1994). Strike-breakers are often labeled "scabs" in union terminology and the cleavage between strikers and non-strikers effectively splits teams, organizations, and sometimes whole communities (Francis, 1985; Getman, 1999; Waddington et al., 1994). The "lack of solidarity," demonstrated by strike-breakers, induces sentiments of "betrayal" in those workers who strike—creating sharp fault-lines between employees.

Theoretically, we argue that the harsh relations between groups of employees after a strike can be explained by the existence of a *solidarity norm*. The solidarity norm explains strikers' contempt for strike-breakers and their strong out-group sentiments towards them. Case study research (Brunsden & Hill, 2009; Waddington et al., 1994) provides indications that strike-breakers indeed break a solidarity norm and, for this reason alone, pose an immediate threat to strikers. The threat is that the success of a strike depends on the degree to which the production process is disrupted, and hence on the number of employees on strike. In addition, because strikers bear considerable costs (e.g. a loss of income), and because they risk future repercussions by the employer, employees who continue to work are considered free-riders. Social disapproval and punishment of free-riders serve to reinforce solidarity norms (Casari & Luini, 2009; Gächter & Fehr, 1999). The punishment of free-riders increases with the extent to which the free-rider deviates from the average investment of the other members (Fehr & Gächter, 2002). In reaction, strike-breakers also may develop strong out-group sentiments towards strikers, fuelling the polarized conflict.

Empirically, we first studied when social relations between workers change due to punishment of non-cooperative behavior by way of a social network case study. This network study shows that the private interactions at work change differently than work-related interaction between colleagues: while one can easily break private ties with colleagues who behave differently, it is less easy (and formally difficult) to escape interaction with colleagues on work-related matters. Thus, breaking social ties to colleagues is not always an option to avoid punishment of deviant behavior. The second empirical study, we report on here, is an experiment and studies the effects of this punishment on the productivity of a team.

Punishment and social relations: a network study

Although previous case studies report the existence of strong cleavages among strikers and "strike-breakers" after a strike, actual changes in social relations before and after a strike have never been studied in-depth. In this section we report on the social network analysis we performed on work relations among employees of a Dutch cleaning firm which suffered a 105-day strike in 2012.[3]

In explaining how deviant behavior and punishment can result in cleavages between team members, we build on the findings of recent social network simulations. Kitts, Macy, and Flache (1999) and Takacs, Janky, and Flache (2008) argue that, in addition to complying to group norms or suffering punishment for deviant behavior, individuals have a third strategy: changing the composition of one's social network strategically in order to avoid punishment and get social approval from other groups—where similar behavior during strikes is the definition of a group. Strategic network adaption can explain why strikes sometimes cause cleavages between workers. However, in work relations, it is not always possible to change the interaction with colleagues at will. Although establishing new network relations with colleagues may not cause trouble, disengaging from interaction with colleagues is less easily done, at least not without potential reprimands from supervisors. Formal and organization restrictions may impede workers' possibilities to apply this particular strategy. Thus, the segregation effect of network adaption is not expected to be complete due to the necessity of work-related interaction, still leaving room for the punishment of deviant colleagues.

To test this explanation we reconstructed the work-related communication network among employees at the beginning of the strike and three months after the strike. We compared this with the changes in the private communication network of the employees after the strike. Both type of relations were reconstructed by way of structured questionnaires which were filled in during a personal interview with 59 of the 66 employees. Seven employees refused to cooperate in the study. Forty-five of the respondents did not participate in the strike, 13 participated throughout the whole duration of the strike, and one went back to work before the strike was settled. The questionnaire contained a list of all the employees' names and respondents were asked to indicate with whom they communicated with on: (a) work-related matters (reflecting a work communication relation); and (b) private-related matters (reflecting a private communication relation). The respondents indicated the intensity of communication on a scale from 0 (no communication) to 7 (daily communication). The respondents completed the questionnaires just after the strike started and again two months after the official settlement of the strike. In addition to the network questionnaires, qualitative questions were asked and field notes were taken.

The formal analysis of the changes in network relations reveals a deep structural cleavage between the former strikers and those who continued working. The behavior during the strike (joining the strike or not) significantly predicts the network ties established and intensified, controlling for other, more natural network changes (such as a tendency towards demographic homophily, transitivity and reciprocity). The deletion of network ties is explained significantly by the behavior during the strike in the private network, but not in the work-related communication network. This "all-or-nothing" strategy in the private network can less easily be adopted in the work-related communication network—largely because of the necessity of (at least minimal) cooperation among workers for their performance appraisal. Another noteworthy finding of this network study is that not only the strikers considered those who did not strike to be free-riders, who may be punished. Strikers themselves were also considered to be free-riders by the non-striking employees. Going on strike, and leaving the rest of the team of workers to perform the tasks necessary to perform well as a company was regarded as a behavior which violated yet another norm: the "team cooperation norm."

Punishment and productivity: an experimental study of reward systems[4]

The social network study showed why and which network relations change due to strike and that norm deviation (whether the norm be to contribute to the strike or to cooperate in the team work) leads to segregation of the employees in a group of strikers and non-strikers. We saw that the avoidance of punishment, and the seeking of approval, changes workers' networks significantly. We also found that the mechanism underlying this process—strategic network adoption—not necessarily leads to complete group segregation. Formal organizational restrictions probably impede the total avoidance of interaction with punishing colleagues. To further study the relation between punishment and productivity we applied a game theoretic experimental design to determine the effect of free-rider punishment—due to strikes—on group productivity.

In this experiment we examined the effect of free-rider punishment on group productivity. We designed an experiment representing two incentive structures: a "weak link game" and a "public good game." The weak link game is characterized by an incentive structure in which the individual reward of each group member is dependent on the effort of the "weakest link," that is: the team member who invests the least effort in the group task (Thommes, Vyrastekova, & Akkerman, 2013). The "public good game" is characterized by an incentive structure in which the individual reward of each group member is dependent on the total output of the group minus their own effort.

The experiments started with five consecutive rounds of cooperation in a team of three team members. In each of the five rounds, each team member chose a level of effort between one and seven. After two minutes, during which efforts could be changed, the efforts chosen were final. After every round all the team members' efforts were made known to the other team members. These rounds were followed by a strike, in which the subjects could decide to participate or not, followed by another five consecutive rounds of cooperation. Those who decided to participate in the strike paid three euro (the show-up fee for the experiments), while all participants would benefit an extra six euro when the strike was successful. The strike was successful when at least four employees participated in it. Before the second set of five rounds of cooperation began, team members were informed about the strike participation of their team members. The pre- and post-strike rounds of cooperation were performed in teams of three members, while the strike concerned all participants in the experiment (that is, the "whole organization"). The "whole organization" consisted of four teams, whose composition remained the same during the experiment. We expected that after the strike the productivity in groups consisting of strikers and non-strikers, would be affected by punishment within teams, while the homogenous teams would continue their level of production of the pre-strike rounds.

The computerized experiments were held in the Nijmegen Decision Lab in November and December 2011. The subjects (N=72), all students of the Radboud University, were randomly assigned to teams. Their payment after the experiments included a show-up fee and a variable part depending on the rewards earned in the games. Those who participated in the strike did not receive the show-up fee. Both the public good and the weak link game, each played with four teams at the time, were played three times, resulting in 12 team level observations for both games.

The experiments showed that during the first five rounds before the strike, team members establish higher level of productivity by each contributing more effort in each consecutive round. After the strike, for some groups their productivity decreased dramatically. Mixed teams—consisting of both strikers and free-riders—lowered their production after the strike, as expected. While productivity recovered somewhat after two or three rounds, total production in the second set of rounds never reached the level of the previous rounds. This negative effect of mixed team composition on productivity is stronger for teams in which strikers are in the majority, compared to teams in which only one member participated in the strike. Remarkably, homogeneous teams—either containing exclusively strikers or exclusively non-strikers—increased their productivity after the strike.

Both empirical studies show that strikes can have a serious negative effect on the social relations on the shop floor. Different choices regarding the participation in strikes may lead to segregation of groups of employees. Especially when strong social norms about participation in strikes are present, punishment of deviant behavior causes segregation between groups that bothers communication and collaboration. When formal and organizational restrictions impede employees to strategically adapt their social network at work, punishment of deviant behavior cannot always be avoided. As shown in the experimental study, punishment of team members can have severe consequences for team productivity. On the other hand, we also found that strikes can positively affect cooperation between team members. For homogenous teams, in which nobody deviates from the group norm—whatever that norm may be—we found that cooperation is higher after the strike.

Conclusion

In this chapter we challenged current explanations of industrial conflict, which consider strikes as being independent and isolated events: the bargaining between negotiation partners is not affected by conflict elsewhere, and the conflict has no influence on other bargaining events. By contrast, we argued that strikes are not isolated in space from other bargaining events, and are not isolated in time from their consequences for relations on the shop floor.

As for contagious conflict between organizations we found evidence that the *outcomes* of labor negotiations in nearby bargaining events do affect both the initial demands as well as the eventual outcomes of collective bargaining. Conflict in nearby bargaining does not affect the outcomes of bargaining. However, when negotiators reach an impasse, they do use information from nearby organizations. Information about employees' readiness for industrial action and the success of industrial conflict then becomes significant. The positive relation between the use of this information and conflict in the bargaining thus suggests that conflict becomes contagious in situations of latent conflict.

As for the contagious effect of strikes within organizations, we also conclude that conflict between management and the union can ignite conflict between other groups in the organization. We showed that strikes, being a collective good, are especially harmful for social relations between employees, when strong, but different, group norms exist about participation in strikes. The punishment of those colleagues who deviate from the dominant group norm sets in group segregation leading to strong social cleavages within organizations that seriously affects cooperation in teams.

Notes

1 This section is based on Lehr, Akkerman and Torenvlied (2012).
2 This section is based on Lehr, Vyrastekova, Akkerman and Torenvlied (2013).
3 This section is based on Thommes and Akkerman (2013).
4 This section is based on Thommes, Vyrastekova and Akkerman (2013).

References

Addison, J. T., & Teixeira, P. (2009). Are good industrial relations good for the economy? *German Economic Review, 10*, 253–269.

Akerlof, G. A., & Yellen, J. L. (1990). The fair wage-effort hypothesis and unemployment. *The Quarterly Journal of Economics, 105*(2), 255–283.

Andrews, K. T., & Biggs, M. (2006). The dynamics of protest diffusion: Movement organizations, social networks, and news media in the 1960 sit-ins. *American Sociological Review,* 71, 752–777.

Babcock, L., Engberg, J., & Greenbaum, R. (2005). Wage spillovers in public sector contract negotiations: The importance of social comparisons. *Regional Science and Urban Economics, 35*, 395–416.

Babcock, L., Wang, X., & Loewenstein, G. (1996). Choosing the wrong pond: Social comparisons that reflect a self-serving bias. *Quarterly Journal of Economics, 11*, 1–19.

Barling, J., & Milligan, J. (1987). Some psychological consequences of striking: A six month, longitudinal study. *Journal of Occupational Behaviour, 8*, 127–137.

Biggs, M. (2002). Strikes as sequences of Interaction: The American strike wave of 1886. *Social Science History, 26*, 297–300.

—— (2005). Strikes as forest fires: Chicago and Paris in the late Nineteenth Century. *American Journal of Sociology, 110*, 1684–1714.

Bohstedt, J., & Williams, D. E. (1988). The diffusion of riots: The patterns of 1766, 1795, and 1801 in Devonshire. *Journal of Interdisciplinary History, 19*, 1–24.

Brunsden, V., & Hill, R. (2009). Firefighters' experience of strike: An interpretative phenomenological analysis case study. *The Irish Journal of Psychology, 30*, 99–115.

Casari, M., & Luini, L. (2009). Cooperation under alternative punishment institutions: An experiment. *Journal of Economic Behavior & Organization, 71*(2), 273–282.

Connell, C., & Cohn, S. (1995). Learning from other people's actions: Environmental variation and diffusion in French coal mining strikes, 1890–1935. *American Journal of Sociology, 101*, 366–403.

De Dreu, C. K. W., & Weingart, L. R. (2003). Task versus relationship conflict, team perfomance and team member satisfaction: A meta-analysis. *Journal of Applied Psychology, 88*, 741–749.

Fehr, E., & Gächter, S. (2002). Altruistic punishment in humans. *Nature, 415*, 137–140.

Fowler, J. L., Gudmundsson, A. J., & Whicker, L. M. (2009). The psychological impact of industrial strikes: Does involvement in union activity during strikes make a difference? *Journal of Industrial Relations, 51*, 227–243.

Francis, H. (1985). The law, oral tradition and the mining community. *Journal of Law and Society, 12*, 267–271.

Frank, R. H. (1984). Interdependent preferences and the competitive wage structure. *The RAND Journal of Economics*, 510–520.

Franzosi, R. (1995). *The puzzle of strikes.* Cambridge, UK: Cambridge University Press.

Gächter, S., & Fehr, E. (1999). Collective action as a social exchange. *Journal of Economic Behavior and Organization, 39*, 341–369.

Getman, J. G. (1999). *The betrayal of local 14.* Ithaca, New York: Cornell University Press.

Gramm, C. L., Schnell, J. F., & Weatherly, E. W. (2006). Remedy-seeking responses to wrongful dismissal—comparing the similarity-attraction and similarity-betrayal paradigms. *International Journal of Conflict Management,* 17, 266–290.

Gruber, J., & Kleiner, S. S. (2010). Do strikes kill? Evidence from New York State. NBER Working Paper 15855.

Heckathorn, D. D. (1996). The dynamics and dilemmas of collective action. *American Sociological Review, 61*, 250–277.

Hicks, J. R. (1932). *The theory of wages.* New York, USA: Macmillan.

Kelloway, E. K., Barling, K., & Shah, A. (1993). Industrial relations stress and job satisfaction: Concurrent effects and mediation. *Journal of Organizational Behaviour, 14*, 447–457.

Kitts, J. A., Macy, M. W., & Flache, A. (1999). Structural learning: Attraction and conformity in task-oriented groups. *Computational & Mathematical Organization Theory,* 5(2), 129–145.

Krueger, A. B., & Mas, A. (2003). Strikes, scabs and tread separations: Labor strife and the production of defective Bridgestone/Firestone tires (No. w9524). National Bureau of Economic Research.

Krueger, R.A., & Mas, M. A. (2004). Strikes, scabs, and tread separations: Labor strife and the production of defective Bridgestone/Firestone tires. *Journal of Political Economy. 112*, 253–289.

Kuhn, P., & Gu, W. (1999). Learning in sequential wage negotiations: Theory and evidence. *Journal of Labor Economics,* 17(1), 109–140.

Lehr, A., Akkerman, A., & Torenvlied, R. (2013). Spillover and conflict in collective bargaining: survey evidence from The Netherlands. Paper presented at the Industrial Relations in Europe Conference, Bucharest, September 12.

Lehr, A., Vyrastekova, J., Akkerman, A., & Torenvlied, R. (2013). Spillover and conflict in wage bargaining: Experimental evidence. Paper presented at the European Sociological Association Conference, Torino, August 29.

MacDowell, L. S. (1993). After the strike. Labour relations in Oshawa, 1937–1939. *Industrial Relations, 48*, 691–711.

Mas, A. (2007). Labor unrest and the quality of production: Evidence from the construction equipment resale market. *NBER Working Paper Series,* no. 13138.

Mauro, M. J. (1982). Strikes as a result of imperfect information. *Industrial and Labor Relations Review, 35*, 522–538.

McCarthy, W., O'Brien, J., & Dowd, V. (1975). *Wage inflation and wage leadership: A study of the role of key wage bargains in the Irish system of collective bargaining.* Dublin: The Economic and Social Research Institute.

McConnell, S. (1989). Strikes, wages and private information. *The American Economic Review,* 79, 801–815.

Meyers, D. T. (2000). The diffusion of collective violence: Infectiousness, susceptibility, and mass media networks. *The American Journal of Sociology, 106*, 173–208.

Reder, M. W., & Neumann, G. R. (1980). Conflict and contract: The cases of strikes. *The Journal of Political Economy, 88*, 867–886.

Rees, A. (1993). The role of fairness in wage determination. *Journal of Labor Economics, 11*(1), 243.

Soule, S. A. (2004). Diffusion processes within and across movements. In D. A. Snow, S. A. Soule & H. Kriesi (Eds.), *The Blackwell Companion to Social Movements*. Oxford: Blackwell Publishing.

Takács, K., Janky, B., & Flache, A. (2008). Collective action and network change. *Social Networks, 30*(3), 177–189.

Thommes, K., & Akkerman, A. (2013). Clean up your network: How a strike changed the social networks of a working team. Sunbelt XXXIII International Network for Social Network Analysis Annual Conference, Universitat Hamburg, Hamburg, May 21–26.

Thommes, K., Vyrastekova, J., & Akkerman, A. (2013). The after effects of strikes on team collaboration – experimental evidence. Paper presented at the 73rd Meeting of the Academy of Management, Orlando, August 9–12.

Waddington, D., Dicks, B., & Critcher, C. (1994). Community responses to pit closure in the Post-Strike Era. *Community Development Journal, 29*, 141–150.

8 Human rights promotion, the media and peacemaking in Africa

Brian Burgoon, Andrea Ruggeri, and
Ram Manikkalingam

Introduction

In the corpus of civil wars, the armed conflict between combatants has frequently been accompanied by widespread violation of human rights that considerably exacerbates the human toll of war. With the rise of mass media, people are now better informed than ever about such violation as the stories and images of atrocities are made public, discussed and debated. This process has sometimes encouraged the international community (e.g. governments, international organizations) to intervene in domestic conflict, by pressuring the actors involved to improve human rights conditions (Lebovic & Voeten, 2006). In more extreme cases, foreign powers (either unilaterally or collectively) have become involved militarily in countries ravaged by civil war, citing the avoidance of further violence and bloodshed as important motivations to do so (e.g. Kaufman, 1996).

Despite the growing involvement of media and governments in protecting human rights in the context of violent conflicts, we know little about how media attention affects the conflicts themselves. Recent scholarship has analyzed the effects of foreign interventions on conflict duration and post-conflict stability, but little attention has been given to the effects of substantive human rights demands often underlying these interventions. And studies on the effects of human rights promotion by media and non-governmental organizations have focused on implications for actual violations of these rights (e.g. Hafner-Burton & Tsutsui, 2005; Franklin, 2008; Hafner-Burton, 2008; Conrad & Moore, 2010). But little theoretical or empirical connection has been established between these issues— attention to human rights violations on the one hand and duration or intensity of conflicts on the other. The few exceptions (Ruggeri & Burgoon, 2012; Schudel et al., 2012), furthermore, have focused on yearly measures of media attention to human rights violations that obscure the possibility and likelihood that any implications such attention might have for conflict is temporally more fine-grained—visible in developments occurring from one month or day to the next.

These shortcomings and silences are a problem, since media attention to human rights has potentially large, but also uncertain, implications for conflicts. Human rights promotion is seen by practitioners of conflict mediation as a way to support justice and to promote long-term peace, or at least to promote justice without worsening conflict. Intuition and anecdotes suggest that such promotion can indeed embolden belligerent parties to make changes in human rights conditions that can serve to improve political legitimacy and stabilize social opposition in ways that promote peaceful transition. But mediation experiences also suggest that promotion of human rights can complicate negotiations to end hostilities or can spark intransigence among leaders who worry about post-conflict revenge for previous human rights abuses. The problem is that we lack systematic investigation to adjudicate between these plausible and competing implications of human rights promotion.

This chapter attempts such adjudication by exploring whether media attention to human rights influences the intensity of civil conflicts. We start by articulating arguments on how human rights promotion by the international media has offsetting effects that in some ways can help resolve and in other ways exacerbate domestic conflict. We then test these competing views in an empirical analysis of newly gathered monthly data on media reporting and conflict in seven African countries between 1988 and 2010. These data focus on detailed coding of reporting of human rights abuses in the context of conflicts in these countries, and provide leverage to isolate the month-to-month effects of media reporting on conflict, net of *ex ante* human rights conditions. This analysis yields modest but important evidence that naming and shaming by the media has a pacifying effect where civil conflicts are ongoing. Such findings suggest that even "soft" interventions in the form of naming and shaming of human rights violations might well help build peace.

Human rights promotion and its implications for conflict

Amidst violent conflict and the many abuses of human rights that often accompany such conflict, many third-party actors frequently seek to improve human rights conditions to establish political stability and justice in such settings. This applies to third-party nation states; to regional international political institutions like the European Union or the United Nations; to economic institutions like the International Monetary Fund or the World Bank; and to a great many non-governmental actors, from mediation organizations to human rights NGOs, to dispersed media and journalists-commentators. The tools these actors use in their promotion of human rights are as diverse as their membership—including symbolic or official political resolutions; legal political and economic conditionality and sanctions; and formal legal proceedings to prosecute and punish human rights violators. But they also include a more diffuse, or "softer," tool of human rights promotion: informational reporting and monitoring that track, that is "name and shame," human rights abuses and abusers.

Such attention to human rights from the media has steadily increased over the past decades. Ramos et al.'s (2007) annual counting of articles in *Newsweek* and the *Economist* suggest a sea-change from less than ten articles annually around 1975 to a ten-fold increase by 2000, with the *Economist* even citing violations 142 times in the year 2000 (Schudel et al., 2012). The question for us, of course, is what if anything such attention yields in the conflict settings where human rights violations are being named and shamed.

The answer has to do, in the first instance, with the contributions that such media attention might make to the development and protection of various kinds of human rights, from individual, to political to social rights—rights that feed into broader notions of justice, as well as more downstream and real political stability and wellbeing. But such human rights promotion may also be relevant for its more indirect implications for conflict itself. Most intuitively, human rights promotion calls attention to justice, stability and wellbeing that may nudge conflicting parties in ways that help quell conflicts. On the other hand, anecdotes abound of instances where human rights promotion appears to complicate more than quell conflict— by taking bargaining chips off of negotiating tables, and by complicating already tense and dense political confrontations.

Unfortunately, more systematic scholarly literatures on human rights and on violent conflict are of little help in judging how human rights promotion affects conflict. They say plenty about related human rights development and about conflicts, but little about their interconnection. The literature focused on war termination says little about any aspects of human rights conditions affecting such termination (Goemans, 2000), but the extensive literature on causes of war says plenty about how broad political and human rights conditions affect incidence of conflict. For instance, the enormous literature on "the democratic peace" explicitly discusses aspects of individual and political rights associated with democratic liberalism tend to promote peace, at least once such liberalism becomes institutionalized (Oneal & Russett, 2002; Snyder & Mansfield, 2000). There is also some insight into how social as opposed to political rights can matter to conflict, where absence of social rights appears to spur violence (Wang et al., 1993). As for specifically individual or civil rights—such as free speech or protection from torture, rape, recruitment of child soldiers, etc.—the literature has focused mainly on how conflict affects such rights (Poe & Tate, 1994; Thoms & Ron, 2007). Missing from this litany of insight, in any event, are ideas about whether human rights *promotion* shapes the incidence, duration, or intensity of armed conflict.

The scholarship giving some attention to such promotion, meanwhile, provides only very limited information on how human rights promotion might influence conflict. The literature on humanitarian intervention by governments and/or the UN or other peacekeeping missions identifies lessons about the conditions under which such interventions meaningfully save lives and promote stability (Seybolt, 2009; Kuperman, 2001; Doyle & Sambanis, 2001; Regan, 2002; Fortna, 2004). But their focus is on military interventions and occupations—rather than explicitly human rights-focused media pressure—to help promote peace. The literature that *does* focus on the effects of diplomatic or economic pressure, meanwhile, has focused on effects for actual observance of human rights rather than conflict. For instance, we know plenty about the efficacy of UN and aid organizations for fighting corruption or violations of human rights (Hafner-Burton & Tsutsui, 2007; Lebovic & Voeten, 2006), or about the effects of naming and shaming in the media and by NGOs in diminishing human rights violations (Franklin, 2008;

Ramos et al., 2007). But none of this knowledge tells us what *human rights promotion* means for violent conflicts.

Even the partial exceptions say more about (particular aspects of) violence rather than the incidence or duration of actual war. A recent study by Murdie & Bhasin (2011), for instance, discusses and empirically establishes a positive relationship between human rights INGO activities and domestic protest. And Krain (2012) finds a negative correlation between naming and shaming and state-sponsored mass murders, though his analysis focuses on violence events (mass murders) and covers only 29 events in 25 different countries. Finally, Poe & Tate (1994) study links between conflict and human rights, but do so by addressing the reverse to our current interest, finding a positive effect of civil conflict on the abuse of causally downstream human rights.

We are left, hence, with intuition and anecdote to judge whether and under what conditions promoting human rights helps conflict resolution. For what they are worth, intuition and anecdote, including those based on our own mediation experience, suggest that promotion of human rights might hinder as well as help conflict resolution. We can briefly inventory these diverse insights to motivate two broad and competing views and accompanying hypotheses about how media attention to human rights violations affects conflict.[1]

The first, intuitive view is that human rights promotion in general, and media-based "naming and shaming" in particular, has a range of pacifying implications for conflict. First, calling attention to human rights conditions and violations in a conflict setting can help inspire conflicting parties privy to such promotion to make improvements in or feel deterred from worsening human rights conditions, changes that often constitute intrinsic lowering of violence but may also defuse and channel political discontents into peaceful interaction. Such changes can, in turn, identify and remedy important root causes of conflict and can help parties to a conflict, as well as mediating groups, to negotiate long-term political stability.

Second, promoting human rights can also contribute indirectly—short of actual improvements in human rights—to a process of interaction within conflict settings that builds peace. Human rights promotion can, namely, invoke legal and ethical standards and rules that are neutral in polarized political settings, and can protect those on both sides of a conflict within conflict zones who are more likely to use their voice to foster political solutions when human rights are being pushed. Such standards and rules could well facilitate the interaction of conflicting parties to move towards peace.

Third and finally, promoting human rights can help foster confidence in building more complicated peace settlements by encouraging other outside actors to commit economic, political and (neutral) military resources to build a peace process. Here the key agents connecting human rights promotion to peacemaking are not the conflicting parties themselves but those outside observers able to use a range of means to promote peace among such parties. And those outside actors might be themselves more inclined to intervene in light of the media attention to human rights surrounding conflicts. And this intervention, or perhaps the threat of intervention, can in turn encourage peaceful accommodation in conflict settings.

These various implications add up to beneficence with respect to peacemaking. This pacifying consequence can be expected whether the human rights promotion is undertaken by media organizations, NGOs, nation states or international organizations, whether such promotion involves simple monitoring or naming and shaming or actual sanctions or interventions. And although such pacifying effects might apply particularly where media attention to human rights violations is targeted at a particular kind of party to a conflict, or to a particular aspect of human rights, even more general, untargeted attention to any human rights problems can be expected to dampen fighting and encourage peace. Combined, hence, we have the basis for a first general hypothesis about the direct implications of media naming and shaming: *Human rights promotion by international media should help hasten an end to conflicts and dampen the intensity of conflict (henceforth H1).*

On the other hand, promoting human rights via naming and shaming or other means may well do more harm than good with respect to conflict. First, such promotion can bog down peace discussions where combatants are already asked to address many contentious issues underlying conflict—as it were raising the transaction costs of bargaining and negotiation towards the establishment or maintenance of peace. Second, human rights promotion by the media or other organizations can spark intransigence by one or another party, because one or both parties may: sense a loss of control over its future; may fear losing face or credibility in dealing with their own constituency or outside interlocutors; or may fear punishment that human rights improvements would entail (Mendeloff, 2004). Third, human rights promotion can delegitimize the process of peace-building and negotiations, particularly the peacemaking efforts of outside (Western) actors, because *ex ante* human rights violations tend to be very one sided, such that attention to such violations can quickly seem like biased intervention, and because the values and rule-of-law standards within which human rights get championed can seem like imposed Western constructions.

By such logic, the promotion of human rights might well backfire, even if the beneficent effects emerge in the context of the same conflict settings. It is possible, hence, that the net effect for peacemaking is negative, or perverse. Such a possibility motivates a second hypothesis that directly contrasts with the first: *Human rights promotion by international media should lengthen and intensify rather than shorten and dampen conflicts (henceforth H2).*

Of course, a number of other hypotheses about the direct effects of media naming and shaming could be articulated in light of the broad logics articulated above. The most obvious is that the offsetting implications of media attention can be expected to cancel one another out, such that such promotion has no significant net effects on war violence. Or, alternatively, human rights promotion could have just no effect on such violence. Such a possibility constitutes the null hypothesis of our study. Our state of knowledge is preliminary enough, and our theoretical priors open enough, that we consider such complexities as an inductive matter. Our analysis is most focused on adjudicating the basic opposition between the Pacifying and the Perversity Hypotheses (H1 and H2, respectively).

Estimating the effects of media attention to human rights on conflict intensity

There are many obstacles to a systematic study of human rights promotion and conflict. The first of these obstacles involves finding or developing valid and reliable measures of such promotion. With respect to media naming and shaming, for instance, it is difficult to know which media sources, which kinds of reporting on which kinds of activities by which perpetrators and victims are relevant to naming and shaming of human rights violations. Such measures, further, should capture detail in terms of time and space to allow judgment of their downstream implications for conflict. Existing data with these characteristics are lacking, with the best and most nuanced data focusing at most on country–year variation— smoothing over intra-year variation that in turn prevents exploration of downstream effects of media naming and shaming for conflict that can be expected to be more fine-grained in time than one year average to the next.

Even if such basic measurement issues are overcome, there are further obstacles to identifying the possible implications of any measure of human rights naming and shaming for conflict intensity. Key among these threats is potential endogeneity bias caused by omitted variables and by reversed causality. The former could well arise given the difficulty of isolating the conflict consequences of human rights promotion from actual human rights conditions or other sources of both media attention and conflict; the latter can emerge from the fact that the severity and duration of conflict not only reflects, but surely also affects, human rights promotion. Our empirical analysis, of course, must tackle these and other measurement and inferential challenges.

We try to overcome these challenges by analyzing the relationship between the intensity of wars and media attention to human rights violations in seven African countries during periods of post-Cold War civil war in those countries: Angola (post-1989 civil war involving government and UNITA), Burundi, Cote d'Ivoire, DRC, Liberia, Nigeria (post-2004 intrastate territorial disputes) and Sierra Leone.[2] We do so by focusing on how monthly naming and shaming as measured by newly-gathered data on *New York Times* reporting of human rights violations in these conflict settings influences the monthly intensity of violence as measured by battle-related deaths.

Independent variable: New York Times *mentions of human-rights violations*

The measure of media naming and shaming of human rights violations comes from a new dataset of our own design that codes extensive information on the reporting of human rights violations in the *New York Times* and in periodic United Nations mission reports. The former provides a useful basis for information on media naming and shaming because the *New York Times* is among the most widely respected and read news outlets in the world, including not only extensive world news reporting (by its own journalists and from AP, Reuters and other wire services) and high-profile Opinion-Editorial (Op Ed) pieces. Even if it is not the "paper of record" that it claims to be, the *New York Times* is an intrinsically influential (at least among international political and business audiences) source of news and opinion, and is a useful proxy for other kinds of media coverage—altogether providing information on both naming and shaming of human rights violations to the extent that such issues get explicit attention in its pages.

To code those pages by focusing on all news and opinion articles that mention any of the conflict countries that are our cases, the articles are identified using Lexis-Nexis news compiling and searches, but the coding of content with respect to possible mention and discussion of human rights violations is done by hand. Computer coding we have found to yield both under and over counting given the many word combinations relevant to human rights violations: a great many kinds of violent acts involving a wide range of perpetrators and victims, not easily reduced to word strings like "human rights" or "civilians." Our coding methodology includes documenting basic information about the reporting's date, placement and character (e.g. news versus Op Ed). And the core information involves coding details of any reporting on various categories of human rights violations, focusing on the UN list and definitions of unlawful, non-combatant killing, imprisonment, questioning, torture, rape, etc. Those details include not just whether such violations are mentioned, but which abuses, by which presumed or accused perpetrators, which victims, and which actions, if any, are recommended with respect to the abuses. After testing for and adjusting to establish inter-coder reliability, the resulting coding provides a basis for valid, reliable and temporally and cross-conflict comparable information on *NYT* naming and shaming to the conflict-day.

For the present analysis we focus on the number of mentions of human rights violations per country-month in our seven cases. We shall call this variable "HR mentions." These mentions apply to distinct human rights violations in a given article, such that some articles will name more than one violation—for instance torture and killing, yielding two mentions for a given article. Across the seven conflict countries, there can be many months where there are no articles appearing about a conflict in a country, and in those months when a conflict is reported there may well be no mention of human rights violations. Hence, in our sample of seven African conflicts the monthly mentions range from 0 to 22 monthly mentions of one or another human rights violations, averaging a modest and widely dispersed 1.203 mentions (s.d. 2.34) across the sample 867 country-conflict months.[3] Tables 8.1a and 8.1b provide summary statistics of this and other features used in the analysis. Table 8.1a provides an overview across our seven African conflict cases of such *New York Times* mentions as well as other features of the country, and Table 8.1b provides the full-sample summary statistics. As can be seen in column 1 of Table 8.1a, the Democratic Republic of the Congo (DRC) is the conflict country about which *New York Times* reporting includes the highest average mentions of human rights violations (two per month), with Cote d'Ivoire the conflict with the lowest such average (0.8 monthly mentions).

Table 8.1a National monthly means of *HR mentions, Battle deaths* and other covariates

	NYT mentions of human-rights violations per month	Battle-related deaths per month	Civilians killed per month	Reporting on conflict per month	Rain pattern per month	Food-price change per month
Angola (1988–2000)	0.8	210.6	8.1	5.5	82.6	0.175
Burundi (1994–2006)	0.9	53.5	46.7	3.6	103.9	0.011
Cote d'Ivoire (2002–2007)	0.5	14.0	9.8	4.5	112.1	0.002
DRC (1996–2010)	2.0	103.7	385.4	6.2	127.5	
Liberia (2005–2011)	0.7	17.7	99.8	4.9	201.7	
Nigeria (2005–2011)	1.8	6.1	2.7	4.6	98.4	0.009
Sierra Leone (1992–2003)	1.7	83.7	69.5	3.9	206.9	0.016

Table 8.1b Summary statistics

Variable	Obs	Mean	Std. Dev.	Min	Max
Battle-related deaths in civil war (monthly)	867	77.50	313.32	0	6964
Non-state plus battle deaths	867	92.64	325.45	0	6964
One-sided violence	867	112.56	681.91	0	14880
All war-related deaths	867	205.20	785.14	0	15203
Human-rights violation mentions	867	1.20	2.34	0	22
Conflict-related articles	867	4.84	8.29	0	89
Rainfall	867	138.78	112.53	0.32	519.26
Change in food prices	497	0.05	0.13	−1	0.9

Figure 8.1 provides a more detailed snapshot of the over-time variation for two of the cases, Angola and the DRC. Graphed are the monthly human rights mentions in the *New York Times* articles over the life of the conflict period, together with the monthly total number of articles addressing the conflict in the country. As can be seen, the monthly human rights mentions are almost always substantially lower than the total number of articles addressing the conflict; but in a few months we can see that the number of mentions is higher than the monthly number of articles—capturing some articles where more than one distinct human rights abuse gets news or Op Ed attention. Most importantly, however, is that we see here very substantial month-to-month variation in the media attention to the

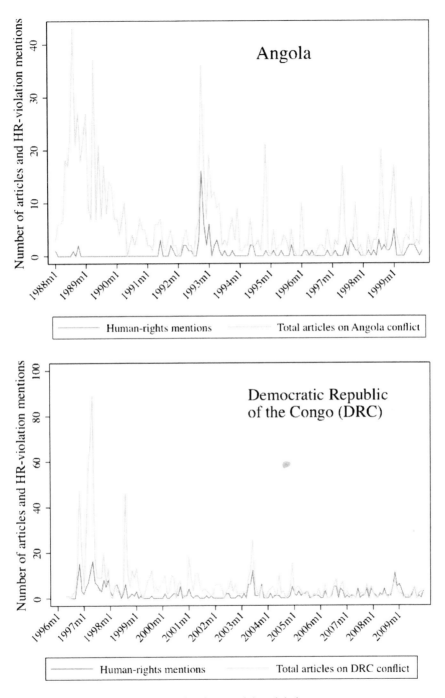

Figure 8.1 Reporting on conflict and on human-rights violations

conflict and to human rights violations. Even within a year the variation can be substantial, affirming an important motivation of this paper, that naming and shaming of human rights violations varies within a given conflict-year and might well have implications that vary likewise.

Dependent variable: battle-related deaths

To see those implications requires systematic information about the intensity of violence across our seven African conflicts and with a similar level of temporal detail—daily or monthly information on violence. We find such data in the Uppsula Conflict Data Program's data on daily battle-related deaths in civil wars involving armed government and rebel groups (UCDP, 2012). The information includes estimates of the intensity of violence on wars, allowing us to better judge whether and how such violence might be influenced by media attention to human rights violations. Alternative measures of the intensity of violence with monthly or daily detail include the ACLED battle deaths measure, but this alternative has narrower temporal and spatial coverage than the UCDP data, and is not qualitatively superior in any event. UCDP also measures related aspects of violence, including rebel-on-rebel violence ("non-state violence") and violence against civilians ("one-sided violence"). But neither of these is a substitute for what we most want to study—how human rights promotion plausibly influences organized violence during civil wars. We do consider in our robustness tests measures of violence that combine UCDP measures of battle deaths, rebel-on-rebel deaths, and one-sided violence deaths (more on this below). But our baseline and principal interest is in battle-related deaths.

Across both conflict countries and time, such battle deaths vary substantially. This is immediately apparent in column two of Table 8.1a, where we see the average monthly battle deaths for the lives of the seven conflicts studied here, ranging from 6.1 in the Nigerian conflict to 210.6 in the Angolan civil war. But these averages obscure the extensive over time variation in the sample, yielding more dispersed patterns for the full sample's 867 conflict-months: ranging from 0 to 6964 monthly deaths in the given country, with a mean of 77.5 and standard deviation of 313.32.

Figure 8.2 provides a more detailed snapshot of this over-time variation within one of the cases, the DRC, with the trends in the battle deaths overlaid upon the patterns of *New York Times* mentions of human rights violations between 1996 and 2009. What is clearest in the snapshot is the very substantial variation in violent intensity not only from year to year but also month to month. This is further a priori reason to consider the possibility that the within-year monthly variation in media attention might have within-year monthly implications for the intensity of conflicts. The arguments and hypotheses above suggest various possibilities with respect to the pattern of such "implications" that we expect to emerge in the data, including the snapshot in Figure 8.2. But to the naked eye there is not a clear pattern suggesting media attention to human rights violations leading or lagging, causing or reflecting, reducing or raising conflict intensity.

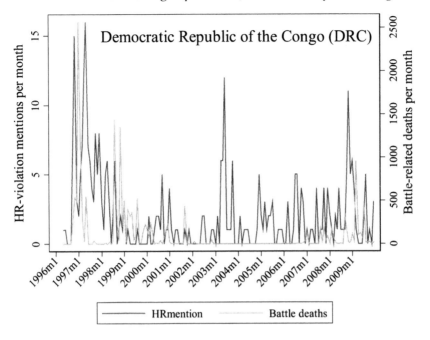

Figure 8.2 Reporting on human rights violations and battle deaths in the DRC

This is a graphic reminder of the complexity of the possible relationships under review, here, and the inferential threats to estimating how media attention to human rights violations might have implications for, rather than simply mirror, the intensity of conflicts. As we shall see below, the relationship here and in the full sample is one where temporally upstream values of conflict tend to positively correlate with downstream *New York Times* mentions of human rights violations, while the upstream values of *New York Times* mentions tend to negatively correlate with the downstream conflict measures.

Controls: general media reporting, one-sided violence, rain, and price shocks

Our more controlled estimation of the latter—of how *upstream New York Times* human rights mentions influence *downstream* conflict intensity—requires controlling for measurable factors plausibly affecting both conflict intensity and media naming and shaming. Finding reliable and valid measures with such features is difficult given the poor quality of data in our seven conflict cases and the fine-grained time dimension of our study. But we are able to directly control for a few important sources of omitted variable bias, and for the rest rely on monthly and country fixed effects. The most important control concerns *ex ante* violence against civilians, based on the UCDP measure of "one-sided violence," a variable we treat as a rough proxy for upstream actual human rights violations that certainly and plausibly affect media attention to such. Because one-sided violence against civilians is likely to disproportionately (more than other conflict measures) influence the violation of human rights of civilians, we see this as the best available substitute for (currently unavailable) reliable monthly data directly measuring human rights violations. As an empirical matter, a series of lags of one-sided violence strongly and positively influence the upstream *NYT* mentions of human rights violations.[4]

The other substantive controls include monthly *NYT* articles giving any attention to the country conflict cases (Ruggeri and Burgoon, 2013, based on Lexis-Nexis search already discussed briefly above). This is important to control away for the effects of general attention to conflicts as opposed to actual naming and shaming of human rights violations. We also control for monthly rain patterns (World Bank/CCKI, 2013), to control for the effects of seasonally varying conditions relevant to fighting intensity. The last of our substantive controls is a measure of month-on-month changes in food prices, standardized by country, to capture the influence of economic shocks on media attention and conflict (World Bank, 2012). As can be seen by the final column of Table 8.1a, this is only available for five of our seven conflict case-countries. Because these various substantive controls do not exhaust possible sources of omitted variable bias, we also consider in all our baseline models the influence of monthly and country dummies.

Estimation approach

Our baseline models are negative binomial regression models, because our dependent variable(s) is a highly dispersed count (visible in the summary statistics but also in the reported dispersion statistics below). In all reported specifications, we consider a lagged dependent variable to address the presence of autocorrelation, and also monthly and case-wise fixed effects to address remaining omitted variable bias (as discussed above) and the presence of heteroskedasticity. All baseline models calculate, further, robust standard errors clustered by country. The reported models consider various constellations of lags of *HR mentions* and various controls, to paint as clear a picture as possible of how *ex ante* media naming and shaming influence conflict intensity.

These models address a number of the most important threats to inferences underlying hypotheses one and two. But there are good reasons to believe that the models do not fully address possible endogeneity (due to measurement error and simultaneity or reverse causation) and in particular omitted variable bias. The direction of such bias is uncertain but likely to be in the direction of overstating any positive correlation (understating any negative correlation) between *HR mentions* and *Battle deaths*. First, upstream conflict intensity can be expected to drive, not just reflect, media attention. This is a pattern that emerges in our dataset, where models of *HR mentions* regressed on various constellations of lagged *Battle deaths* reveal the latter to be positively and highly significant predictors of *HR mentions*.[5] Our estimates of how lagged *HR mentions* influence *Battle deaths* can hence be expected to be endogenous in a positive direction (creating a bias in favor of the perversity hypothesis, H1). Second, although our models with measures of fixed effects and one-sided violence against civilians should partly address how *HR mentions* partly pick up the effects of *ex ante* human rights violations, remaining bias in this direction should also be in the positive direction (again biased against Hypothesis 1 and in favor of Hypothesis 2). With these issues in mind, we can consider the various estimations and robustness and sensitivity tests.

Findings

Table 8.2 summarizes the main results. The first two models estimate *Battle deaths* as a function of a number of monthly lagged measures of *HR mentions* in the same model (we consider various constellations, from one to 12-month lags, but we report the one-month through seven-month lags). Model 1 is a minimalist model of this form, including no substantive controls beyond the lagged dependent variable plus monthly and country dummies. Model 2 then introduces three substantive controls with full seven-conflict coverage. These models help identify the general pattern of how upstream *HR mentions* influence downstream *Battle deaths*.

The pattern to emerge from these first two models is one of modest negative relationships between *HR mentions* and *Battle deaths*. The minimal Model 1 yields significant results for *HR mentions* at five-month and six-month lags, and these results are negative. Controlling for monthly and country-specific fixed effects, we see a modest but broadly negative correlation suggesting a pacifying effect of media attention to human rights violations. Adding the substantive controls for *ex ante* and monthly violence against civilians, total articles devoted to the country-specific conflicts, and rainfall modestly strengthens the portrait— where also the one-month lag of *HR mentions* reaches standard levels of significance. In these models multi-collinearity is not a problem, but considering substantive controls to address possible omitted variable bias, particularly with respect to *ex ante* conflict and human rights violations, is something that needs to be specified to be upstream from the lags of *HR mentions*.

The remaining models, hence, consider individual lags, focusing by way of illustration on the results for the first, third, and sixth monthly lags of *HR mentions*, respectively. First (models 3–5) with most full-sample controls then (6–8) also controlling for food-price change. The results generally reinforce the portrait offered in the first couple of specifications, with only the third lag yielding no significant results. The one-month and, particularly, the six-month lags are significantly negative, suggesting that, net of substantive and the monthly and country controls, *HR mentions* may reduce the *Battle deaths* in the African conflicts. The other individually estimated lags of *HR mentions* corroborate this pattern (not shown). The last estimations add a final control for monthly *Food-price changes*, which drop the DRC and Liberian cases. Doing so reduces the significance of the one-month lag effect of *HR mentions* but *increases* the significance of the six-month lag. Altogether, then, we see some instability in the results with respect to statistical significance across the various specifications. But the pattern emerging is one of a more negative than positive or non-existence effect of *ex ante HR mentions* for conflict intensity.

Table 8.2 Conflict intensity and human rights naming and shaming in Africa

	(1)	(2)	(3)	(4)	(5)	(6)	(7)	(8)
Battle deaths $_{t-1}$	0.002***	0.002***	0.002***	0.001**	0.000*	0.001*	0.002**	0.000
	(0.000)	(0.000)	(0.001)	(0.001)	(0.000)	(0.001)	(0.001)	(0.000)
HR mentions $_{t-1}$	−0.016	−0.178***	−0.130**			−0.118		
	(0.059)	(0.046)	(0.057)			(0.074)		
HR mentions $_{t-2}$	0.040	0.008						
	(0.060)	(0.056)						
HR mentions $_{t-3}$	0.089	0.107*		0.006			−0.168	
	(0.064)	(0.064)		(0.066)			(0.119)	
HR mentions $_{t-4}$	0.030	0.054						
	(0.060)	(0.093)						
HR mentions $_{t-5}$	−0.101**	−0.092***						
	(0.049)	(0.033)						
HR mentions $_{t-6}$	−0.123**	−0.155***			−0.141***			−0.178**
	(0.052)	(0.054)			(0.029)			(0.081)
HR mentions $_{t-7}$	0.189	0.139						
	(0.158)	(0.169)						
Civilian deaths $_{t-1}$	0.0003	0.0003	0.0003	0.0002	0.0003**	−1.104***	0.001*	0.002**
	(0.000)	(0.000)	(0.000)	(0.000)	(0.000)	(0.336)	(0.001)	(0.001)
Total conflict news $_{t-1}$	0.062	0.062	0.073	0.028	0.000	0.033	0.102	0.056
	(0.042)	(0.042)	(0.063)	(0.038)	(0.037)	(0.048)	(0.093)	(0.062)
Rain-fall $_{t-1}$	−0.002	−0.002	−0.002	−0.002	−0.001	−0.000	−0.000	0.000
	(0.002)	(0.002)	(0.001)	(0.002)	(0.002)	(0.001)	(0.001)	(0.001)

	(1)	(2)	(3)	(4)	(5)	(6)	(7)	(8)
Food-price change $_{t-1}$						0.546	−1.158	−1.357
						(0.477)	(1.378)	(1.229)
Monthly dummies	Yes	Yes	Yes	Yes	Yes	Yes	Yes	Yes
Country dummies	Yes	Yes	Yes	Yes	Yes	Yes	Yes	Yes
Constant	4.832***	4.755***	5.355***	5.456***	6.122***	5.654***	4.816***	6.005***
	(0.252)	(0.274)	(0.386)	(0.365)	(0.270)	(0.558)	(0.682)	(0.374)
Log alpha	1.776***	1.751***	1.829***	1.837***	1.856***	1.489***	1.473***	1.469***
	(0.366)	(0.358)	(0.349)	(0.349)	(0.360)	(0.414)	(0.390)	(0.408)
Log pseudolikelihood	−3001	−2993	−3094	−3067	−3030	−1959	−1926	−1907
Observations	832	832	862	856	847	495	491	485

DV: *Battle deaths*: Total monthly battle-related deaths (UCDP, 2012)

Negative binomial regression coefficients with robust standard errors (in parentheses) clustered by country. Monthly and country dummies included but not shown.

*** p<0.01, ** p<0.05, * p<0.1

Gauging the substantive meaning of these effects is difficult from the raw coefficients and significance in Table 8.2. Figure 8.3 reports the results of counterfactual simulations based on the results from Models 3 and 5, respectively— the significant results from the estimations with the most and most targeted controls. They take the other parameters at their means while allowing *HR mentions* to vary the full range of the sample values (0 to 22 monthly mentions in a conflict). That full range of increase in monthly *NYT* mentions of human rights violations predicts, in both estimations, a drop of as many as 40 *Battle deaths*. This can be seen as a substantial increase in so far as such a drop would be close to tracing the drop from the sample's 75th percentile to its lowest percentile in *Battle deaths*. A more realistic monthly variation, however, is from 0 to 2 or 3 monthly articles mentioning human rights abuses. Such an increase predicts a much more modest drop in the intensity of the conflicts, on the order of 3–5 monthly battle deaths. Of course, such numbers are very theoretical judgments, in

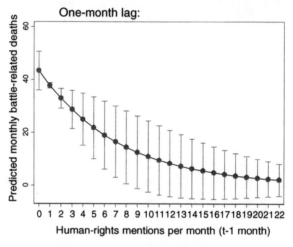

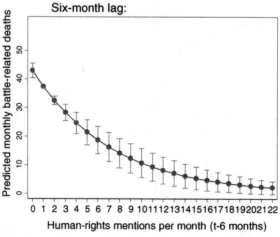

Figure 8.3 Predicted battle deaths as function of reporting on human rights violations

any event. But they give us a sense that the substantive results are modest, though still meaningful in the direction of lowering violence—modest support for the Pacification Hypothesis (H1) and against the Perversity (H2) or null hypotheses.

These results hold in the face of a range of sensitivity and robustness tests. The results are similar should one consider alternative specifications of violence intensity—for instance taking either a combination of battle-related and non-state violence (i.e. among non-state actors) or a combination of battle-related, non-state and one-sided violence (i.e. against civilians). They also are robust to other mixes and specifications of the controls, such as dropping any one of the controls or measuring absolute food prices, monthly temperature, counts for number of events wherein civilians were killed. More importantly, the results also hold up to jackknife analysis of step-wise dropping of conflict countries, periods of time, and censoring-out extreme values on *HR mentions* or *Battle deaths*. And alternative estimators yield similar results in a pacification direction, such as left-censored Tobit regression for the baseline dependent variable or Logit for dummies of substantial death counts, yield similar results where various lags of *HR mentions* correlate more negatively and in any event not positively with *Battle deaths* across lags.

Altogether, the descriptive and econometric results suggest modest support for the Pacification Hypothesis 1, where *NYT* naming and shaming of human rights violations appear to reduce rather than raise the intensity of conflict violence. We put somewhat more stock in such a conclusion given the direction of the results in light of the possible remaining endogeneity and omitted-variable bias. As discussed above, either source of bias that may well remain in the reported or other specifications we attempted can be expected to overstate any positive correlation between *HR mentions* and *Battle deaths* in the conflict cases. The tenor of the evidence pointing in the opposite direction can, in light of such a direction of bias, imply that our estimates understate the negative, pacification effects of media attention for violence.

Conclusion

These patterns shed substantial light on the question on which this study focuses: Does the promotion of human rights by international media dampen or intensify conflicts? As we have seen, attention to human rights violations in the context of civil contexts can have both pacifying and perverse effects on such conflicts. On the one hand, focusing on human rights may foster stability and cooperation by defusing political discontent and stimulating peaceful interaction. On the other hand, highlighting abuse and violation of rights in the media may deter combatants and/or governments from striking a peace deal in the prospect of future legal prosecution. So even though the protection of human rights is widely considered to be an essential aspect of a just world, it may stand in the way of creating a peaceful one. Our empirical analysis, however, shows modest support for the former of these views. In the net, "naming and shaming" by international media appears to modestly lower conflict intensity, measured as battle deaths. And these results may well be *underestimating* the pacifying effects of media-based naming and shaming.

Although such findings are theoretically and empirically important, further research is necessary to draw stronger and more nuanced inferences on the relationship between human rights promotion and conflict. A major limitation in our analysis is that data on media reports is limited in terms of depth and content. Future research on this topic could benefit from better information in order to capture variation in different regions, kinds of conflicts, time periods, different cases of human rights violations, and "targets" of naming and shaming. Such detail might reveal more about how human rights promotion can facilitate rather than undermine conflict resolution. In the meantime, our exploration of the best, new, temporally fine-grained data suggests a finding of clear interest to students and practitioners of conflict. With respect to recent civil conflicts and for at least one important kind of human rights promotion—the naming and shaming activity of media coverage of human rights abuses—outside human rights promotion appears to promote more than complicate peacemaking.

Notes

1   The following arguments about how human rights promotion can defuse or exacerbate conflict draw on Manikkalingam 2008, which provides fuller discussion of anecdotal evidence supporting those arguments.
2   The conflict periods vary across the cases: Angola (post-1989 civil war involving government and UNITA), Burundi (post-1993-election ethnic conflict), Cote d'Ivoire (post-2001 MPCI rebellion), DRC (post-1996 civil war), Liberia (post-1989 civil war), Nigeria (post-2004 intrastate territorial disputes) and Sierra Leone (post-1991 civil war).
3   See Table 8.1 for the summary statistics of this and all other variables used in the analysis.
4   In these models (not shown but available upon request) we regress *NYT HR mentions* on seven monthly lags of one-sided violence, plus monthly and country dummies. Six of the seven lags are positively signed, four significantly so. The one negative exception is no where near standard significance. And the joint-significance of the lags is extremely high (Chi-square of 5924.4).
5   In these extra models (not shown but available upon request) we regress *NYT HR* mentions on seven monthly lags of *Battle deaths*, plus monthly and country dummies. Four of the seven lags are positively signed, the first three highly significantly so. The negatively signed lags are no where near standard significance. And the joint-significance of the lags is high (Chi-square of 58.5).

References

Balch-Lindsay, D., & Enterline, A. J. (2000). Killing time: The world politics of civil war duration, 1820–1992. *International Studies Quarterly, 44*, 615–642.

Box-Steffensmeier, J. M., & Jones, B. S. (1997). Time is of the essence: Event history models in political science. *American Journal of Political Science, 41*, 1414–1461.

—— (2004). *Event history modeling.* New York: Cambridge University Press.

Burgoon, B., & Ruggeri, A. (2013) Human-rights promotion in African conflicts. Paper presented to the Encore (European Network for Conflict Research) Spring Workshop, Amsterdam (April 2013).

Cingranelli, D. L., & Richards, D. L. (2010). The Cingranelli-Richards (CIRI) Human Rights Dataset. Accessed April 1, 2011. http://ciri.binghamton.edu/.

Cleves, M. A., Gould, W., Gutierez, R. G. & Marchenko, Y. V. (2008). *An Introduction to survival analysis using stata* (College Station: Stata Press).

Collier, P., Hoeffler, A., & Soderbom, M. (2004). On the duration of civil wars. *Journal of Peace Research, 41* (3): 256–276.

Conrad, C. R., & Moore, W. H. (2010). What stops the torture? *American Journal of Political Science,* 54, 459–476.

Cox, D. R. (1972). Regression models and life-tables (with discussion). *Journal of the Royal Statistical Society,* Series B, 34, 187–220.

Cunningham, D. E., Gledtisch, K. S., & Salehyan, I. (2009). It takes two: A dyadic analysis of civil war duration and outcome. *Journal of Conflict Resolution, 53*(4): 570–597.

DeRouen, K. R., & Sobek, D. (2004). The dynamics of civil war duration and outcome. *Journal of Peace Research, 41,* 303–320.

Doyle, M., & Sambanis, N. (2000). International peacebuilding: A theoretical and quantitative analysis. *American Political Science Review,* 94, 779–801.

Elbadawi, I. (2000). External interventions and the duration of civil war. World Bank Policy Research Working Paper 2433.

Fearon, J. D. (2004). Why do some civil wars last so much longer than others? *Journal of Peace Research,* 41, 275–301.

Fearon, J. D., & Laitin, D. D. (2003). Ethnicity, insurgency, and civil war. *American Political Science Review,* 97, 75–90.

Fortna, V. P. (2004). Does peacekeeping keep peace? International intervention and the duration of peace after civil war. *International Studies Quarterly,* 48(2): 269–292.

—— (2005). Interstate peacekeeping: Causal mechanisms and empirical effects. *World Politics,* 56(4): 481–519.

Franklin, J. C. (2008). Shame on you: The impact of human rights criticism on political repression in Latin America. *International Studies Quarterly,* 52, 187–211.

Frieden, G., Lake, D. A. & Schultz, K. A. (2009). *World Politics: Interests, Interactions, Institutions.* New York: WW Norton.

Gleditsch, N. P., Wallensteen, P., Eriksson, M., Sollenberg, M. & Strand, H. (2002). Armed conflict 1946–2001: A new dataset. *Journal of Peace Research,* 39, 615–637.

Goemans, H. (2000). *War and Punishment: The Causes of War Termination and the First World War.* Princeton, N. J.: Princeton University Press.

Goertz, G., & Diehl, P. F. (1993). Enduring rivalries: Theoretical constructs and empirical patterns. *International Studies Quarterly,* 37, 147–171.

Hafner-Burton, E. M. (2008). Sticks and stones: Naming and shaming the human rights enforcement problem. *International Organization,* 62, 689–716.

Hafner-Burton, E. M, & Ron, J. (2009). Seeing double: Human rights impact through qualitative and quantitative eyes. *World Politics,* 61, 360–401.

Hafner-Burton, E. M., & Tsutsui, K. (2005). Human rights in a globalizing world: The paradox of empty promises. *American Journal of Sociology, 110,* 1373–1411.

—— (2007). Justice lost! The failure of international human rights law to matter where needed most. *Journal of Peace Research,* 44, 407–425.

Kaufman, C. (1996). Possible and impossible solutions to ethnic conflict. *International Security, 20,* 136–175.

Krain, M. (2012). J'Accuse! Does naming and shaming perpetrators reduce the severity of genocides or politicides? *International Studies Quarterly,* 56.

Kuperman, A. (2001). *The limits of humanitarian intervention: Genocide in Rwanda.* Washington: Brooking Institution.

Lebovic, J. H., & Voeten, E. (2006). The Politics of shame: The condemnation of country human rights practices in the UNCHR. *International Studies Quarterly,* 50, 861–888.

Long, S., & Xu, J. (2011). Predicted values with confidence intervals for regression models. www.indiana.edu/~jslsoc/spost.htm (Accessed February 1, 2011).

MacCulloch, R. (2004). The impact of income on the taste for revolt. *American Journal of Political Science, 48* (4): 830–848.

Manikkalingam, R. (2008). Promoting peace and protecting rights: How are human rights good and bad for resolving conflict? *Essex Human Rights Review, 5*(1): 1–12.

Mendeloff, D. (2004). Truth-Seeking, truth-telling, and postconflict peacebuilding: Curb the enthusiasm? *International Studies Review, 6*(3): 355–380.

Murdie, A., & Bhasin, T. (2011). Aiding and abetting: Human rights INGOs and domestic protest. *Journal of Conflict Resolution, 55*(2): 163–191.

Olson, M. (1993). Dictatorship, democracy, and development. *American Political Science Review, 87*(3): 567–576.

Oneal, J. R., & Russett, B. (2001). *Triangulating peace: Democracy, Interdependence and International Organization.* New York: Norton.

Poe, S. C., & Tate, C.N. (1994). Repression of human rights to personal integrity in the 1980s: A global analysis. *American Political Science Review, 88,* 853–872.

Ramos, H., Ron, J., & Thoms, O. (2007). Shaping the Northern media's human rights coverage, 1986–2000. Journal of Peace Research, 44(4): 385–406.

Regan, P. (2002). Intervention and durations of conflicts. *Journal of Conflict Resolution, 45.*

Roberts, A. (1993). Humanitarian war: Military intervention and human rights. *International Affairs, 69,* 429–449.

Ruggeri, A., & Burgoon, B. M. (2012). Human rights "naming & shaming" and civil war violence. *Peace Economics, Peace Science, and Public Policy, 18*(3): 1–12.

Schudel, W., Burgoon, B., Manikkalingam, R., & Schudel, W. (2012) From naming and shaming to negotiated peace: Civil war duration and media coverage of human rights violations. Paper prepared for the Annual Meeting of the International Studies Association, San Diego (CA).

Seybolt, T. (2009). Harmonizing humanitarian aid: Adaptive change in a complex system. *International Studies Quarterly, 53,* 1027–1050.

Snyder, J., & Mansfield, E. (2000). *From voting to violence: Democratization and nationalist conflict.* New York: Norton Books.

Sovey, A. J., & Green, D. P. (2011). Instrumental variables estimation in political science: A reader's guide. *American Journal of Political Science, 55*(1): 188–200.

Thoms, O. N. T., & Ron, J. (2007). Do human rights violations cause internal conflict? *Human Rights Quarterly, 29:* 674–705.

UCDP (2012). *UCDP Battle-Related Deaths Dataset v.5-2012.* Uppsala Conflict Data Program, www.ucdp.uu.se, Uppsala University, and, when applicable, the UCDP Battle-Related Deaths Dataset Codebook.

Voeten, E., & Merdzanovic, A. (2009). United Nations General Assembly voting data. http://hdl.handle.net/1902.1/12379 UNF:3:Hpf6qOkDdzzvXF9m66yLTg== V1

Walter, B. F. (2006). Building reputation: Why governments fight some separatists but not others. *American Journal of Political Science, 50*(2): 313–330.

Wang, T. Y., Dixon, W. J., Muller, E. N. &Seligson, M. A. (1993). Inequality and political violence revisited. *American Political Science Review, 87,* 977–994.

Wooldridge, J. M. (2002). *Econometric analysis of cross section and panel data.* Cambridge: MIT Press.

World Bank (2012). Data on monthly precipitation. Climate Change Knowledge Portal http://data.worldbank.org/developers/climate-data-api. Downloaded March 2013.

9 New lines of conflict

European integration and immigration

Wouter van der Brug, Daphne van der Pas, Marc van de Wardt, Marijn van Klingeren, Claes de Vreese, Sarah de Lange, Catherine de Vries, Hajo Boomgaarden, and Rens Vliegenthart[1]

Introduction

"At the root of all politics is the universal language of conflict" (Schattschneider, 1960, p. 2). Consequently, much research in political science focuses on conflicts. Different groups of citizens have different interests, values and ideologies and will therefore have different views on the most appropriate actions of governments, on policies that should be implemented and legislation that should be adopted. That political conflicts arise as a consequence of these differences in interests and worldviews is a logical and inevitable consequence of the freedom of speech and association. We therefore use the term "conflict" in this chapter descriptively, and we do *not* take any normative view, implying that conflict would be normatively bad and cooperation good.

If conflicts represent one side of the coin, cooperation reflects the other side. Conflicts divide those on different sides of a conflict line, but they stimulate cooperation between those who are on the same side (De Dreu, Aaldering, & Saygi, this volume). If this cooperation is satisfactory, the different partners will have an incentive to sustain the cooperation. This is one of the reasons why conflicts over new issues are often organized along the same lines as previous ones. A second reason is that positions on new issues are often taken on the basis of deeper-rooted ideological principles (Harinck & Ellemers, this volume). Positions on stem cell research, euthanasia and abortion tend to be related, because some people take restrictive positions on all of these issues on the basis of religious morality, while others take liberal positions because they value individual freedom. Political conflicts thus become structured along a limited number of dimensions, such as left vs. right in most European and Latin American countries and liberal vs. conservative in the United States.

The largest political changes occur when new issues are politicized which are not (strongly) correlated with existing conflict lines, because the politicization of these new issues might break up existing coalitions and stimulate cooperation between groups that were on the opposite sides of previously existing conflict lines. Political scientists speak of "realignment" when substantial changes occur in the way political conflicts are structured in a society. In this chapter we present a selective set of results from a large-scale cross-national comparative research project on the politicization of two "relatively new" issues, which have the potential of causing a realignment: the issue of European integration and the issue of migration and civic integration of immigrants.

In democratic politics, there are three aspects of conflicts over issues, and we will provide results on each of these in this chapter. The first aspect pertains to the *salience of the issue*, i.e., how prominent the issue appears on the agenda of parties, citizens or the media. Some actors may want to get an issue high on the political agenda, while others may try to keep the issue off the agenda altogether. Reasons why parties would not want an issue high on the agenda could be that their supporters are internally divided, that it would threaten coalitions they are part of, or that it would hurt them electorally. A second aspect of conflicts over (new) issues is positional. Conflicts could arise over the appropriate actions to take, so that political actors take different *positions on an issue*. A third aspect of conflict over an issue is in the way problems are being *framed*. Framing refers to the process by which a particular problem becomes defined (e.g., Entman, 1993; de Vreese, 2005). For example, one may define problems related to migration as being essentially socio-economic, whereas someone else may define it as a socio-cultural issue. This chapter provides examples of research on all three aspects of conflict.

A somewhat naive model of political conflict would expect all conflicts to arise directly from discontent among specific groups of citizens with certain developments. If social tensions arise from the fact that many low skilled migrants settle in a neighborhood, resulting in discontent among the native population, such discontent could trigger political actions of native citizens. However, very few political scientists or sociologists would assume that political actions are spontaneous reactions to discontent that require no political organization. Our research is part of a much broader tradition of research, which focuses instead on the strategic actions of collective actors in politicizing or depoliticizing issues. Ample research exists on the role of various types of (collective) actors in processes by which an issue politicizes. In our study we focus specifically on the role of the media, political parties and the public (see Figure 9.1). More specifically, while taking into consideration that each of these actors may be influenced by real world developments, we study the various ways in which the agendas of the media, parties and the public are interrelated. Does the salience of an issue on one of the agendas affect the salience on the other? How about positions on issues, or the way the issues are framed? Most importantly, can we detect circumstances in which these effects are more or less likely to occur? We will present results focusing on each of the three relationships presented in Figure 9.1, and we will introduce the relevant theoretical expectations, the data and results in each of the separate sections.

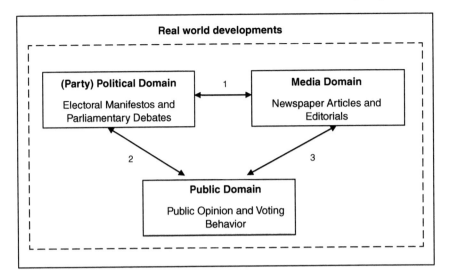

Figure 9.1 The triadic relationship between the political, media and public domain

Media responding to the party agenda

Anyone who reads the newspaper or watches the news on television will notice that the media often report on debates in Parliament and about discussions waged by politicians beyond the parliamentary arena. So, at face value, one would be inclined to conclude that the media agenda is largely determined by political parties. However, that conclusion would be oversimplified, because the media report only on a very limited part of the discussions in Parliament. Many of those discussions are highly technical and may not be seen as having "news value"—i.e. not regarded as being worth reporting upon. So, it is important to assess how the media select the items that are considered newsworthy. Only recently have political and communication scientists increased their efforts to study the complex relationships between the party and media agenda when it comes to the emergence of attention and conflict over policy issues (Walgrave and Van Aelst, 2006; Vliegenthart and Walgrave, 2011).

This section presents evidence from an article, which focuses on the extent to which the media tend to pay more attention to issues when there is more conflict over the issue (Van der Pas, De Vries and Vliegenthart, forthcoming). The study focuses on two types of conflict: positional and discursive. Discursive conflict among parties is conflict over the interpretation of an issue. This builds upon the thesis put forward by Chong and Druckman (2007, p. 100) that "virtually all public debates involve competition between contending parties to establish meaning and interpretation of issues." So, the hypothesis was that the media would pay more attention to an issue when there was more disagreement among parties about the interpretation of an issue. The other form of conflict considered was positional conflict based on varying policy stances of parties—the more those varied, the higher the level of positional conflict.

Data

Time series data were collected on 13 EU sub-issues from 1987 to 2006 in the UK, the Netherlands and Germany.[2] Party manifestos were employed as a source to measure the agenda of parties and national quality newspapers (*The Guardian, NRC-Handelsblad* and the *Süddeutsche Zeitung*) and were used as a basis for the media data. A content analysis of party manifestos was conducted by trained coders to arrive at measures for positional conflict, framing conflict, negativity and salience of each sub-issue. In each manifesto the coders isolated the statements that concern the EU, and coded which EU sub-issue the statement was related to. In addition, the coders indicated the position the statement expressed towards the European integration process, ranging from favorable (+1) to unfavorable (−1) with neutral in between (0), and which frame was used by the party. For each statement, the coders could choose five non-mutually-exclusive frames: the peace frame, the prosperity frame, the pride frame, the profit frame and the politics frame. Table 9.1 provides examples of how these frames were coded.

So, for each sub-issue distances were computed between two parties. If one party has mainly negative statements in its manifesto and the other mainly positive, the *positional distance* is large. The more they relied on different frames, the larger are their *discursive distances*. On the basis of all distances between the parties, the authors computed the average positional and discursive distances, weighted by party size. This was done for each combination of election year, sub-issue and country, thus providing them with a data set of 144 cases.

Based on the manual coding of the party manifestos as outlined above, we developed search strings for any of the 13 sub-issues. Using the search strings, the newspaper database was searched in order to determine the total number of articles mentioning each issue starting two months before an election (the moment most party manifestos were published) until two months before the next election

Table 9.1 Examples of statements on sub-issue "agriculture" with different frames

Party	Frame	Statement
Labour Party	profit	"Because of our success in achieving extensive reforms in the Common Agricultural Policy (CAP), 2005 will be the first year for decades when farmers will be free to produce for the market and not simply for subsidy."
Liberal Democrats	prosperity	"We will insist on the enforcement of maximum time limits and for transporting live animals in the EU, a stricter timetable for banning veal crates and improved rearing conditions for pigs and chickens across the EU."
Conservative Party	politics	"We will continue to play a leading part in European Community negotiations to reform the CAP."

(when new party manifestos were published). This way, the independent variables, taken from the election periods, always precede the dependent variable in time. The score that was used in the analysis is the *share* (i.e. percentage) of the attention for the EU as whole that is devoted to a certain EU sub-issue in a given period. These relative scores reflect the substantive interest at the sub-topic level.

Results

We computed various models that estimate the change in attention for any of the 13 sub-issues in the media. In addition to various control variables, these changes were predicted by:

1   a change in salience among parties;
2   a change in the average distances among parties; and
3   the interaction between the change in salience and the change in distance.

All effects were positive, but only the interaction turned out to be statistically significant. This was true for the effect of positional distances as well as for the effect of framing distances. When estimating the effects of both kinds of conflict simultaneously in one model, only the interaction between salience and discursive conflict turned out to be significant.

The results show that the media are indeed more likely to report on an issue when the issue has become more salient on the party agenda, but *only* when there is conflict among parties. This dovetails with findings by Schuck et al. (2011) showing how news about Europe is more visible in places where there is elite contestation on the issue. Apparently, political conflict increases the news value of an issue and is an important moderator of "agenda setting" effects. This is not just positional conflict, but discursive conflict appears equally important. Particularly, this latter finding has important consequences for how we conceptualize party competition and its effects on media reporting. The framing of policy issues is a central feature in communication science (see Entman, 1993), but is largely neglected within the literature on party competition (for an exception see Helbling et al., 2010). The widespread approach within agenda studies has been to focus on the transfer of salience from the party to the media agenda and vice versa. Our results suggest that emphasizing salience alone may lead to an incomplete understanding of how party and media agendas interact. Discursive conflict over the frames employed has important consequences for media reporting.

Parties responding to the media agenda

The causal arrow that runs the other way—from the agenda of the media to the agenda of parties—is equally important for the functioning of representative democracy. To which extent are the mass media able to dictate the political agenda? The scholarly work on *mediatization, mediamalaise,* and *media-logic* seems to suggest that media have a large and growing influence on the workings and the content of competition between parties (Altheide & Snow, 1979; Mazzoleni et al., 2003). Yet on the other hand, studies on the effect of the media agenda on political agendas have produced conflicting findings and scholars have now come to the conclusion that the magnitude of mass-media's agenda-setting power varies (Walgrave & Van Aelst, 2006). The differences in media influence on political agendas can partly be explained by the nature of the issues on the table (e.g., sensational or non-obtrusive), the type of media outlet (e.g., TV or newspaper, quality or tabloid), and the time (campaign or routine times), but also an important part of the explanation lies in the strategic behavior of political actors. The strategic interests of political parties form "a crucial gate-keeping mechanism in terms of mass media influence on macro-politics," as noted by Green-Pedersen and Stubager (2010, 664).

In this section, we discuss a study that examined whether parties selectively discuss issues when the media framing is to their advantage, and remain silent about the issues when it is not (Van der Pas, forthcoming). The theoretical argument is that parties are strategic actors and take advantage of the opportunities the media environment offers. Parties prefer issues to be framed in a particular way because a frame entails a problem definition and suggests appropriate solutions. As a consequence, parties themselves use the frame that most closely suits their policy program, but it is also rational for parties to talk about an issue when the framing in the media is how the party likes to frame the issue. In other words, the frame preferences of political parties should moderate the agenda-setting power of the media.

Data

The hypothesis was tested using the issues of European integration and immigration in newspapers and the parliaments of the Netherlands and Sweden in the period from 1995 to 2010. To gauge the framing of the issues among political parties and in the media, trained coders manually coded newspaper articles and parliamentary questions and speeches. For the newspapers, 9 (EU) or 12 (immigration) articles per quartile were randomly selected from all articles in the database containing at least one mention of EU or immigration related words in the header. Similarly, for political framing, four parliamentary questions were randomly sampled from the question hours in which the EU and immigration search strings yielded at least three hits, and off-topic questions were discarded manually. In addition, for the Dutch parliament in each year the two debates containing most EU or immigration related words were selected, and from these debates the first entry of each party was coded. This is the speech MPs prepare completely beforehand, so it reflects the carefully chosen framing of the party best. For each issue, the coders could choose six non-mutually-exclusive frames: the economic frame, the social frame, the cultural frame, the judicial/legal frame, the international security frame and the political frame.

A measure of discursive distances between parties and the media was computed for each three-month period. For each party the preference for a frame was assessed by calculating the fraction of questions and speeches in which the frame was used over all coded parliamentary questions and speeches. For every quarter of a year in the research period, the fraction a frame was used by the media was calculated from the coded newspaper articles. An overall framing proximity measure was computed for each issue and each quartile between each party and the media, via a Euclidean distance formula. When the framing used in the media is similar to that of the party, the distance is small, so the proximity is high. When the framing is different, the distance is larger, so the proximity is low. For each of the four issues of immigration and European integration and both countries (Sweden and the Netherlands) a separate model was built with the issue attention of parliamentary parties in the question hour as the dependent variable. This gives the data a time-series cross-sectional structure, with panels being parties which are followed over time, measured in quarters from 1995 till 2010. The number of cases ranges from 287 to 413.

Results

Theoretically, no effects were expected for the issue of immigration in Sweden and the issue of the EU in the Netherlands, because these issues were hardly politicized in this period in these countries. Effects of discursive proximity between the media and parties were expected in the Netherlands regarding the immigration issue and in Sweden regarding the EU issue, because there is quite substantial variation there in the attention to the issues. For the issue of the EU in Sweden a significant interaction between media salience and framing proximity was found, which means that parties react to the frames in the media more when the issue is more visible in the media. On the other hand, for immigration in the Netherlands only a main effect of framing proximity was found, so for this issue the amount of media attention was of no importance. It therefore appears that, at least in the period from 1995 till 2010, Dutch parties were *always* sensitive to the framing in the media, whereas for Swedish parties media framing only mattered if the visibility was high enough. A possible explanation for this difference is that the attention for immigration in Dutch newspapers was always high while it varied for the EU in Sweden, or alternatively, that the immigration issue was such a game changer for Dutch politics that parties were constantly watching the framing, even if it was not on the front pages. As mentioned though, this is a small difference in results, as for both cases a closer resemblance to the media framing led to a greater issue emphasis in Parliament.

The findings demonstrate that parties decide strategically when to respond to the media and when not to. These findings contribute to the recent set of studies that stress that the transfer of salience to politics is not automatic, but that parties strategically filter media attention according to their interests (Green-Pedersen & Stubager, 2010; Thesen, 2013). This way, the study also adds to our wider understanding of the conditionality of the media's political agenda-setting power (Walgrave & Van Aelst, 2006).

Parties (not) responding to public opinion

Mainstream parties have several reasons for not wanting to politicize new issues, such as immigration or European integration. Particularly, their potential supporters are often divided on these issues and their official positions on these issues are not always very popular (e.g., Van der Brug & Van Spanje, 2009; De Vreese, 2006). Furthermore, when these issues are politicized, it threatens existing coalitions (e.g., Green-Pedersen & Stubager, 2010). When these issues are not on the political agenda, new so-called "niche parties" may be formed, which try to mobilize support on these kinds of issues (e.g., Meguid, 2005; Adams et al., 2006). The most notable examples are green parties that have emphasized the issue of the environment and radical right parties that have emphasized immigration. Mainstream parties may respond in different ways when these new issues come up, especially when niche parties are successful in mobilizing support around these issues. They may ignore the issue, they may respond by taking opposing positions, or they may co-opt the position of the niche parties. In this section we present results from a study by Van de Wardt (forthcoming), in which he investigates the conditions under which some of the mainstream parties are prepared to take the risk of responding to niche parties by raising attention for these issues. This strategy involves a risk since mainstream parties have no prior knowledge of the electoral consequences. If the strategy fails, mainstream parties may lose electoral support to niche parties who put the issue originally on the agenda. Furthermore, he examines whether parties respond to rising concern among the public regarding these new issues. These questions are answered on the basis of the case of Denmark, with a focus on two issues: immigration and European integration. Note that this study focuses only on the attention parties give to an issue, not on changes in their positions.

In much of the existing literature (cf. Meguid, 2005; Adams et al., 2006), a distinction is made between niche parties (i.e., radical right, radical left and green parties) and mainstream parties (i.e., Social Democrats, Liberals, Conservatives, Christian Democrats). Van de Wardt proposes an analytical distinction between mainstream opposition parties (MOPs) and mainstream government parties (MGPs) (de Vries & Hobolt, 2012). The main goal of all mainstream parties is to be in office. Therefore, MOPs are dissatisfied with the current situation, while MGPs are happy with the status quo. Van de Wardt predicts that MOPs will be more inclined to accept the risks of responding to niche parties on new issues such as immigration or European integration. MGPs, on the other hand, wish to maintain the status quo and will therefore behave risk averse. These parties are therefore most reluctant to address these issues.

Data

The hypotheses are tested on the politicization of the immigration and EU issue in Denmark, using annual data between 1974 and 2003. The salience of immigration and European integration among MOPs and niche parties was determined by their yearly percentage of parliamentary questions. In turn, declaration of government speeches delivered at the opening of each parliamentary year were used to measure the issue attention of MGPs. For each year, the percentage of sentences devoted to the EU/immigration issue was calculated. The salience of immigration/EU on the public agenda was determined by the percentage of people mentioning the issue as important relative to the total number of issues mentioned by all respondents.[3] In addition, Van de Wardt controlled for the yearly number of newly arriving immigrants (measured in ten thousands),[4] and for the Danish net contribution to the EU (relative to the country's GDP).[5]

The extent to which different groups of parties react to each other and to public opinion was estimated by means of Vector Auto Regression (VAR) models. These models enable the researcher to simultaneously treat each of the time series as exogenous and as endogenous. So, it leaves open the possibility for causality to run both ways. Two models were specified: one examining agenda-setting on immigration and the other the same dynamics on the EU.

Results

A first important result is that shifts in public attention exert no significant influence on political attention. Moreover, trends in the numbers of migrants are not relevant for the attention to the issue of immigration, while there is also limited evidence that attention to the EU responds to shifts in Denmark's net contribution. Attention does, however, increase around some important events (such as 9/11 and referendums on the EU). So, the political parties seem quite unresponsive to the public when shaping the political agenda. By the same token, the public itself is irresponsive to saliency shifts among political actors. Parties are, however, responsive to each other. Specifically, Mainstream Opposition Parties (MOPs) increase their attention for both issues in response to greater emphasis by niche parties. Mainstream Government Parties (MGPs), on the other hand, do not respond to niche parties, while they do respond when the issues are brought forward by MOPs. This means that niche parties play an important role in getting these kinds of issues on the political agenda. So, indirectly, citizens can influence the political agenda through their vote.

The reciprocal relationship between the media and public opinion

The relationship between news media and public opinion has been the focus of many studies in political communication. Various studies show that the public responds to changes in news coverage (e.g., Balmas & Sheafer, 2010; Kim & McCombs, 2007), but also the role of the public in shaping the news has received some attention in the field (e.g., Behr & Iyengar, 1985; Zhou & Moy, 2007). The combination of the two, that is the *reciprocal* relationship between the media domain and public opinion, remains however relatively underexplored. In this section we present results from a study by Van Klingeren et al. (forthcoming), which focuses on this reciprocal relationship. Specifically, the paper asks whether a "spiral of negativism exists" in the mutual way in which the media and the public affect each other.

Extant literature has found that the media find negative news more attractive than positive news, so that they are inclined to select negative news (e.g., Soroka, 2006; Keplinger, & Weißbecker, 1991). In addition, negatively valenced messages are perceived by the public as more attractive, more important and more newsworthy than a positively valenced message, even when it displays the exact same information (i.e., the asymmetry bias, see Soroka, 2006). Hence, a negativity bias regarding EU news messages causes the audience to receive a relatively large share of negatively valenced information, which allegedly makes them more skeptical towards the EU and causes the negativity bias in the media to increase. In other words, a "negativity spiral" could arise that leads to a steady increase in Euroscepticism across time (see Slater, 2007).

Data

Data were collected in five political and media systems in four countries: the Netherlands, Denmark, Sweden and the two Belgian areas that both have their own systems, Flanders and Wallonia. These systems are in several ways very similar. Each are long-term EU members, all have multiparty systems, media systems consisting of a combination of public and private television broadcasters and newspapers that offer a mixture of quality and popular newspapers.

Data on the media and public opinion were collected and aggregated on the basis of six-month periods over 12 years (1997–2008). This means the data contain 120 observations (24 time periods × 5 regions). To measure Euroscepticism in the media, one tabloid and one quality newspaper were collected in each of the regions, when available. For each month and each region, a random selection was made of three articles on the European Union, with the aid of a search string. These articles were manually coded by native speakers. This resulted in a total of 3,075 coded articles, 1.02 percent of the total number of articles (302,008) about the European Union. These stem from the same dataset as the one used by Van der Pas et al. (forthcoming). The units of analysis were full newspaper articles. To measure Euroscepticism, coders were instructed to read the full article and then to answer the question: "From the perspective of a Europhile: How would you say the EU is discussed? In a negative way, a balanced way, a positive way, or a neutral way." The inter-coder reliability with regard to tone question was satisfactory (Krippendorf's-alpha: 0.61; pairwise percentage agreement of 67 percent).

To measure public opinion towards the EU, multiple rounds of the Eurobarometer were employed (Eurobarometers 47 through 70). The measure relies on one single indicator, which is interpreted to measure *general support for the European Union*: "Generally speaking, do you think that (YOUR COUNTRY'S) membership of the European Union is a good thing, bad thing, or neither good nor bad?"

Results

The study employs pooled time-series data, which enabled us to test whether, for example, the valence in newspaper articles in the first six months affects public opinion in the six subsequent months, and vice versa. The data were analyzed by fixed effects models, which means that the effects are estimated on the basis of the over-time variation within each region, but that the variation between regions is controlled for. So, effectively, we control for level differences in Euroscepticism, which are due to factors such as regional characteristics, but also characteristics of the newspapers.

The results show that negatively valenced news increases the relative presence of Euroscepticism among the public, while the effect of positive news is not significant. These results thus support the hypothesis of an asymmetry in the effect of news, where the negative effect of negative news is stronger than the positive effect of positive news. Negatively valenced news about the EU increases Euroscepticism. The effects of public opinion on the content of the media are in the opposite direction of what was expected. Increases in Euroscepticism among the public generates a decrease of negatively valenced news messages about the EU, while EU support reduces the relative presence of positive messages. Both effects are, however, insignificant. So there is no evidence that the media respond to public opinion.

In sum, we may conclude that there is no support for a spiral of negativism (see Slater, 2007). However, the study does support the supremacy of negativity thesis: negatively valenced media increased Euroscepticism, while positively valenced media produced no effect. This supports the work of social psychologists who have argued that people are generally more responsive to negative than to positive information (e.g., Helson, 1964; Ju, 2008; Lang, Bradley, & Cuthbert, 1997; Sherif & Sherif, 1967; Shoemaker, 1996). This does not create an ongoing spiral of negativism, but media do have the ability to make the public somewhat more skeptical about the European Union.

Conclusion and discussion

In the introduction to this chapter we explained that there are three different aspects of conflicts on issues:

1   the salience of issues;
2   the positions taken on issues; and
3   the ways in which issues are framed.

In our research project we addressed each of these three aspects of politicization and de-politicization of issues. In doing so, we focused in particular on different ways in which the agendas of the public, parties and media influence each other, and we presented results for the dynamic relationships between the agenda of the public, the media and political parties.

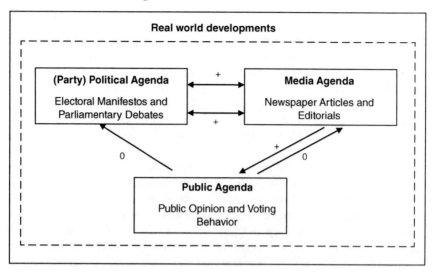

Figure 9.2 The triadic relationship between the political, media and public domain

Figure 9.2 shows five arrows, which denote a causal relationship between two agendas. The agendas of parties and the media were found to influence each other, yet not unconditionally. Parties are more likely to emphasize an issue when the media frame the issue in a way that is advantageous to them. The media are more likely to pay attention to an issue when there is conflict between parties on the issue. The media influence the public, but only a significant effect was found on negative news, which fuels Euroscepticism. No significant effect was found from positive news about the EU.

Our studies also produced two very important null-findings. We did not find any evidence that changes in attitudes had an effect on the tone of the news, nor that the salience of an issue among the public had any effect on the amount of attention parties pay to an issue. In our chapter, we did not pay attention to one theoretically interesting effect. Yet, it would be difficult to imagine a direct effect by parties which is not mediated through the media (although changes in the media landscape and the rise of social media make direct communication between political parties and candidates and their followers or potential electorate easier). In addition to these null-findings, we found very limited evidence of the party agenda responding to real world developments. There were some events that had an impact on the attention of parties for issues. For instance, 9/11 increased the attention for the issue of immigration and the referendum on the Maastricht Treaty increased attention to the EU issue. But the attention to the immigration issue is unrelated to the number of migrants.

So, if we sum up the evidence, we may conclude that the political and media agenda are largely shaped through the strategic interactions between political parties and journalists. Parties are unlikely to pick up concerns from citizens, whose only channel of influencing the agenda is through their vote. By voting for "new" parties that call attention to issues that were previously somewhat ignored, voters can make sure issue such as environmentalism (green parties) or immigration (anti-immigration parties) are addressed. The most likely route by which the issue gets a more prominent position on the agenda is the following. A niche party mobilizes electoral support around an issue. When it is successful, mainstream opposition parties will also start paying attention to it, after which it is also addressed by governing parties. Yet, even though some rather indirect ways exist in which the public can influence the political agenda, we should conclude that the process by which the agendas are formed, is highly top-down. These findings largely support earlier results that also pointed to the limited responsiveness of the political and media agenda to the priorities of citizens (e.g., Kleinneijenhuis and Rietberg, 1995; Green-Pedersen and Stubager, 2010).

Notes

1 The authors would like to acknowledge the financial support of the Netherlands Organization of Scientific Research, as part of its program "Conflict and Security" (NWO 432-08-130).
2 The 13 sub-issues are: 1) EU general issues, 2) accession of new member states, 3) economy, 4) foreign policy, 5) social policy, 6) crime, 7) the environment, 8) agriculture, 9) immigration, 10) democracy, 11) education, 12) culture, 13) moral issues.
3 The author expresses his gratitude to Christoffer Green-Pedersen for sharing this dataset and Jens Wagner from the Danish Data Archive (DDA) for providing the public opinion surveys.
4 Gathered from the website of the Danish National Bureau of Statistics.
5 Based on EU Budget Financial Report 2008, and GDP data from Eurostat website.

References

Adams, J., Clark, M., Ezrow, L., & Glasgow, G. (2006). Are niche parties fundamentally different from mainstream parties? The Causes and the electoral consequences of Western European parties' policy shifts, 1976–1998. *American Journal of Political Science, 50*(3), 513–529.

Altheide, D. L., & Snow, R. P. (1979). *Media logic.* Beverly Hills, CA: SAGE.

Balmas, M., & Sheafer, T. (2010). Candidate image in election campaigns: Attribute agenda setting, affective priming, and voting intentions. *International Journal of Public Opinion Research, 22,* 204–229.

Behr, R., & Iyengar, S. (1985). Television news, real-world cues, and changes in the public agenda. *Public Opinion Quarterly, 49,* 38–57.

Chong, D., & Druckman, J. N. (2007). A theory of framing and opinion formation in competitive elite environments. *Journal of Communication, 57*(1), 99–118.

De Vreese, C. H. (2005). Framing: Theory and typology. Document Design.

—— (2006). Political parties in dire straits? Consequences of national referendums for political parties. *Party Politics, 12*(5), 581–598.

De Vries, C. E., & Hobolt, S. B. (2012). When dimensions collide: The electoral success of issue entrepreneurs. *European Union Politics, 13*(2), 246–268.

Entman, R. M. (1993). Framing: toward clarification of a fractured paradigm. *Journal of Communication, 43*(4), 51–58.

Ezrow, L., De Vries, C. E., Steenbergen, M. R., & Edwards, E. E. (2010). 'Mean voter representation and partisan constituency representation: Do parties respond to the mean voter position or to their supporters?, *Party Politics, 17*(3), 275–301.

Green-Pedersen, C., & Stubager, R. (2010). The political conditionality of mass media influence: When do parties follow mass media attention? *British Journal of Political Science, 40*(3), 1–15.

Helbling, M., Hoeglinger, D., & Wüest, B. (2010). How political parties frame European integration. *European Journal of Political Research, 49*(4), 495–521.

Helson, H. (1964). *Adaption-level theory.* New York, NY: Harper.

Ju, Y. (2008). The Asymmetry in economic news coverage and its impact on public perception in South Korea. *International Journal of Public Opinion Research, 20,* 237–249.

Kepplinger, H. M. & Weißbecker, H. (1991). Negativität als Nachrichtenideologie, *Publizistik, 36,* 330–342.

Kim, K., & McCombs, M. (2007). News story descriptions and the public's opinions of political candidates. *Journalism & Mass Communication Quarterly, 84,* 299–314.

Kleinneijenhuis, J., & Rietberg, E. (1995). Parties, media, the public and the economy: Patterns of societal agenda-setting, *European Journal of Political Research, 28:* 95–118.

Lang, P. J., Bradley, M. M., & Cuthbert, B. N. (1997). Motivated attention: Affect, activation and action. In P. J. Lang, R. F. Simons, & M. Balaban (Eds.), *Attention and orienting: Sensory and motivational processes* (pp. 97–136). Hillsdale, NJ: Erlbaum Associates.

Mazzoleni, G., Stewart, J., & Horsfield, B. (2003). *The media and neo-populism: A contemporary comparative analysis.* Westport, CT: Praeger Publishers.

Meguid, B. M. (2005). Competition between unequals: The role of mainstream party strategy in niche party success. *The American Political Science Review, 99*(3), 347–359.

Schattschneider, E. E. (1960). *The semisovereign people: A realist's view of democracy in America.* Hinsdale: The Dryden Press.

Schuck, A. R. T., Xezonakis, G., Elenbaas, M., Banducci, S. A., & Vreese, C. H. de (2011). Party contestation and Europe on the news agenda: The 2009 European Parliamentary Elections, *Electoral Studies, 30*(1): 41–52.

Sherif, M., & Sherif, C. W. (1967). Attitudes as the individual's own categories: The social judgement approach to attitude change. In C. W. Sherif, & M. Sherif (Eds.). *New attitude, ego involvement, and change* (pp. 105–154). York: Wiley.

Shoemaker, P. J. (1996). Hardwired for news: Using biological and cultural evolution to explain the surveillance function. *Journal of Communication, 46*(3), 32–47.

Slater, M. D. (2007). Reinforcing spirals: The mutual influences of media selectivity and media effects and their impact on individual behavior and social identity. *Communication Theory, 17,* 281–303.

Soroka, S. N. (2006). Good news and bad news: Asymmetric responses to economic information. *The Journal of Politics, 68,* 372–385.

—— (2012). The gatekeeping function: Distributions of information in media and the real world. *Journal of Politics, 74,* 514–528.

Thesen, G. (2013). When good news is scarce and bad news is good: Government responsibilities and opposition possibilities in political agenda-setting. *European Journal of Political Research, 52*(3), 364–389.

Van de Wardt, M. (forthcoming). Desperate needs, desperate deeds. Why mainstream parties respond to the issues of niche competitors. Under review.

Van der Brug, W., & Van Spanje, J. (2009). Immigration, Europe, and the 'New' Cultural Dimension. *European Journal of Political Research, 48*(3), 309–334.

Van der Pas, D. (forthcoming). Making hay while the sun shines: Do parties only respond to media attention when the framing is right? Accepted by the *International Journal of Press/Politics*.

Van der Pas, D., De Vries, C., & Vliegenthart, R. (forthcoming). Do media respond to party conflict? Debates on European integration in British, Dutch & German election campaigns, 1987–2006. Under review.

Van Klingeren, M., Vliegenthart, R., Boomgaarden, H.B. & De Vreese, C.H. (2014). A spiral of negativity: The reciprocal influence between negative news media and Euroscepticsm. *Under review*.

Vliegenthart, R., & Walgrave, S. (2011). When the media matter for politics: Partisan moderators of the mass media's agenda-setting influence on parliament in Belgium. *Party Politics, 17*(3), 321–342.

Walgrave, S., & Van Aelst, P. (2006). The contingency of the mass media's political agenda setting power: Toward a preliminary theory. *Journal of Communication, 56*(1), 88–109.

Zhou, Y., & Moy, P. (2007). Parsing framing processes: The interplay between online public opinion and media coverage. *Journal of Communication, 57*, 79–98.

10 Bystander conflict

Training interventions for teams in high-stake professions

Evangelia Demerouti, Kim J. P. M. van Erp,
Josette M. P. Gevers, and Sonja Rispens

Introduction

Paramedics, policemen, nurses, the fire brigade; they all carry out their duties in stressful situations characterized by high urgency and uncertainty. Public and patient safety, security, and well-being play a pivotal role in their jobs in which they regularly encounter possibly traumatic events. The possibility of severe consequences for individuals (i.e., service recipients like patients, citizens) or society as a whole requires public service employees to perform at the highest level possible. Not surprisingly, such high-stakes occupations put high psychological and physical demands on public service employees.

In addition to the demands their jobs inherently entail, public service employees are frequently exposed to an additional demand, as recent research reveals, that public service employees are frequently exposed to conflict situations at work, ranging from disagreements to verbal and physical aggression (Abraham, Flight, & Roorda, 2011; Bakhuys Roozeboom, Koningsveld, & Van den Bossche, 2010). Customers, patients, or colleagues are not the only source of discord. Random bystanders that are not directly involved in the task at hand are a frequent source of feelings of conflict as well, for example when paramedics providing medical service to a patient, are being intimidated by a passer-by. We label the situation of an employee feeling frustrated in the achievements of his/her work goals by an external party *bystander conflict* (Van Erp, Gevers, Rispens, & Demerouti, 2013a).

Bystander conflicts may thus generate a demand overload that poses a threat to employees' overall well-being, to their ability to concentrate and, eventually, to their level of performance. In order to effectively cope with these high demands and to successfully carry out their jobs, public service employees need to possess sufficient resources. According to Hobfoll (2001) individuals strive to obtain or maintain things that they value ("resources"), which include objects (e.g., food, housing), conditions (e.g., safety, health), personal characteristics (e.g., self-esteem, personal skills), and energies (e.g., money). Because resources are means to the achievement or protection of other valued resources (Hobfoll, 2001), we suggest that resources can help public service employees to maintain their optimal functioning and well-being even when they are confronted with bystander conflict.

The question that still remains unanswered is which resources are relevant for these professionals to deal with bystander conflict and how these resources can be enhanced.

In this chapter we argue that a training intervention is a suitable instrument to equip public service employees with the relevant resources to deal with the additional stressor of bystander conflict. We outline the possibilities and advantages of training interventions to empower public service employees in bystander conflict. Starting with a short introduction on the issue of bystander conflict, we elaborate on its potentially harmful consequences, and the need to deal with this undesirable demand. Next, we give a review on the training intervention literature, thereby drawing from two largely independent movements that can be distinguished in this literature. First, we explore the development of the *individual interventions* that aimed to reduce the negative consequences of stressors, either by teaching individuals how to handle the stressor and the stress symptoms, or by enhancing individuals' strengths. Second, we review *team training interventions* aimed at developing teamwork knowledge, skills and attitudes required for effective team functioning, especially in high-stake, stressful situations. The chapter will continue with the presentation of a bystander conflict training that combines both research traditions and is tailored to the specific situation of dealing with bystander conflict. Finally, the chapter will conclude with research implications to further our insight into the phenomenon of bystander conflict.

Bystander conflict

Bystander conflict refers to the process that begins when an employee acting in the primary process perceives differences and opposition between him/herself and another individual who is not directly involved in the primary process about interests, resources, beliefs, values, or practices that matter to them (Van Erp et al., 2013a). Bystanders may wittingly or unwittingly cause perceptions of conflict in public service employees. For instance, firefighters on duty, trying to extinguish a fire, may be confronted with bystanders that swear at them and threaten them. Also, paramedics helping a patient may be confronted with an upset family member who is so distressed that he/she keeps demanding attention or refuses to let go of the patient in order to let the paramedics do their job. Whether caused on purpose or unknowingly, bystander conflicts are problematic because they likely have a huge negative impact on several facets of the public service being provided. A bystander conflict disconcerts employees and, demanding employees' attention, it places an extra burden on their cognitive capacities. Specifically, a bystander conflict requires energies and cognitive means of the public service employee, for example, to answer, reassure, or try to ignore the bystander (see Van Erp et al., 2013a). As a result, employees may experience difficulties concentrating on their (important and urgent) tasks. They may struggle to remember the correct procedures and they may lose sight of situational changes, as conflict induces rigidity of thinking (cf. Carnevale & Probst, 1998; Rafaeli, Erez, Ravid, Derfler-Rozin, Treister, &

Scheyer, 2012). In short, bystander conflict stands in the way of excellent performance, therewith interfering with patient or public safety.

Additionally, bystander conflict has a potentially devastating effect on work-related affective reactions. Conflict at work has been reported to contribute to reduced job performance, higher absenteeism rates, and increased staff turnover (Hoel, Einarsen, & Cooper, 2003). Similarly, repeated encounters with bystander conflict may stir negative affectivity, and increase feelings of depression and emotional exhaustion while at work. Employees may experience reduced psychological well-being, and job satisfaction may decline. Consequently, employees will be less motivated to aim for high levels of performance and may become less willing to remain with the company and more often absent (cf. Arnetz & Arnetz, 2001; Hogh, Sharipova, & Borg, 2008; Hershcovis & Barling, 2010; Van Erp, Rispens, Gevers, & Demerouti, 2013b).

Empowerment and training

To equip public service employees with resources to deal with the additional stressor of bystander conflict, a training intervention is a suitable instrument. Training programs are an important way for employees to learn skills and knowledge in order to perform tasks more effectively (Goldstein & Gilliam, 1990). They play a crucial role in improving individuals' adaptability and flexibility in challenging task situations. We do not argue that training employees will reduce the amount of bystander conflict experiences, but rather focus on the empowering effect training interventions have to increase the ability of employees to effectively deal with bystander conflict such that the harmful *consequences* of bystander conflict are minimized. We argue that training interventions should be aimed at enhancing employees' resources. Having sufficient resources at one's disposal is of great importance in order to cope with unexpected, adverse, and/or stressful events (Hobfoll, 1989). Resources become increasingly important the more demanding or stressful the circumstances are (see Bakker, Demerouti, & Euwema, 2005; Bakker, Hakanen, Demerouti, & Xanthopoulou, 2007).

Furthermore, because bystander conflict typically manifests itself in public areas (Abraham, Flight, & Roorda, 2011), outside the physical walls of the company, and therefore the possibilities for organizations to prevent bystander conflict—and eliminate the extra demands—are limited (cf. Barling, Rogers, & Kelloway, 2001). Reinforcing resources offers additional opportunities to maintain or restore the equilibrium between employees' demands and resources, and as such protect employees' well-being and performance (Bakker et al., 2005). We suggest that two kinds of resources are relevant to counteract the effects of bystander conflict among public sector professionals: personal resources and job resources.

Personal and team resources

For the specific situation of bystander conflict employees may benefit from two types of resources: first, they may benefit from personal resources involving confidence in dealing with and understanding of bystanders and bystander conflict situations. However, in addition to personal resources, team resources are of great importance for public service employees. A second type of resource that may be of crucial importance are therefore resources that protect the optimal execution of the primary task by the team despite whatever interruption.

Personal resources are lower-order, cognitive-affective aspects of personality; developable systems of positive beliefs about one's "self" (e.g., self-esteem, self-efficacy, mastery) and the world (e.g., optimism, faith) which motivate and facilitate goal-attainment, even in the face of adversity or challenge (Van den Heuvel, Demerouti, Bakker, & Schaufeli, 2010, p. 129). Increasing public service employees' personal resources may help them cope more easily with adverse situations like bystander conflict.

Furthermore, public service employees often carry out their jobs in teams. They may therefore benefit from interventions aimed at enhancing *team resources.* Team resources can be defined as the psychological, social, or organizational aspects of the team that are functional in achieving work-related goals, reducing job demands, and stimulating personal development (cf. Xanthopoulou, Bakker, Demerouti, & Schaufeli, 2007). Team resources are of particular importance to teams in the public service sector, given that team members strongly depend on each other for excellent performance, and given the high-stakes nature of their jobs.

Personal and team resources may counteract the negative consequences of bystander conflict. First, the extent to which bystander conflict leads to feelings of stress will be attenuated when employees have enough resources at their disposal. Second, personal and team resources may provide employees with the behavioral and cognitive abilities to deal with bystander conflict in a constructive and de-escalating way. Next we review in further detail previous research on the reinforcement of personal resources as well as the training interventions aimed at effective teamwork.

Personal interventions

In the past few decades several types of interventions have tried to improve the way employees cope with stressors and experiences of stress at work from an individual perspective. First, *stress management interventions* aimed at reducing the stress symptoms. Later on, *positive psychology interventions* turned away from this prevention focus, and instead aimed at increasing individuals' strengths. Over the years such intervention became increasingly directed to the specific context and the specific problem at hand, such as *conflict management interventions* in *healthcare settings.* We will now discuss the development of these personal interventions.

Stress management interventions

Since the 1970s, *stress management interventions*—aiming at the reduction of (the severity of) *stress symptoms* (Giga, Cooper, & Faragher, 2003)—have been increasingly applied in organizations in order to help employees cope with stressors at work. Stress management interventions have been primarily oriented at the individual level (Richardson & Rothstein, 2008), for instance by changing employees' appraisal of stressful situations, and alleviating their negative reactions to stressors (Richardson & Rothstein, 2008). Examples of such interventions are cognitive-behavioral skills training (e.g., Bond & Bunce, 2000) and relaxation techniques (Shapiro, Astin, Bishop, & Cordova, 2005).

In general, stress management interventions have been found to be effective in decreasing levels of stress and anxiety and increasing well-being and mental health. A recent meta-analysis including 50 individual-level stress management interventions revealed that in comparison to no-treatment control groups stress management interventions have a medium to large effect on symptoms of stress in terms of psychological and physiological outcomes (Cohen's d =0.526; Richardson & Rothstein, 2008). However, these results are not straightforward. First, the effectiveness of the interventions was mainly measured in very general terms of psychological outcomes (e.g., anxiety, mental health, job satisfaction) whereas only six studies measured more specific organizational outcomes (i.e., absenteeism and productivity). As such, these studies provide very little insight into the overall, organization-wide effectiveness of stress management interventions or to behavioral outcomes like individual performance.

Second, mixed results were found depending on the type of intervention, of which Richardson and Rothstein distinguished four. During relaxation intervention individuals receive breathing, relaxation and mediation techniques. Cognitive-behavioral interventions aim to alter individuals' appraisal of stressful situations by providing insight into the role of their thought and emotions in stressful situations. Multimodal interventions combine relaxation techniques with cognitive-behavioral techniques. Finally, a collective of intervention that could not be classified as relation or cognitive-behavioral, received the label "alternative." Examples are "journal writing about recent stress reactions," "active learning experience designed to increase participant's personal resources," "classroom management skills training" for teachers and "personal development skills." Much more effective than the multimodal and relaxation interventions, this collective of alternative interventions emerged as the second most effective intervention type, after the cognitive-behavioral interventions. Interestingly, the interventions in this category seem to be less general, and better geared towards the specific stressor under investigation. They aimed to enhance resources that were of particular interest to the target group.

In conclusion, on the one hand, stress management interventions are an effective means to reduce individuals' stress and anxiety and increase their well-being. On the other hand, stress management interventions seem to be a very general solution to a very general problem, making them less suitable for tackling more specific and complex dilemmas, like bystander conflict situations (cf. Briner & Reynolds, 1999). Furthermore, up till now no conclusive evidence exists regarding the effect of stress management interventions on organizational and work-related outcomes such as performance, motivation, and withdrawal tendencies.

Positive interventions

Whereas stress management interventions have been specifically aimed at preventing negative experiences and unconstructive qualities, positive interventions aim at building strengths and positive emotions. About a decade ago, several researchers proposed a more positive approach to organizational behavior (e.g. Fredrickson, 2001; Luthans, 2002; Seligman and Csikszentmihalyi, 2000). They emphasized that, rather than a focus on weaknesses and deficiencies, there is a need for building strengths in individuals for better well-being, higher levels of satisfaction, and eventually better performance. A focus on weaknesses and deficiencies "does not move psychology closer to the prevention of these serious problems. Indeed the major strides in prevention have come largely from a perspective focused on systematically building competency, not correcting weaknesses" (Seligman & Csikszentmihalyi, 2000, p. 7).

As a result, in the last decade many researchers have focused on the development and evaluations of Positive Psychology Interventions (PPIs). PPIs aim to cultivate positive feelings, behaviors or cognitions and focus on building individuals' strengths rather than remedying their weaknesses (Sin & Lyubomirsky, 2009). Consequently, PPIs could contribute to positive outcomes like employee health, well-being, and satisfaction by increasing the *personal resources* individuals have at their disposal. For example, Luthans and colleagues have focused on increasing individuals' positive psychological state of development, consisting of self-efficacy, hope, optimism and resilience, which they refer to as Psychological Capital. Additionally, studies have reported on interventions aiming, among other things, at enhancing positive emotions through goal setting and planning (Macleod, Coates, & Hetherton, 2008; Ouweneel, Le Blanc, & Schaufeli, 2013; see also Cohn & Fredrickson, 2010), assertiveness, self-efficacy and self-awareness (e.g., Demerouti, Van Eeuwijk, Snelder, & Wild, 2011; Macleod et al., 2008; Ouweneel, Le Blanc, & Schaufeli, 2013) and have outlined the strategies human resource departments should follow to develop resilience (Luthans, Vogelgesang, & Lester, 2006; see Cohn & Fredrickson, 2010). Overall, prior studies have convincingly shown the effectiveness of training in developing psychological capital and increasing personal effectiveness through changes in participants' cognitions, behavior, and emotions and tension control (e.g., Demerouti et al., 2011; Luthans, Avey, & Patera, 2008). Furthermore, not only do PPIs enhance resources, there is strong evidence that PPIs benefit individual and work-related outcomes as well. For instance, Psychological Capital has been found to positively influence specific work-related outcomes like performance, commitment, absenteeism and OCB (e.g. Luthans et al., 2008).

More evidence can be found in two recent meta-analytical studies demonstrating the effectiveness of PPIs on well-being and depression (Bolier et al. 2013; Sin & Lyubomirsky, 2009). Bolier et al. (2013) included 39 intervention studies and found that the interventions had small positive effects on well-being and decreased depression. Subjective well-being and psychological well-being had increased (Cohen's d, 0.34 and 0.20 respectively), whereas feelings of depression had slightly decreased (Cohen's d, 0.23) directly following the intervention. Three to six months after the intervention the effect of the intervention seemed to have faded somewhat, but still effect sizes were significant for subjective and psychological well-being.

Sin and Lyubomirsky (2009) reported stronger meta-analytical effect sizes, but they applied qualitatively less strict inclusion criteria. They explored the effectiveness of 51 intervention studies, and revealed that, compared to control groups, the PPIs were significantly more effective; PPIs increased well-being (r= .29) and reduced the levels of depressive symptoms (r =.31).

However, PPIs as well as stress management interventions have primarily focused on enhancing very general personal resources, in order to influence general constructs (e.g., increase well-being and decrease depression) and to "making people (lastingly) happier" (see Seligman, Steen, Park, & Peterson, 2005; see also the meta-analytical reviews mentioned earlier). From an organizational perspective, one would be additionally interested in the effect of (more specific) PPIs on more specific work-related outcomes. Recent research suggests that the effect of PPIs on performance are rather limited, compared to the established positive results for well-being (Meyers, Van Woerkom, & Bakker, in press). Furthermore, many PPIs aim at general personal resources (e.g., hope, optimism, gratitude; Meyers et al., in press). To counteract the main threats to performance in public service occupations such general resources may be helpful in some instances (e.g., in the case of resilience) but will not always suffice to tackle the problems (e.g., in the case of hope). That is, there is a need for interventions aimed at strengthening personal resources that are more specifically geared towards the (undesirable) situation (bystander conflict in this case), in order to eventually protect or even increase employees' performance.

Conflict interventions in healthcare

In the healthcare sector an increasing amount of interventions aim at reducing conflict escalating into violence and aggression, which is in line with findings that demonstrate that health professionals run an increased risk of facing violence and aggression (Abraham et al., 2011; Bakhuys Roozeboom et al., 2010).

Rather than following the general approach of stress management interventions, these healthcare interventions aim at a specific stressor. Therefore one would expect that their effectiveness should increase. However, studies investigating the effectiveness of so-called aggression management interventions report mixed results. In a study by Nau, Halfens, Needham and Dassen (2010) nursing students improved their de-escalating skills following an extensive aggression management training, but other studies have reported no effect on outcomes like nurses' attitudes towards patients' motives for and tolerance of aggression and violence (Needham, Abderhalden, Halfens, Dassen, Haug, & Fischer, 2005). A review of nine interventions, revealed that often research designs were weak and the results inconclusive (Runyan, Zakocs, & Zwerling, 2000)

The focus on aggression and violence which is prevalent in healthcare sector interventions can be seen as a drawback. Although many of these interventions aim at the de-escalating of the conflict situation, aggression and violence are already escalated forms of conflict. In that sense it comes as no surprise that attitudes towards aggressive patients do not change through interventions. In order for de-escalating techniques to be effective, they should be applied much earlier in the conflict process. Aggression and violence are often preceded by disagreements, incompatibilities and friction. Once a conflict escalates, hostility may increase, and conflict parties will be less inclined to use constructive solutions (Pruitt, 2008). Employees should possess resources that they can employ already in these early phases of conflict in order to prevent escalation, and maintain a positive, understanding attitude.

Recommendations for bystander conflict interventions

PPIs have up till now proved effective in increasing personal resources and consequently increasing positive outcomes like well-being and satisfaction and decreasing negative outcomes like stress and depressive symptoms. In the same vein, interventions aimed at reducing the negative consequences of bystander conflict for public service employees may benefit from a positive psychological perspective. However, to tackle the specific consequences of bystander conflict for safety issues, performance, motivation and withdrawal intentions, bystander-conflict intervention should be geared more specifically at those personal resources that are applicable to the specific situation. As already indicated, next to personal resources also team resources are relevant for bystander conflict. In the next section we will elaborate on the advancement of team training interventions that aim to enhance relevant team resources.

Team training interventions

About 30 years ago, team training interventions were initially developed in the aviation industry who at that time struggled to reduce fatal accidents due to human errors. When the aviation industry came to realize that the majority of air transportation accidents are caused by human failures, this was the first step towards the development of non-technical team training interventions (Helmreich, Merritt, & Wilhelm, 1999). In order to reduce the errors made in the cockpit *Cockpit Resource Management* aimed to improve interpersonal behaviors (e.g., open communications, assertiveness) and cognitions (e.g., situational awareness, decision making) between crew members. Soon the CRM acronym came to stand for *Crisis Resource Management* and the training interventions were introduced in other high-reliability organizations, including the healthcare sector (e.g., McCulloch, Rathbone, & Catchpole, 2011; see also O'Connor, Campbell, Newon, Melton, Salas, & Wilson, 2008). The intervention studies demonstrated that *teamwork* (i.e., the way in which teams interact to achieve team goals; Salas, Sims, & Burke, 2005) is an important, team-based resource for teams working in high-demand, urgent, and stressful situations to achieve excellent performance (and to prevent costly failures; see, for example, Gaba, Howard, Fish, Smith, &

Sowb, 2001 or Reznek, Smith Coggins, Howard, Kiran. Harter. Sowb et al.. 2002). Nowadays, team training is a widely applied strategy to enhance team effectiveness and performance through increasing effective teamwork (Salas. Burke, Bowers, & Wilson, 2001; Salas, DiazGranados, Weaver, & King, 2008; Weaver et al., 2010; O'Connor et al, 2008; Salas, Nichols, & Driskell, 2008). Salas and colleagues (2005) extracted the key team components of effective teamwork. Five key factors (shared leadership, mutual performance management. back-up behavior, team orientation, team adaptation) and three supporting coordination mechanisms (mutual trust, shared mental models, closed-loop communication) that are important for effective team functioning were distinguished (Salas, Rosen, Held, & Weissmuller, 2009; Salas et al., 2005).

Because the engagement in effective teamwork is cognitively demanding in itself (Driskell, Salas, & Johnston, 1999), it is of great importance that the abovementioned team resources are well established and thoroughly embedded in the team's functioning. Research has shown that in increasingly demanding situations, team members' attentional focus becomes more constrained (Driskell et al., 1999). Instead of an integrated team perspective, individuals tend to focus on their own, individual task. As a consequence, the individual team members lose sight of what happens within the team and the environment and team functioning may deteriorate. When, however, team resources are internalized, teams will be able to employ the team resources without much effort, even in the face of urgent. high-demand situations. In effect, more energy and cognitive resources will be available for dealing with other demands, such as attending to a patient or responding to a bystander. As such, effective teamwork allows the team to preserve valuable cognitive capacity, so that team members will have the energy and cognitive means available to cope with the extra demands of bystander conflict.

Effectiveness of teamwork interventions

The effectiveness of teamwork interventions has been validated in an extensive meta-analysis including 22 studies on teamwork interventions. The results showed that teamwork interventions have a positive effect on team performance ($\rho = .38$). Furthermore, cognitive outcomes (e.g., declarative knowledge gains). affective outcomes (e.g., trust, confidence, positive attitudes), and behavioral outcomes (e.g., decision making, coordination, situation assessment) were enhanced following a teamwork training ($\rho = .52$, $\rho = .41$, $\rho = .44$, respectively; Salas, DiazGranados, Klein, Burke, Stagl, Goodwin, & Halpin, 2008).

Additionally, Salas and colleagues compared the effectiveness of teamwork training with the effectiveness of taskwork training. Whereas teamwork training focuses on team-resource enhancement, taskwork training aims to develop the technical skills of team members (e.g., cross-training; Salas et al., 2008; Cannon-Bowers, Tannenbaum, Salas, & Volpe, 1995). Teamwork and taskwork training have been found to positively affect performance to the same extent. However. cognitive and affective outcomes benefitted most from teamwork training. Behavioral outcomes improved least following taskwork training and most following a training targeting both taskwork and teamwork. These results emphasize the importance of good teamwork for team effectiveness. Indeed, Salas, Nichols, and Driskell (2008) found that the implementation of a teamwork component into team training strongly strengthens its effectiveness. From their meta-analytic results they conclude that "the most potent contribution to effective team training appears to include a focus on coordination and adaptation" (Salas, Nichols et al., 2008, p. 471).

How teamwork interventions empower public service employees in bystander conflict

As mentioned before, public service employees usually work under circumstances of high demand, that are urgent, and where the consequences of errors may be severe. For instance, paramedics need to attend to a patient as soon as possible, in order to save his/her life, and the fire brigade has to know exactly what type of extinguishing agent to use, in order to prevent an industrial fire from becoming a (national) disaster. Bystander conflict entails an additional demand, or even a threat, to the team's effectiveness, as it increases the chances of failure. We therefore argue that, in order to empower public service teams, teamwork will offer an important team resource. Teamwork training may help public service employees facing bystander conflict to maintain the highest possible levels of performance and strong levels of affective, cognitive, and behavioral outcomes (cf. Salas, Nichols et al., 2008).

Dual-focus: personal resources and team training intervention

Judging from these reviews on interventions, there seems strong empirical support for the usefulness of training intervention in reinforcing both positive personal resources and team resources. Surprisingly, however, the deployment and evaluation of such resource-enhancing interventions in conflict settings is limited, especially when it comes to high-stakes conflict situations.

Bystander conflicts are considered high-stake conflicts in that:

1 they put at stake something highly valued by not only the parties involved but also more generally by the society (e.g., patient and public safety);
2 the occurrence and development of bystander conflict is accompanied with great uncertainty and unpredictability; and
3 bystander conflicts are experienced as intense and urgent by employees (see e.g., Abraham et al., 2011, Giebels et al., forthcoming).

The execution of employees' primary task often does not allow for any delay or interruption and given this high-stake nature of bystander conflict, negotiation techniques that may work in less urgent situations, that will carry less severe consequences, (e.g., at "the office") are unlikely to be applicable to the high-stakes conflict situation in the public arena.

Interventions aimed at resource enhancement, on the other hand, may be of particular value to high-stake conflict situations such as bystander conflict. First, when resources become internalized they will require less time, energy and cognitive resources. This way, the primary task of the public service employee (extinguish the fire, bringing patient in safety) is less severely interrupted or delayed by the conflict handling or negotiation episodes. Second, bystander conflict often lacks the presence of a joint goal shared by both conflict parties. Whereas a joint mission encourages conflict parties to resolve the conflict or at least find a workable, de-escalated state (e.g., when the individual team members share the mission to meet the project deadline) the absence of a joint mission may increase the probability that the conflict will continue and even escalate (see, for example, De Dreu, Kluwer, & Nauta, 2008; Ufkes, Giebels, Otten, & Van der Zee, 2012). Without the bystander's support for one's goals (e.g., patient safety) it will be increasingly difficult to reach a cooperative situation, and conflict management strategies like problem solving and negotiation techniques may not always suffice. Third and relatedly, in contrast to, for instance, negotiation strategies, employees can use their resources independently of the conflict party, the bystander. In order to start a negotiation, the other party should at least to some extent acknowledge the conflict (otherwise, why negotiate?) and be willing to find a solution. In the bystander conflict situation, the bystander may not acknowledge the need to reach a workable situation, and may even be focused on intentionally disturbing the situation.

Another recommendation that follows from the reviews on personal and team interventions concerns interventions' specificity: aiming at the specific resources that may be of particular value in the face of the problem concerned (in our research bystander conflict situations) seems to be important. Past research has shown that general interventions lead to general and often mixed results (e.g., stress management), and often do not lead to actual improvement of organizational outcomes (e.g., job performance). This is important because implementation of interventions is a very costly matter. In order to be cost-effective, interventions that benefit employees' performance and motivational attitudes, and diminish withdrawal intentions such as absenteeism and turnover are more appropriate.

A resource enhancement intervention for paramedics facing bystander conflict

The potential benefits of resource-enhancing training intervention for public service employees facing bystander conflict can be demonstrated with a recent research project among paramedics. The project involved a randomized simulation-based pre-test/post-test control group design and was conducted among ambulance drivers and ambulance nurses of a Dutch ambulance care organization. We developed and evaluated a training intervention that combined the reinforcement of both personal and team resources of the employees. Employees all participated in two role play practice sessions, where their medical service to a patient was being hindered by a bystander (played by an actor). Unlike the control group, the intervention group received an educational session about the value of employing personal and team resources in bystander conflict situations. Employees were randomly appointed to either the intervention or the control condition.

With regard to personal resources, and in line with the definition of a personal resource, the training aimed to enhance specific systems of positive belief about oneself and about the world. Specifically, the training aimed at building participants' belief that they are able to handle conflict situations effectively and to resolve conflicts easily, that is, conflict management efficacy (cf. Bandura, 1994, 1989). Additionally, the training focused on participants' perspective-taking, their ability to adopt the psychological perspective of the other party. This resource may help them to arrive at a more accurate evaluation of the bystander conflict situation, which in turn may help them cope with the situation more constructively. To this end, the training provided insight in and information on bystander-conflict situations, how they could be handled constructively, and how escalation of the conflict could be prevented. Furthermore, employees were acquainted with the possible motives for bystanders' behavior, and the strategies that could prevent and/or evoke certain reactions. Second, regarding team resources, the training aimed at strengthening teamwork as well as mutual emotional support among team members. Emotional support refers to sharing feelings with, encouraging of and showing respect to other team members and is of great importance to alleviate the negative effects of stressful situations. Furthermore, primarily based on the aforementioned work of Salas and colleagues, the educational session introduced employees to several important components of teamwork. The intervention specifically aimed at those components that could be easily understood, mastered and put into practice: closed-loop communication, performance monitoring, back-up behavior and team adaptability.

Results of the bystander conflict intervention

The results of this study suggest that, two months after the intervention, employees reap the fruits of the intervention, in that overall, improvement in the availability of resources was confirmed. Specifically, employees that had received the training intervention were engaged more in taking the psychological perspective of the bystander and they perceived themselves better able to deal with conflict situations at work. This increase in conflict management efficacy was also visible in the control condition, suggesting that the mere practice of a bystander conflict situation actually helps employees' conflict management efficacy. With regard to team resources, teamwork increased following the training intervention but not in the control condition. Emotional support within the team was maintained at stable levels in the intervention group, but decreased in the control condition. The research project furthermore showed that these personal and team resources were strongly associated with performance and work-related affective outcomes. Therewith, this research project has been one of the first to establish the importance of personal and team resources in (bystander) conflict situations, suggesting that the deployment of resources can counterbalance the negative effect of bystander conflict (Van Erp, Rispens, Gevers, & Demerouti, 2013b).

Conclusion and future research

In this chapter we reviewed the existing literature on stress management, positive psychology, aggression management and team training interventions, and illustrated the particular usefulness of (a combination) of these types of training for empowering public service employees facing bystander conflict. Our main conclusions are that, first, in order for public service employees to deal with bystander conflict, resource enhancing interventions are a potentially valuable solution. Second, studies on positive psychology interventions have confirmed the positive effects of interventions aiming at increasing resources. However, future research should focus more on interventions that are specifically geared towards the specific situations, such as bystander conflict. Third, team training interventions have been identified as an effective means to reduce human failure in high reliability environments such as aviation and surgery. We are of the opinion that team training has a much larger applicability. Many public service organizations operate in urgent situations where errors or failures have large consequences and performance relies heavily on team collaboration effectiveness. In such conditions, teamwork interventions will be valuable. Fourth, in order for personal resources to become fruitfully employable team resources should be available. If team members fail to work together as a team, their individual capacities will not have the ability to be employed. Finally, future research is needed to further our knowledge on the possibilities of intervention in public service occupations. We provided a first encouraging example, but much more work is needed to explore the effect of specific applied resource enhancement interventions and the combination of increasing personal and team resources in an intervention. Finally, more insight is needed regarding the effect of such interventions, not only on resources but also on individual and organizational outcomes such as well-being, performance, commitment, and turnover.

References

Abraham, M., Flight, S., & Roorda, W. (2011). *Agressie en geweld tegen werknemers met een publieke taak. Onderzoek voor Veilige Publieke Taak 2007 – 2009 – 2011.* Amsterdam, the Netherlands: DSP-groep BV. Opgevraagd bij de Rijksoverheid: www.rijksoverheid.nl/onderwerpen/agressie-en-geweld/documenten-en-publicaties/kamerstukken/2011/10/03/aanbieding-onderzoek-naar-agressie-en-geweld-tegen-werknemers-met-een-publieke-taak.html

Arnetz, J. E., & Arnetz, B. B. (2001). Violence towards health care staff and possible effects on the quality of patient care. *Social Science & Medicine, 52*(3), 417–427.

Bakhuys Roozeboom, M., Koningsveld, E., & Van den Bossche, S. (2010). *Agressie afgerekend. Een onderzoek naar de kosten en baten van maatregelen tegen agressie en geweld in de publieke taak.* TNO Kwaliteit van Leven, Hoofddorp.

Bakker A. B., & Demerouti, E. (2007). The job demand-resources model: State of the art. *Journal of Managerial Psychology, 22*, 309–328. doi: 10.1108/02683940710733115.

Bakker, A. B., Demerouti, E., & Euwema, M. C. (2005). Job resources buffer the impact of job demands on burnout. *Journal of Occupational Health Psychology, 10*, 170–180. doi:10.1037/1076-8998.10.2.170.

Bakker, A. B., Hakanen, J. J., Demerouti, E., & Xanthopoulou, D. (2007). Job resources boost work engagement, particularly when job demands are high. *Journal of Educational Psychology, 99*, 274–284. doi: 10.1037/0022-0663.99.2.274.

—— (1989). Regulation of cognitive processes through perceived self-efficacy. *Developmental Psychology, 25*, 729–735.

Bandura, A. (1994). Self-efficacy. In V. S. Ramachaudran (Ed.), *Encyclopedia of human behavior* (Vol. 4, pp. 71–81). New York: Academic Press. (Reprinted in H. Friedman [Ed.], *Encyclopedia of mental health*. San Diego: Academic Press, 1998).

Barling, J., Rogers, A. G., & Kelloway, E. K. (2001). Behind closed doors: In-home workers' experience of sexual harassment and workplace violence. *Journal of Occupational Health Psychology, 6*(3), 255–269.

Bolier, L., Haverman, M., Westerhof, G. J., Riper, H., Smit, F., & Bohlmeijer, E. (2013). Positive psychology interventions: A meta-analysis of randomized controlled studies. *BMC Public Health, 13*(1), 119.

Bond, F. W., & Bunce, D. (2000). Mediators of change in emotion-focused and problem-focused worksite stress management interventions. *Journal of Occupational Health Psychology, 5*(1), 156–163.

Briner, R. B., & Reynolds, S. (1999). The costs, benefits, and limitations of organizational level stress interventions. *Journal of Organizational Behavior, 20*, 647–664.

Cannon-Bowers, J. A., Tannenbaum, S. I., Salas, E., & Volpe, C. E. (1995). Defining team competencies and establishing team training requirements. In R. Guzzo, E. Salas, & associates (Eds.), *Team effectiveness and decision making in organizations* (pp. 333–380). Palo Alto: JAI.

Carnevale, P. J., & Probst, T. M. (1998). Social values and social conflict in creative problem solving and categorization. *Journal of Personality and Social Psychology, 74*, 1300–1309. doi: 10.1037//0022-3514.74.5.1300.

Cohn, M. A., & Fredrickson, B. L. (2010). In search of durable positive psychology interventions: Predictors and consequences of long-term positive behavior change. *Journal of Positive Psychology, 5*, 355–366. doi:10.1080/17439760.2010.508883.

De Dreu, C. K., Kluwer, E. S., & Nauta, A. (2008). The structure and management of conflict: Fighting or defending the status quo. *Group Processes & Intergroup Relations, 11*(3), 331–353.

Demerouti, E., Van Eeuwijk, E., Snelder, M., & Wild, U. (2011). Assessing the effects of a 'personal effectiveness' training on psychological capital, assertiveness and self-awareness using self-other agreement. *Career Development International, 16*, 60–81. doi:10.1108/13620431111107810.

Driskell, J. E., Salas, E., & Johnston, J. (1999). Does stress lead to a loss of team perspective? *Group Dynamics: Theory, Research, and Practice, 3*(4), 291.

Fredrickson, B. L. (2001). The role of positive emotions in positive psychology: The broaden-and-build theory of positive emotions. *American Psychologist, 56*(3), 218–226.

Gaba, D. M., Howard, S. K., Fish, K. J., Smith, B. E., & Sowb, Y. A. (2001). Simulation-based training in anesthesia crisis resource management (ACRM): A decade of experience. *Simulation & Gaming, 32*(2), 175–193.

Giebels, E., Ufkes, E. G., & Van Erp, K. J. M. P. (forthcoming). Understanding high-stakes conflicts. In N. Ashkanasy, O. B. Ayoko, & K. A. Jehn (Eds.), *The handbook of research in conflict management*, London: Edward Edgar Publishing.

Giga, S. I., Cooper, C. L., & Faragher, B. (2003). The development of a framework for a comprehensive approach to stress management interventions at work. *International Journal of Stress Management, 10*(4), 280.

Goldstein, I. L., & Gilliam, P. (1990). Training system issues in the year 2000. *American Psychologist, 45*(2), 134.

Helmreich, R. L., Merritt, A. C., & Wilhelm, J. A. (1999). The evolution of Crew Resource Management training in commercial aviation. *International Journal of Aviation Psychology, 9*(1), 19–32.

Hershcovis, M. S., & Barling, J. (2010). Toward a multi-foci approach to workplace aggression: A meta-analytical review of outcomes from different perpetrators. *Journal of Organizational Behavior, 31*, 24–44. doi:10.1002/job.621.

Hobfoll, S. E. (1989). Conservation of resources: A new attempt at conceptualizing stress. *American Psychologist, 44*, 513.

—— (2001). The influence of culture, community, and the nested-self in the stress process: advancing conservation of resources theory. *Applied Psychology: An International Review, 50*, pp. 337–370.

Hoel, H., Einarsen, S., & Cooper, C. L. (2003). Organisational effects of bullying. Bullying and emotional abuse in the workplace. *International Perspectives in Research and Practice 2*, 145–161.

Hogh, A., Sharipova M., & Borg, V. (2008). Incidence and recurrent work-related violence towards healthcare workers and subsequent health effects. A one-year follow-up study. *Scandinavian Journal of Public Health, 36*, 706–712. doi:10.1177/1403494808096181.

Luthans, F. (2002). Positive organizational behavior: Developing and managing psychological strength. *Academy of Management Executive, 16*, 57–72.

Luthans, F., Avey, J. B., & Patera, J. L. (2008). Experimental analysis of a web-based training intervention to develop positive psychological capital. *Academy of Management Learning & Education, 7*, 209–221.

Luthans, F., Vogelgesang, G. R., & Lester, P. B. (2006). Developing the psychological capital of resiliency. *Human Resource Development Review, 5*(1), 25–44.

MacLeod, A. K., Coates, E., & Hetherton, J. (2008). Increasing well-being through teaching goal-setting and planning skills: Results of a brief intervention. *Journal of Happiness Studies, 9*, 185–196.

McCulloch, P., Rathbone, J., & Catchpole, K. (2011). Interventions to improve teamwork and communications among healthcare staff. *British Journal of Surgery 2011, 98*, 469–479.

Meyers, M. C., van Woerkom, M., & Bakker, A. B. (in press). The added value of the positive: A literature review of positive psychology interventions in organizations. *European Journal of Work and Organizational Psychology.*

Nau, J., Halfens, R., Needham, I., & Dassen, T. (2010). Student nurses' de-escalation of patient aggression: A pretest–posttest intervention study. *International Journal of Nursing Studies, 47*(6), 699–708.

Needham, I., Abderhalden, C., Halfens, R. J. G., Dassen, T., Haug, H. J., & Fischer, J. E. (2005). The effect of a training course in aggression management on mental health nurses' perceptions of aggression: A cluster randomised controlled trial. *International Journal of Nursing Studies, 42*(6), 649–655.

O'Connor, P., Campbell, J., Newon, J., Melton, J., Salas, E., & Wilson, K. (2008). Crew resource management training effectiveness: A meta-analysis and some critical needs. *International Journal of Aviation Psychology, 18*(4), 353–368.

Ouweneel, E., Le Blanc, P. M., & Schaufeli, W. B. (2013). Do-it-yourself: An online positive psychology intervention to promote positive emotions, self-efficacy, and engagement at work. *Career Development International, 18*(2), 173–195.

Pruitt, D. G. (2008). Conflict escalation in organizations. In C. K. W. De Dreu, & M. J. Gelfand (Eds.) *The psychology of conflict and conflict management in organizations. The organizational frontiers series,* (pp. 245–266). New York, NY: Taylor & Francis Group/Lawrence Erlbaum Associates.

Rafaeli, A., Erez, A., Ravid, S., Derfler-Rozin, R., Treister, D. E., & Scheyer, R. (2012). When customers exhibit verbal aggression, employees pay cognitive costs. *Journal of Applied Psychology.* Advance online publication. doi:10.1037/a0028559.

Reznek, M., Smith-Coggins, R., Howard, S., Kiran, K., Harter, P., Sowb, Y., & Krummel, T. (2003). Emergency Medicine Crisis Resource Management (EMCRM): Pilot study of a simulation-based crisis management course for emergency medicine. *Academic Emergency Medicine, 10*(4), 386–389.

Richardson, K. M., & Rothstein, H. R. (2008). Effects of occupational stress management intervention programs: A meta-analysis. *Journal of Occupational Health Psychology, 13,* 69–93.

Runyan, C. W., Zakocs, R. C., & Zwerling, C. (2000). Administrative and behavioral interventions for workplace violence prevention. *American Journal of Preventive Medicine, 18*(4), 116–127.

Salas, E., Burke, C. S., Bowers, C. A., & Wilson, K. A. (2001). Team training in the skies: Does crew resource management (CRM) training work? *Human Factors: The Journal of the Human Factors and Ergonomics Society, 43*(4), 641–674.

Salas, E., DiazGranados, D., Klein, C., Burke, C. S., Stagl, K. C., Goodwin, G. F., & Halpin, S. M. (2008). Does team training improve team performance? A meta-analysis. *Human Factors: The Journal of the Human Factors and Ergonomics Society, 50*(6), 903–933.

Salas, E. DiazGranados, Weaver, S. J., & King, H. (2008). Does team training work? Principles for health care. *Academic Emergency Medicine, 15,* 1002–1009.

Salas, E. Nichols, D. R., & Driskell, J. E. (2008). Testing three team training strategies in intact teams: A meta-analysis. *Small Group Research, 38,* 471–488.

Salas, E., Rosen, M. A., Held, J. D., & Weissmuller, J. J. (2009). Performance measurement in simulation-based training. A review and best practices. *Simulation & Gaming, 40*(3), 328–376.

Salas, E., Sims, D. E., & Burke, C. S. (2005). Is there a "big five" in teamwork? *Small group research, 36*(5), 555–599.

Seligman, M. E., & Csikszentmihalyi, M. (2000). Positive psychology: an introduction. *American Psychologist, 55*(1), 5.

Seligman, M. E. P., Steen, T. A., Park, N., & Peterson, C. (2005). Positive psychology progress: Empirical validation of interventions. *American Psychologist, 60,* 410–421.

Shapiro, S. L., Astin, J. A., Bishop, S. R., & Cordova, M. (2005). Mindfulness-based stress reduction for health care professionals: Results from a randomized trial. *International Journal of Stress Management, 12*(2), 164–176.

Sin, N. L., & Lyubomirsky, S. (2009). Enhancing well-being and alleviating depressive symptoms with positive psychology interventions: A practice-friendly meta-analysis. *Journal of Clinical Psychology: In Session, 65,* 467–487.

Ufkes, E. G., Giebels, E., Otten, S., & van der Zee, K. I. (2012). The effectiveness of a mediation program in symmetrical versus asymmetrical neighbor-to-neighbor conflicts. *International Journal of Conflict Management, 23*(4), 440–457.

Van den Heuvel, M., Demerouti, E., Bakker, A. B., & Schaufeli, W. B. (2010). Personal resources and work engagement in the face of change.In J. Houdmont &S. Leka (Eds.), *Contemporary occupational health psychology: Global perspectives on research and practice*, 124–150. London: Wiley.

Van Erp, K. J. P. M., Rispens, S., Gevers, J. M. P., & Demerouti, E. (2013a). When bystanders become bothersome: The negative consequences of bystander conflict and the moderating role of resilience. *Under Review [revised & resubmitted], European Journal of Work and Organizational Psychology.*

—— (2013b). Enhancing resources to empower public service workers facing bystander conflict. *Paper presented at the 26th Annual IACM Conference, Tacoma, Washington.*

Weaver, S. J., Lyons, R., DiazGranados, D., Rosen, M. A., Salas, E., Oglesby, J., Augenstein, J. S., Birnbach, D. J., Robinson, D., & King, H. B. (2010). The anatomy of health care team training and the state of practice: A critical review. *Academic Medicine*, *85*, 1746–1760.

Xanthopoulou, D., Bakker, A. B., Demerouti, E., & Schaufeli, W. B. (2007). The role of personal resources in the Job Demands-Resources model. *International Journal of Stress Management*, *14*, 121–141. doi: 10.1037/1072-5245.14.2.121.

Index

Page numbers in **bold** indicate tables and in *italic* indicate figures.

CPSIA information can be obtained at www.ICGtesting.com
Printed in the USA
LVOW08s1454071014

407668LV00005B/63/P